Wild Flowers

Francis William Bessler

ISBN: 1499727860
ISBN 13: 9781499727869
Library of Congress Control Number: 2014910128
CreateSpace Independent Publishing Platform
North Charleston, South Carolina

Featuring
Blog Entries
from my website -
www.una-bella-vita.com

Dedicated to
ALL OF US
because
ALL OF US
are the same.
It is only
thinking we are different
that causes
most of our ills.

Introduction

The essays found in this work were first written as blog entries within my original writings website - www.una-bella-vita.com. Not all of the blogs of that website are included here, but many of those written from December, 2012, when I started my writings website, to July, 2014 are featured in this work. The reason for that is to provide a printed edition of some of my latest writings - for some who might find it useful to have a printed book in hand, rather than have to review a work via some electronic medium.

For what it's worth, this work represents much of the end of 50 years of writing about life. In a way, then, it is like a 50th anniversary - marking a celebration of being a student of life in some written form for 50 years - from my first recorded work in 1963 to the present, mid 2014. None of my earlier works have been published via a noted publisher, but all of them are found now in the *OUT IN THE OPEN* feature of my website. If you find the writings in this compilation of latter works interesting, consider yourself welcome to review other of my writings within my website. In terms of form, my writings of the past have been a mixture of essay (over 50), philosophical story (7), and song (about 180). Find it all in my website - as well as essays and songs (lyrics) in the entries of this work.

Briefly about myself, I was born on a small farm outside of Powell, Wyoming on December 3rd, 1941 - the seventh of eight children of Leo and Clara Bessler. I was raised Christian Catholic and even spent 6 years after high school graduation in 1960 from Powell High studying for the Catholic ministry - starting in the Fall of 1960 at St. Lawrence Seminary in Mount Calvary, Wisconsin, to learn Latin - as a

vi | Francis William Bessler

requirement to continue studies at St. Thomas Seminary in Denver, Colorado. In the Fall of 1961, with a Latin education behind me, I entered St. Thomas Seminary.

I loved all of my seminary years, but in the Spring of 1966, I was "discontinued" from further studies at St. Thomas because "my thinking is not that of a Catholic priest." At least, that is what I was told by the Rector of St. Thomas - one, Father Danagher - when I was told I was being terminated from further study. My main offense was that I argued that *Faith must be subject to Understanding* - or else we could never be certain of any dogma upheld as truth. My Church disagreed with that and my Dogma professor even labeled me as a "heretic" for making Faith subject to Understanding; but I still believe it today.

Subsequent to my seminary training, I have led quite a life - bearing out what Father Danagher told me long ago - that "my thinking is not that of a Catholic priest." As my writings below will attest, Father Danagher was right. If you wish to know more about me, I will refer you to my website (see above and below) - which will bear more of my biography.

In general, however, I consider my thoughts and writings like "wild flowers" - in that they are "flowers" that perhaps grow on the wild side. Thus, the title of this work - *WILD FLOWERS*. In fact, I could even be considered as a bit of a "wild flower" myself - like perhaps was my Dad as well.

In the parish pastor's eulogy for my dear Dad, who passed suddenly from an auto accident at the age of 59 in 1966, Father Prado offered that Dad was like a single "wild flower" on a hill because he led such a quiet, informal life. In that light, Dad and I are both "wild flowers." Dad did not pay much attention to what could be called "formal doctrines and dogmas" - like perhaps those taught in some prescribed form like the *TEN COMMANDMENTS* - but he loved life and revered God in his own attentive way. I guess I am a lot like my Dad. I will let my writings tell the "rest of the story."

Keep in mind, too, that each of the articles below were presented as a single article. Among those articles there will be a lot of repetition - simply because each article is its own argument. Since my thoughts are basically based on the same ideal - *that an Infinite God must be Everywhere and in Everything* - expect that theme to be repeated quite a bit.

Let me also say, that though I do claim copyright for all my writings (including songs), feel welcome to print or publish my works - and use them as you wish, given you remain true to their intent. My songs were written with my own melodies, but it's the lyrics, not the melodies, that are most important. Feel welcome to attach your own melodies - and sing away! *Be my guest!*

And while I am Inviting you to be my guest, I want to say Thanks to all of those in my life who have invited me to be their guest. Many come to mind, but especially dear to me have been those like *Dad & Mom* who encouraged me to pursue the truth in my own way. Then there is a childhood sweetheart named *Kika* Burke who has encouraged me down through the years to never stop searching - even when I was telling myself that I needed to quit due to pain of frustration. In 1980, I felt rather discouraged because I was not finding the truths of the soul for which I was seeking; but Kika told me that I should not be discouraged. I would find the answers, she admonished, if I just kept searching. Later that year, I did - find the answers for which I was searching, that is.

Then there was a former neighbor by the name of *Nancy* Remmenga who invited me to live with her husband, Rich, and herself after my first divorce - while ex-wife, Dee, and daughter, Anita, lived just across the street. Nancy and I discussed many of the soulful issues that I have written about in life; and without a friend like Nancy, who loved to walk with me in a park in Denver, Colorado, I may not have "discovered" some of the ideas about the soul that I have. It was walking in that park that Nancy and I loved that led me to my ideas about the soul.

Then there was a gentle man named *Emmett* Needham, in Georgia where I lived for 21 years, who insisted that when I visited him and his teenaged children that I act in his home just as I do in my own - meaning that my clothes would come off to sit at the dining room table. Emmett died from a heart attack at the age of 53 in 1985, but it is friends like Emmett who have allowed me to act in life like all should act - and thereby confirm that we really are "all alike."

And now there is another Nancy, *Nancy* Shaw, who is the widow of a good friend named Joce, who passed from Parkinson's Disease at the age of 88 on February 29th, 2012. Since Joce's passing, this other Nancy and I have become very close; and it is partly because of this Nancy that I am producing this work. This Nancy suggested this work by offering that I should compile some of my latter writings into a book that could be read in hand - and not just reviewable on a pc. So, with this Nancy as a "partner," *WILD FLOWERS* is being produced.

I would be remiss, too, to not mention my "legal" daughters, Anita Marie Bessler (born 5/23/1970) and Melissa Dawn Bessler (born 10/12/1978). Anita and Melissa arrived in different homes and from different wives, but they know their Dad in their own ways - and have stood by me as I have followed my own ways. Ex step-children, Tammy, Terry, Marie, and Jimmy, need credit too. They know that when I divorced their mothers that I did not divorce them too; and we are all good friends today - long after various divorce decrees separated us.

There have been many others, too, who have been part of my life and have been there as I have found the truths of life for which I have searched - including friends and ex-wives, Dee, Pat, and Ann - and all my lovely grandkids: Desiree, Kelisha, London, Brittany and Aiden - and my one great grandkid: Jaelaun. If you are reading this work now, you know who you are.

Thanks to One & All! Indeed, *"We"* are all part of this *WILD FLOWERS* project. I hope that you can be proud of the effort - to some degree - even if you disagree with some of the ideas; and that includes my siblings, none of whom agree with me and probably wonder how we ever had the same parents. In email jargon - LOL (Lots of Laughs)!

Perhaps, Siblings, we are "strangers in thought," but we remain "brothers in the light" - even if none of you can figure out what your brother "Sonny" is about.

Thanks to Everyone who have been sparks along the way; and Thanks to All who choose to read this effort. For sure, we are all in this wonderful thing called Life together. *Brothers and Sisters are we all! Don't you agree?*

Gently,

A "Wild Flower"

Francis William Bessler
Laramie, Wyoming
www.una-bella-vita.com
July 7th, 2014

Foreword

(Two Reviews - and a Song)

Note:

As part of the publication of this work by Createspace.com (which I would gladly recommend as a publishing source), I was offered to have my work reviewed by two professional review sources - Kirkus and Clarion. Those two reviews are featured below - to be followed by a song I wrote several years ago that I call IT'S A LOVELY DAY TODAY.

Let me say that I appreciate those reviews for their honesty, but I think they may give a false impression that I may have intentionally violated public nakedness indecency laws - perhaps out of protest against laws banning public nudity. Yes, I have been arrested several times for so called "public indecency" by being caught au natural in public in several instances in my past life, but I have always "gone naked" when I thought no one else was around or when I believed no one could see. As offered in some articles of my work below, I admit to being arrested for being caught going naked, but in no instance when I have been caught in that state did I "expect" an audience, so to speak.

Having said that, yes, I do believe that public nudity should be embraced for reasons I will state in many of my works below, but I do agree that laws should be changed to allow for that before I would do it. I believe in "advocacy" to change law, not "protest." Let me advocate a change in law by arguing for such, but I do not believe in simply violating a law in order to protest against it.

I think a judge in Atlanta, Georgia said it best when I was brought before her on a public indecency charge in 1985. In that instance, I was riding my bike au natural in what I thought was an abandoned parking lot. I did not expect anyone else was around, but it turned out I was wrong. I was detained on a Saturday and had to appear before a judge the following Monday. The Judge surprised me by saying that she agreed with me that we should be allowed to ride our bikes au natural - as well as go natural just walking down a street - but she said that I had to gain consent for that via the "legislative way."

No one agrees with that more than I do. Legislatures have made laws to prevent this or that according to a consensus of legislators, and legislatures can change those laws when they see fit to do so. It is really a matter of general consensus - or should be; but with this work, *WILD FLOWERS,* I am "advocating" that we humans change our vision to pay attention to that which really matters - an embrace of our wonderful world and ourselves within it.

I think we need to realize that God has not legislated any of our laws simply because God is within us and not an "individual" outside of us to legislate anything. We need to come to realize that only man has legislated that which we call "morality"; and as we have legislated our own morality, we can change that morality when we come to realize it is we who have decided our own morality - not God.

In the end, it is a "we the people" not a "I, a person" that can change anything in this world. We must change things - not I must change things. In the meantime, it is I as a person who must conduct my life the best I know how - and that does not depend upon any general consensus - as long as I remain private. I need no law to regulate my doing right on my own - in my own space. In that way, I can live "independent of law" - and the more that I do that, I do believe the healthier as a soul I will be.

As I will be arguing in my work below, it is not a general public I will be inheriting in this life or any life I may come to know in the future, but it is a "me" that I will be inheriting. It is then up to "me" to assure myself that the person I want to know in some future is the same person that is living now. No law can change the real me. Only I can do that.

With that, let me leave you to the reviews I requested - to be followed by a song that tries to sum my views in rhyme. Enjoy it all - and all that I "advocate" in this entire work as you will.

Thanks!
Francis William Bessler
August 23rd, 2014

KIRKUS REVIEW:

Debut author Bessler offers a collection of essays and songs about life and religion.

Born in 1941, this former seminarian, divorcee and avid blogger has a lot of opinions to share. Raised Catholic, though by no means adherent to Catholic dogma as an adult, he has a particular interest in the nature of God. He argues in this collection that God should not be thought of as an individual, but as a divine force found in all things. He goes on to say that no one needs to be saved or baptized to be part of God's presence, "*BECAUSE ALL OF US ARE BORN IN GOD* and there is nothing about us that should be considered shameful." He also argues against shame, power and other forms of control, and often focuses on the importance of appreciating the now and of counting others as equal (particularly with the equalizing power of nudity). Not all his thoughts are of unrestrained liberty, however: "Many—and maybe most—may disagree with me on this one, but I think coitus should be restricted to making babies." How do readers reconcile this view of intercourse with an openness to being photographed naked? The author, who claims to have been arrested for public nudity, is more than happy to explain. But what will readers make of this collection's frequent citing of the Gospel of Thomas, and its somewhat meandering personal letter to Pope Francis? If nothing else, it's clear that the author has taken the time to forge his own beliefs. Concepts such as "*shame is the foundation of all evil*" may not appear extremely insightful, but taken as a collection, they form a picture of an intriguing individual who doesn't simply regurgitate the beliefs of others. Instead, his opinions come across as well-thought-out and earnest.

Readers interested in a unique belief system will enjoy many of this author's musings.

CLARION REVIEW:

Four Stars (out of Five)

There is a certain beauty in sameness—picture endless rows of red tulips or fields overflowing with sunflowers—but sometimes wisdom reveals itself on the scraggly edges of such displays, in the wildflowers that refuse to conform. In this aptly titled collection, *Wild Flowers,* self-described "wild flower" Francis William Bessler enthusiastically broadcasts his musings on everything from the afterlife of the soul to right-wing politics. Bessler's expansive writing reflects the evolving philosophy of a former seminary student who challenges his traditional religious education with an unconventional view from the edge.

Twenty-seven essays and twenty-six songs or poems make up this volume, a collection of Bessler's work drawn from pieces he has published on his blog (www.una-bella-vita.com) over the past two years. He's been writing for far longer—he calls this book a fiftieth anniversary celebration of his writing life—and is quite prolific. Indeed, even though he limits the scope of this book to entries from December 2012 to July 2014, his musings run to nearly three hundred pages. Bessler loves life and is eager to share his inclusive view of the world.

The enthusiasm comes through in Bessler's writing; an abundance of exclamation points and frequent phrases rendered in all caps make his optimism clear. Although he takes on many individual topics—the authenticity of the Gospels, the meaning of near-death experiences, and the likelihood of reincarnation, for instance—each essay celebrates his central theme: "An Infinite God must be Everywhere and in Everything."

This thesis is supported with a variety of arguments, some more powerful than others. For instance, when Bessler discusses homosexuality, he rationally argues that if one is created a certain way by God, that cannot, by definition, be ungodly. At other times, though, he resorts to circular logic, often supporting his point of view by the very fact that it is the way he sees things, as when he writes, "I see ONLY GOOD in life because nothing in a Creation from God can be bad."

Bessler's poems, or songs (they're offered up as both), offer lighter fare for the most part, with familiar rhyming patterns and themes that focus on love, acceptance, and light. They're most interesting read as adjuncts to the accompanying essays, as they offer a variation on the themes Bessler has focused on in his prose.

Some thoughts and themes are repeated throughout the book, creating a rhythm that suggests a series of Sunday sermons. Bessler's thoughts can be followed from cover to cover but can also be dipped into one essay/poem at a time. Along the way, the message might begin to seem repetitious, but be on the lookout for Bessler's surprising take on things like the role of the soul in mental illness and the spiritual glory of nakedness. *Wild Flowers* is at heart a devotional to diversity, and there's truly something here for everyone.

Along the way in this essay collection, be on the lookout for Bessler's surprising take on things like the role of the soul in mental illness and the spiritual glory of nakedness.

Sheila M. Trask

It's A Lovely Day Today

By
Francis William Bessler
12/20/2008

Refrain:
It's a lovely day today – as I wander all about.
I look at life with wonder – but I wonder without a doubt
that it's all lovely – from the old to the new.
It's a lovely day today – and you are lovely too.

I thank my lucky stars – for being here with you.
I thank the God that's in them – for the wondrous Moon.
I thank the Earth for the dirt – that makes up your flesh and bones.
I thank you, Dear, for being here – in this wondrous home.
Refrain.

The time is now to appreciate - the mystery of life.
There's no better time than now – to embrace what's right.
And what is right is all there is – because all is Divine.
And that includes you, My Friend, for your soul of light.
Refrain.

I'd like you to be My Darling – and share with me today.
I'd like you to know, My Friend – my love in every way.
But all you need to love me – is first to love the one that's you.
Since we are the same, to love yourself – is to love me in truth.
Refrain.

So, come along with me, My Dear – and share with me what's yours.
Because what is yours is mine – underneath our sparkling stars.
We all own the world that's here – because that world belongs to us.
We are children of a single God – and in each other, we should trust.
Refrain.

HAVE A WONDERFUL LIFE, EVERYONE!
THANKS FOR LISTENING!

Francis William Bessler

Contents

Featuring about 26 essays and 27 songs

Joy To The World!

By
Francis William Bessler
Laramie, Wyoming
12/12/2012

As I begin this "blogging business" of adding a bit of a note to an ongoing journal of my website, it is the season to be jolly - as it is said; and it is too. I have come to realize, however, with each succeeding year that I live - and I have just turned 71 - that there in so such thing as a season to not be jolly. I do not know of a single season that should not be accompanied with joy, Why? Because all seasons have one thing in common - *God is Present in them All!*

We humans are often filled with "folly" which is the exact opposite of *"jolly"* because we insist on seeing one day different than another day in terms of blessedness and one place different than another place in terms of blessedness and one life different than another life in terms of blessedness; and that is the "folly" that keeps all days and all times and all places from being filled with *"jolly."*

To each, his or her own, but for the life of me, I cannot imagine an Infinite God missing from anyplace or anyone. It is simply beyond the rank of possibility. Everywhere I look, I see God because everywhere I look I see Life - or even just Existence. Let others divide the world into Good and Evil if they want, but wanting it does not make it so.

I do not believe there can be any evil in the world in terms of a "missing God"; however I do believe that evil can happen because of

1

a failure to see God in everything. If I see you as lacking God, then it will be quite easy for me to "dismiss" you from among the worthy; and when I have declared you as unworthy, then you, Dear One, are "expendable."

I do not believe that anyone is "expendable" - no matter what he or she has done because by "dispensing" of one for any reason is to "dispense of life" and not just some one considered unworthy because of what he or she may have done. If I dispense of you, I cannot do that unless I dispense of all of your life; and therein is the great tragedy of so called justice. In doing justice by claiming to "eliminate" some considered unworthy individual, it is Life itself that is eliminated.

Well, that's the way I look at it - though I may well be among a minority who do see it that way. Personally, I treasure Life itself for being a fantastic, majestic, and honorable gift of Creation - and God. It is hard for me to insist on punishing someone with life by treating the life they have with contempt. I have a hard time differentiating a person from the life they have.

I admit to being somewhat of an "idealist," however - perhaps in the light of another "idealist" - one we call *Jesus*. I think Jesus was an idealist too - and not many heard his idealism because they were too caught up in their world - or worlds - of civilized reality.

For what it's worth, I pride myself on being a *"Holistic" Christian,* but not a "Messianic" Christian. The former is one who believes that all life is holy because it is blessed of the presence of God. The latter is one who thinks that life itself needs to be "saved" because it has become inherently lacking in goodness for whatever reason. I do not believe that life needs saved because I see no evidence that life itself is guilty of anything - and I am convinced that Jesus did not believe life needs to be saved either. In that, Jesus and I are one. At least, I think so.

Thanks (FWB)

I Own The World

By
Francis William Bessler
1/1/2013

I own the world -
and I don't need a gun.
I'm one with the Moon
and I'm one with the Sun.
No one on Earth is
having more fun.
I own the world -
and I don't need a gun.

I'm one with the squirrels
and I'm one with the birds.
The rabbits and I
love the same world.
None of us possess a thing
but we all own it all
Being one with it
is just having a ball.

I own the world -
and I don't need a gun.
Rifles and bullets
appeal to me none.
Just let me be free
and with the wind run.
I own the world -
and I don't need a gun.

As it is with me,
it can be for you.
You need fear no one
to see your life through.
You can have it all
knowing Life itself is the Truth.
It only depends
upon your attitude.

You own the world -
and you don't need a gun
to stand tall
and know your God's son.
We are all the same -
each and everyone.
You own the world -
and you don't need a gun.

Repeat last verse twice, Then:
Ending:
You own the world -
and you don't need a gun.
We own the world -
and we don't need guns.
Yes - we own the world -
and we don't need guns.

What Is Life?

By
Francis William Bessler
Laramie, Wyoming
1/31/2013

Note:

This article deals somewhat with the human soul. I realize that it is an extremely difficult idea with which to deal because if it exists at all, the human soul is invisible - making it impossible to measure in any scientific way - as well as almost impossible to analyze in some philosophical or spiritual way. It is like the human soul is an enigma. Still, I have chosen to attempt to analyze the human soul in my life - even though I will not do so much in this article.

I think it worthwhile, however, to point out that in the late 1980s, I did write an analytical work on the soul that I call UNMASKING THE SOUL. You can find that work in volume 2 of my OUT IN THE OPEN writings - found elsewhere in my una-bella-vita website. In the meantime, consider this selection below as a bit of a peek into my general thinking about the subject. What a marvelous entity - the human soul! Welcome to a glimpse of it here. Thank You! FWB.

What is Life? I am prompted to ask that question by virtue of the opening lines of a marvelous stage play called *A FEW GOOD YEARS* by Penny & Ron Petersen and Linda Signer about a couple of middle age friends conspiring to bring their various mom and dad together for a "few good years" after each has lost his or her spouse to a passing from life. As it is, some fellow senior thespians of Laramie - as members of a seniors theatrical group called "The Unexpected Company" - will be performing that play in mid February. As narrator, I will open the performance with these lines: *What is life? Why are we here? What part is love? What part is fear? What causes smiles? What brings a tear? Things are not always as they appear.*

Indeed, *"things are not always as they appear,"* but on the other hand, I think that we humans have been so confused about life for the very practice of insisting on looking away from life as it is as if life itself is a prelim for tragedy. I think it is precisely because we humans refuse to look at life that most of us live our entire lives without knowing anything much about them - that is anything worthwhile. Then we choose to offer pure fiction and speculation about some life we can't see - otherwise called the "spiritual life" - as the only real worthwhile knowledge; however, we separate the spiritual from the material and offer that one cannot lead to the other.

Many a claimed "teacher about life" would argue that we can't know about the unknown by looking at what is known - especially if it is a so called "spiritual life" that is being taught - or being taught about. The argument there is that the so called "spiritual" is not the "material" - and thus, we cannot know about the spiritual except through unique spiritual channels. Accordingly, we cannot know about the spiritual except if it is revealed to us by a spiritual agent, in the end supervised by God - the leader of the Spiritual World.

In reality, however, that is probably not so because the difference between the spiritual and the material may only be a dimensional thing. In reality, the so called "spiritual life" is probably an invisible replica of what is non-spiritual - or material; and, in reality, the ONLY way we can know about the hidden spiritual life is to see it through the visible world. In reality, that is probably the way it really is. Souls are probably born into physical bodies simply because a physical body is a visible agent that can be maneuvered for a soul's advantage. The body is probably a chosen vehicle for a soul to seek adventure - and not at all the "trap" that many so called spiritual leaders want us to believe it is.

None of us souls who have bodies probably know the truth for sure, however. I am stating opinion, not truth - though I do believe that what I offer is probably the truth; but none of us know just how we come to occupy our physical bodies - given that we are souls in the first place that can occupy physical bodies. It stands to reason, however, that none of us would choose to occupy a body if there were not some advantage in doing so. In my trust that my soul probably chose my body for some advantage a body could offer, I choose to equate what truth I find in a physical body as some "spiritual or soulful truth" for which I am seeking.

Accordingly, not only should I embrace my body as necessary for my personal health. I should embrace my body as necessary for my "spiritual health." In that, the only way I can find "spiritual truth" is by finding it through observation of my physical body - or, in general, through observation of the physical or material world. Indeed, the material world and my physical body become a requirement for spiritual truth - not an impediment for finding such truth - as many who would have me deny the material world for the sake of my soul would have me believe.

Personally, I believe those who claim that they have knowledge of some spiritual life based only on hearsay and speculation about what can't be seen are probably as dumb as their intended students. My question is - why listen to those who teach about what can't be seen by declaring what can be seen is of no value? How likely is it that such a teacher is going to be right in what he or she teaches? Specifically, I focus on that question because, in fact, most who declare about some unseen spiritual life in the future, almost to a "teacher," claim they treasure something that is unseen over that which is seen. They claim to love the Heaven of the Future that they cannot see over the Paradise on Earth that they can see - though admittedly, they do not see the Earth as a paradise.

In other words, almost everyone who asserts some belief in an existence more wonderful than a current life precedes such a belief with a former belief that this life is lacking. In hoping for a better life sometime in the future, they have to declare the current life is lacking. That is just the way it is; but is it right?

Is it right to deny the wondrous present? And let us never forget that the wondrous present is exactly that - a "present," a gift. Is it right to deny a current gift and simply ignore what we have now under the guise that some future gift might be better? Where is the sense in that? Should not a grateful son - or daughter - be grateful for a current gift and not waste his or her time pining for some other gift?

In actuality, as souls, when we pass from one body, we probably look for another body to continue, as it were, our "education." So of what value would it be to deny one body just to have to pass in death from that body and, in some soulful time, reenter the world we left behind? That would be to say that if we leave the world in a mess, in all likelihood, we will have to deal again with the same mess we thought we left behind.

Talk about true fate; but that may be exactly what happens. When we die, we may find ourselves wandering about the same location of our death in search for another vessel to incarnate simply because that is the process - or may be. A soul without a body may be like a person without a home. Thus, when a soul leaves one body behind, becoming homeless, that soul may have to search for another body to find another home - and repeat the same ole process all over again. How about that?

Of course, I could be wrong. Many believe that I am wrong; but I doubt I am wrong because I cannot look at life - any life - and see anything but wonder and mystery and perfection. The key idea there is "perfection." If I did not see life itself as perfect, then as a soul within life, I guess I might feel somewhat of a stranger in a foreign land, but wherever I look, I see perfection - natural wise. Accordingly, I think my soul will always be at home in this land of perfection. *I guess you could say, then, that for me - Life on Earth is really Heaven on Earth!*

Look at a flower! Is it anything but perfect? Look at a graceful antelope! Is it anything but perfect? Look at a flowing brook as it finds its way over rocks and things in its path! Is it anything but perfect? Look at a mountain side scattered with grass and cactus flowers! Is it anything but perfect? Look at that glorious sunrise or sunset! Are they not perfect - or at least, a reflection of perfection? Look at me! Look at you! Are we anything but perfect - as natural entities, that is?

Others do not see it that way, of course. Many believe their souls belong somewhere else - and this life on this land of the Earth is only some mistake that has to be overcome. To each, his or her own; but If there was some evidence that what I can see is somehow less than what it should be, then maybe I would have reason to doubt that all life really is perfect; but as long as I see no evidence that there is imperfection in life in general, then it makes no sense to believe that my life in particular is less than what it should be; and it makes no sense that a future life is likely to be any different or better than a current life. *If life really is perfect now, how can it be any more perfect later?*

What do I mean there is no evidence of imperfection in life? Some would ask that. Some would counter and claim that there is nothing but imperfection in life - and that would be testimony that I am all wrong. What about the poor baby who is born with some kind of body defect? Surely, that baby is not perfect. How can I claim that all in Nature is perfect when confronted with constant disease?

My answer: *Perceived Perfection is a matter of Vision.* Yes, if I were born with a body defect, I might consider myself as an imperfect creation, related to other creatures of like origin; however Nature - which is the true parent - might not consider one of us being born different than others of us as an expression of imperfection. Why? Because of the aspect of variety. There are many varieties in Nature. That is one of the Obvious Truths that one can find when looking at Nature.

Sadly, however, many humans look at "being different" as perhaps "being defective." From a purely Natural Standpoint, being different is not being defective. It is simply being "other." That' s all. Granted, within society, there is "normal" and "abnormal," but abnormal should not be treated like it is other than normal - from a viewpoint of true compassion. When Jesus touched the lepers, he was not so much "touching defective ones" as he was "treating diseased ones like they are normal"; and that, in my opinion, is the ideal. Treat everyone the same. There can be no better an expression of true compassion than that.

It is difficult to treat a leper like he or she is normal, however, if we insist on seeing Life In General as somehow less than what it should be. In following a path of expecting deficiency in life, we are apt to find deficiency in many ways - simply because we are "programmed" to look for expressions of deficiency. I think that is true. Thus, in a way, I think, we demand that there are ill ones among us to confirm our sense of the necessary defectiveness of the material world. The lepers are not only ill unto themselves; they are satisfaction for those of us who are healthy that life itself is defective by nature. We humans take great pride in seeing ourselves as defective. Otherwise, we could not hope for a better world elsewhere that lacks illness.

Could we?

So, what is life? Why are we here? Each of us needs to answer those questions for ourselves, but personally, I have tried to answer those questions by looking at Life Itself and trying to find the answers in Life Itself - not in the dictates of some who think they know the answers but who have committed themselves to dissecting the material from the spiritual - strictly on hearsay because they refuse to see all life as Good. I can trust Life Itself because Life Itself is my real parent. I cannot trust some who would declare Life Itself as unacceptable because personally I do not find it unacceptable. On the contrary, not only do I find it acceptable; I find it very, very pleasing as well. To each, his or her own, but I trust Life Itself for all the answers I need; and in such Trust, I will find the fulfillment of soul - for which I seek - in this incarnation and in all incarnations to come.

Thanks (FWB)

My Two Trees

By
Francis William Bessler
Laramie, Wyoming
started 2/4/2013; finished 2/8/2013

Refrain:
My two trees - are standing there;
and as they stand, they are so fair.
One's like the other;
twins they seem to be.
I'm in love with my two trees.

My two trees do not belong to me.
They belong to a local Burger King;
but as I see them through a plain window,
I see the story of my body and soul.
I think my body should look at my soul
as my soul should look at my body to know.
Body and soul should be partners in life
so the person that is can find Paradise.
Refrain.

My two trees - in winter - lack leaves,
but so very soon, there will come Spring.
Then they will flower and turn to green
and be as beautiful as I've ever seen.
It's that way, too, I think, with my soul.
One Fall, I will leave this body I know.
But just like the tree, my soul will go on,
to know another person and season to love.
Refrain.

My two trees are just like me,
reaching for light and being free.
We do not pine about what others are -
for we know we are as gracious by far.
We're all the same in life's blessedness.
To know this is to live without stress.
So, why not join my two trees and me
and acclaim life, love, and liberty?
Refrain (twice).

The Best Teacher
Of All!

By
Francis William Bessler
Laramie, Wyoming
2/15/2013

Note:

When I was a kid, I grew up on a small farm in Powell, Wyoming. My family thrived on a little farm of 66 acres. Being that our farm was such a small farm, we had to rely on every acre to produce in order to sustain our rather large family of two parents and eight kids. One of our crops was pinto beans - and it was crucial that we harvest those beans when it was ready to harvest them.

In the normal harvest month of August one year, our bean plants had been cut out of the ground and were lying in what were called "winnows" - or rows of uprooted plants to be fed into a machine called a combine. Leastwise, that is how I remember it. Anyway, while awaiting to be harvested in those winnows, our small bean crop was extremely vulnerable - especially to a hail storm.

One time, when I was about 14 or so, I remember sitting in our living room and not wanting to go to the living room window for resistance about seeing what looked like a huge storm coming in. I was not terrified of the storm, being inside, but I was well aware of what hail could do to our meager and necessary crop of beans - drying out in a field in winnows. I expressed a sense of peril to my Dad. I was so sorry, I offered, that his (and our) crop of beans could be wiped out in an instant by the storm at hand. I will never forget how Dad reacted.

He said: *It will do no good to worry about such things, Francis. Come over to the window with me and watch God's Wonderful Works in process!*

You see, for Dad, all that terrible lightning and terrible thunder - and potential imminent hail - was only part of *"God's Wonderful Works."* I was encouraged to enjoy it - and not be dismayed by it. As it happened, no hail came that year, and all my worry had been for naught, but the lesson I learned from that little event has stayed with me all of my years.

As Dad would say it, *Nature is God's Great Handiwork*, but, in effect, Nature is really equal to God. That is how I have lived my life - seeing Nature as equal to God since, in a way, Nature cannot exist outside of God and God cannot exist outside of Nature. Where one is, the other must be. If that is not an expression of true equality, what can be?

Seeing God and Nature as really one makes it really easy for *Divine Naturists* like me, however. We do not have to rely on someone claiming to be a prophet of God to learn about God. All we have to do is look at what is about us because what is about us is the God many would seek elsewhere. If Nature - and all that is Natural - is really of God, why look elsewhere?

Indeed, *why look elsewhere* - unless what you see is not what you want to see? I do believe it is that "want" factor that allows people to both - overlook the magnificence of what they see - and dream about something a whole lot better than what they have.

I think it is a lot like being able to choose classrooms. I can go into one classroom that is teaching one subject and then decide I don't really care about that subject and "want" to change classes. So, I might leave an unwanted classroom behind and go searching for another; but what I should not dismiss is that the classroom I left behind is still just fine for those students who want to learn the subject taught in that class.

For example, say that I am thinking about going to Spain. Accordingly, I choose to attend a Spanish Class - or a class that teaches Spanish. Then I change my mind and decide I do not want to go to

Spain. I decide I want to go to France instead. Thus, I drop out of the Spanish Class and join the French Class. That's just fine, but it is good to realize that just because I decide I do not want to learn Spanish does not mean that all the students in that Spanish Class were not right in staying there.

Now, what would happen if I decided that I did not want to attend any class available to me? Say that I decided I "wanted" to attend a whole different class, but not knowing what classes might be available in another area, all I could do is speculate about what I might learn in another class. Still, my heart would yearn for that other class and my mind would think of nothing else - even though, in reality, there is no other class. Wanting another class - and another school - will not make it happen. Will it?

Then consider this scenario. In my discontent, after rejecting all the classes available to me, I run into a fellow discontent in the hallway; and this fellow discontent tells me that he heard of another class in another land far away - and that the Master of that far away class wants students as much as students want him. Whoopee! I exclaim to myself. I knew it! I don't really have to mind all these classes here available to me! Another Master is waiting for me - far, far, away!

And thus, I chuck what is at hand out the window. I did not want it. I do not want it; and I will not accept less than the Great Class of that Wonderful Master a fellow discontent told me about. For the rest of my life, then, I live to ignore the classes at hand while yearning for that "much better class" awaiting me if I simply present some evidence to the Master of that far away class that I want to be his student.

In a manner of speaking, I think this is what has happened to the whole human race. I think it really finds itself in a True Paradise - and all we have to do is recognize it is a True Paradise to be happy within it; but in not recognizing we are really in a True Paradise, we simply spend our lives wanting another paradise somewhere else. That paradise at hand, however, is like a University or School. We have to study it to appreciate what it has to offer.

People like Dad and Me don't really have to study intently, however, to be good students. In reality, just wanting to be in a class is quite enough for Dad and Me. Why? Because we see too much majesty in what is around us to suspect that such majesty is not right. People like

Dad and Me don't really have to be meteorologists to appreciate the weather. In fact, we don't much care about the details of what makes a wind blow or rain to form and fall - or snow to happen about us. Still, we are good students of the Paradise at Hand because we see it as such.

People like Dad and Me can look at a rabbit - and be amazed. We can study the rabbit and watch it hop about and watch it trying to find a mate, but beyond that, we don't really need to know any more about the rabbit in order to "appreciate" it. Why? Because we see ourselves as like the rabbit. There "ain't" no real difference as far as we can see. That rabbit and us are the same; but in studying the rabbit, we "appreciate" ourselves - and conversely, in studying ourselves, we "appreciate" the rabbit.

Now, other people might be passing along the same trail as Dad and Me. There is the same rabbit hopping about - the same wonder that Dad and Me want to watch; but they are so focused on being part of some far away paradise that they don't even see the rabbit - and instead, find themselves stumbling over some rock in the path, causing them to damn the rock and wish all the more that they just weren't here.

In one of my favorite works, *THE GOSPEL OF THOMAS* (sometimes referred as *THE GOSPEL ACCORDING TO THOMAS*) - and I deal more with that gospel in other of my writings in my website - in Verse 3 of that work, *Jesus said: If those who lead you say to you: "See, the Kingdom is in heaven," then the birds of the heaven will precede you. If they say to you, "It is in the sea," then the fish will precede you. But the Kingdom is within you and it is without you. If you know yourselves, then you will be known and you will know that you are sons of the Living Father. But if you do not know yourselves, then you are in poverty and you are poverty.*

As Jesus offered in that verse, the key to being in Paradise is Knowing you are in Paradise. Look about you and wonder about what you see - and enjoy it. If there are birds in the air, that is their heaven. If there are fish in the sea, the sea is their heaven; and if you are a "son of the Living Father," heaven is right where you stand.

If you know yourselves, he says, you will be known - by however you see yourself, of course - and by those who see themselves in like manner. If I think I am a "son of the Living Father," but you do not see yourself likewise, then you will not know me as a "son of the Living Father." Why? Because it takes one to know one.

And therein is the true tale of life, I think. Discontents know discontents. And contented ones know contented ones - even in the midst of a general discontent among others. That is just the way it is.

In the light of "it takes one to know one" and my belief that Jesus knew he was a "son of the Living Father," I wonder if ones like Peter really knew Jesus. If Peter - or any of the alleged disciples of Jesus - really knew Jesus, they would have known themselves as "sons of the Living Father." Otherwise, they could not have really known Jesus.

If Peter saw himself as a "son of the Living Father," he could not have seen himself as other than "deserving." I see myself as a "son of the Living Father" and I see myself as "deserving" of that class as well. Granted, I am not responsible for making it happen, but I am "entitled" to the Gift of Life I have been given - merely because I have been given it. If Peter thought likewise, why did he act like he was a "man of sin" that had to be redeemed to be deserving? And if Peter really believed that he was a "son of the Living Father" - like Jesus and Me - why did he go forward and preach that life is not really as it is supposed to be? Why did he go forward and offer that there is another heaven someplace else that the "worthy" will attain and achieve? Based on that, I really wonder if Peter - or any of the alleged disciples of Jesus - really knew Jesus.

In the end, however, it is up to each of us to choose the paradise we want - or want to see. If we insist on a paradise far away, then I suppose we will spend our lives dreaming about that hoped for paradise - even if, in fact, no such paradise exists. But if we decide we are going to be apt students of this world and let another world be for itself, then we are apt to be good students of this life and see wonder in a hail storm that might even destroy our livelihood. For ones like Dad and Me, Nature is our Teacher - even if the details of the class we are attending we miss. In the end, perhaps, it is not "passing a class in life" that is so important. It is merely attending it - and wanting to be there.

Thanks! (FWB)

Hello,Brother Francis!

By
Francis William Bessler
Laramie, Wyoming
3/17/2013

Pope Francis, let me begin this letter by congratulating you on being chosen the pope - or principal leader - of your church. When I decided to write you this letter, originally, it started *HELLO, POPE FRANCIS* - but I changed my mind after beginning it and changed it to what you see above - *HELLO, BROTHER FRANCIS*. I decided on this change because you are not my "pope," but you are my "brother" - human wise. So, for others, you are their "pope." For me, you are only my "brother." Thus, I start as I have.

Brother Francis, I am also a Francis. In a way, that says it all. You are now Francis - and have chosen the name of Francis - and I have always been a Francis. In a way, you are just "catching up to me." You are only "becoming Francis" after a life of being Jorge - or probably as we would call you in English, George. But be you a George of the past or a Francis of the present, in real terms, you are no different now than you have ever been before; but I am not telling you anything new. Am I? In a way, you have always been a Francis - like I have always been a George. The truth is - regardless of name, we are really the same.

Brother Francis, we have a common love - or loves. We both love God - and we both love Jesus; though our impressions of both are quite different. You have followed a trail of Jesus that has Jesus admiring authority and making the value of life dependent upon authority - or perhaps, better put, hierarchy. I have followed a trail of Jesus that allows me to relate to Jesus - and to our other common love, God - without any need of going through authority. You have believed that a Peter was right in claiming a right to "organize Christianity" according to strict dogma and doctrine. I have - for the most part in life - believed that a Peter was never a right course for Christianity because Jesus never emphasized authority while he lived.

As I see Jesus, Brother Francis, I see a man who taught that organization and law and rules are not important in life. In fact, it was his claiming that no one needs law or some social order to be saved that got him killed - by a crowd of Jews who depended on law and order to exist. It was "law and order" that Jesus actually opposed - and that which also got him executed. Yet it was another "law and order" instituted by Peter that carried on Christianity after Jesus died.

So, we see Jesus quite differently - you and I, Brother Francis; but I guess that's ok - as long as we both embrace the *REAL TEACHING* of Jesus - which seems to be two-fold: *to love God with all our hearts and minds and souls and to love one another as if each of us is God.* I think that is what Jesus was all about - regardless of how we get there to say it. You can say it from a pulpit - and I can say it from just being Francis; but now that you are a Francis too - or realize it - then maybe you can somehow de-emphasize law and order and just go right to the heart of the matter - and be yourself without need for any social trappings.

When I awake in the morning, Brother Francis, I am first aware of one thing - a thing I think of as "Creation." I look out my window and see trees and clouds and mountains and rabbits and squirrels - and I see "Creation." There is no evidence of any social order - or law - in any of that - "Creation"; and I do believe that the key to really loving life is simply to by step all of "human creativity" and focus on being part of "Natural Creativity." I think it is doing that - just emphasizing Creation in general - that allows us to rid ourselves of any boogey men or devils - or Satans.

In my opinion, Brother Francis, devils and Satans are really a product of the minds of souls (in and out of bodies) that are intent on trying to control things; and so they "create divisions" to make control possible. But those divisions cannot exist if we see Creation without looking for anything else. It is our looking at created things as if they are separate from Creation that allows some among us to "divide created things" into good and evil things; but if we look at ourselves as only part of CREATION, then we could not so easily be misled. *Creation, as a Whole, must be Good because it must be of God; and each member of Creation has to be Good because it is part of a Good Creation.* How simple can it be?

As we probably both realize, Brother Francis, no thing in life is "all of Creation," though every thing in Creation reflects All of Creation! It is one of the Great Wonders of Time - and Eternity. At least, that has been my focus in life - to try and know CREATION and my being part of CREATION, not my being some isolated "created thing" as if the GOOD CREATION of which I am a part does not exist.

You know, Brother Francis, speaking of "good," it is good I am writing this letter now because it reminds me of a paper I wrote on CREATION way back in the mid '60s or so. I have written quite a bit in life, for what it's worth, and one of the things I wrote while a student of philosophy at St.Thomas Seminary in Denver, Colorado in 1965 or so was an essay work I called *THE THEORY OF CONSTANT CREATION.* Sadly, this work is one of many writings that I have lost throughout the years - and in a moment, I will explain why this one was lost - but my idea then was that it is unlikely that Creation could have ever been completed because the evidence is that it is something "going on" - not having been completed.

The gist of my *"theory of constant creation"* as I can try to recall it now, Brother Francis, is that it is unlikely the story of *GENESIS* in the *BIBLE* has creation right. In that story, God "creates" the world in 6 days - and IT IS DONE! But the truth is, IT IS NOT DONE. The guy who wrote that story looked at Creation as something that was over - not going on - but the evidence is just the opposite.

As I saw it back when I wrote my initial paper on Creation, Brother Francis, Creation could not have been a "done deal" or "done deed" back in the alleged time of Adam & Eve. Of course not! Creation has to be an ONGOING thing. The very idea that God "created the world" and then stepped back and said IT IS DONE has to be nonsense. How obvious can it be? I was not "created" back when Adam & Eve were "created." Am I not a member of Creation? You were not created when Adam & Eve were created, Brother Francis. Are you not a member of Creation? That should tell us in an instant that God could not have "created the world" and that was the end of that. Anyway, that was the gist of my *THEORY OF CONSTANT CREATION*.

I must admit, though, that there was more to my paper than that. In it, I also theorized that matter itself is being constantly created - not just life forms within matter. I do not remember now the details of my thought, but I do remember that in my paper I argued that it is likely that matter itself is constantly being created; but because I have no record now of my thought, sad to say, that thought is lost.

I remember being so proud of that paper, Brother Francis, and in my joy to share it with my philosophy professor, Father Connolly, I took my only copy of it to him. I asked him if he would review it - and I thought he would be as proud of me as a student of his for writing it as I was in writing it; but he shocked me and told me I AM NOT INTERESTED IN YOUR THEORY and closed his door on me.

In one of the single most immature moments of my life, Brother Francis, I retreated to my living quarters and tore up the only copy I had of my work and threw it into the waste basket. I guess you could say I was really angry that a philosophy professor could so easily and rudely discount a "philosophical treatise" of a student. In my anger and frustration, I just erratically tore up my paper and threw it away. How idiotic that was - in retrospect!

It was very unwise of me for doing that, of course, Brother Francis. I should not have cared what anyone else might have thought of my work. I should have taken my essay and given it away - not destroyed it as I did. But I did learn from that, Brother Francis, to try and ignore objection and get on with living my life as I think it should be lived.

I have often wondered what student, Francis, wrote in that paper he so ruefully destroyed, Brother Francis; but I have never lost sight of my reason for thinking about it and writing it - a TREMENDOUS LOVE FOR CREATION. That love has allowed me to see past so many divisions that so many see in life; and it is that kind of love that I urge everyone to pursue - just a love for CREATION as if nothing else matters; and in the end, Brother Francis, that is probably true. Nothing else really does matter. Does it?

Hey, Brother Francis, I could say a lot more - and I really planned on saying a lot more when I sat down to write this - but I think I will leave it at that.

I will leave you, though, with a definition that you might find quite interesting. You probably already know it, having chosen the name, but the definition of "Francis" is "Free." Maybe it is partly because of being named Francis by a loving family that I have actually been "free" most of my life - and perhaps it is partly because of being Francis that I have been "free" to act in reality as I have in my dreams.

It is quite a heritage, you know, Brother Francis, to be a Francis. I urge you to simply be that as you go forward in your everyday activities as pope - and my guess is, if you do that, the lights will come on for so many in your audiences and life can become as our fellow hero, Jesus, really imagined it to be - *ONE BIG BROTHERHOOD OF CREATION!*

Good Luck, Brother Francis, Good Luck!

Thanks! (FWB)

Not A Cloud

In The Sky

By
Francis William Bessler
Laramie, Wyoming
3/31/2013
(Easter)

Not a cloud in the sky,
but I'm wondering why
mankind is still so full of fear?
Why does it insist
that it's so full of sin
and why does it love all its tears?

Not a cloud in the sky,
but northern warriors say nigh -
there's enemies on the flank in the south.
We've got to go where they are
and commit ourselves to war;
and we've got to wipe those devils out.

Not a cloud in the sky,
but southern warriors can't abide
all their enemies up there in the north.
Never mind they're all the same;
they have to find another to blame
in order to know some better worth.

Not a cloud in the sky,
but mankind doesn't like
to see things all peaceful and still.
There's no joy in rest,
but there's joy in wiping out a pest.
So, making war becomes our will.

Not a cloud in the sky,
but if mankind is to survive,
it has to invent a reason to go on.
So, it predicts storms on the way;
and we must ignore our sunny days
to give us a reason to belong.

Not a cloud in the sky,
but if rain is in our sight,
then we must look out for a flood.
Never mind we could go nude;
but nude doesn't quite suit our mood;
we'd rather deny each other's good.

Not a cloud in the sky
and I believe Jesus tried
to tell us that long, long ago.
There's nothing wrong with life,
except if we choose strife
and create our own storms to know.

Not a cloud in the sky,
but I'm still wondering why
so many choose the way of storm.
It makes no sense to me,
but then maybe that's why I am free
and that's why I'll always love my form.

Not a cloud in the sky,
but I'm still wondering why
mankind chooses the way of fear?
Why does it insist
on loving what is risk
and why does it love all its tears?

Spiritual Reward

&

Punishment

By
Francis William Bessler
Laramie, Wyoming
4/5/2013

A friend, Pat Ivers, asked me to address the notion of *"What happens to mean souls after they die?"* Pat knows, however, that I do not believe that God will do any punishing because I believe that God is IN everything and everyone - thus making it an irrational idea to have God punish - or reward - anyone. How can something that is INSIDE of you be OUTSIDE of you as an agent to punish - or reward?

I realize that my thinking on that is somewhat abnormal because I think many - and maybe most - have an idea that God is a person that can and will deal with all subjects. I will be addressing that notion that God can't be a person in the first place in my next blog that I call *THE UNIVERSALITY OF GOD;* but given such a belief that no one need fear punishment - or reward - by God because God is not a reality to do such, do I believe that any punishment will be forthcoming? And if so, by whom?

Thanks for asking for my opinion, Pat. Let me begin by saying *I DON'T KNOW* for sure, but then no one does - regardless of many being absolutely sure of their minds on such a subject. No, I do not know; and I do not mind admitting that; but I do have an opinion - and that is what I am offering to Pat - and anyone who cares to listen.

First of all, do I believe in sin - in order that a sinner might need or receive punishment for it? No, I do not believe in sin as "separation from God," a somewhat traditional view of sin; but I do believe in sin as just plain "meanness." Oh, yes I do! Given a definition of sin as being "meanness," yes I do believe in sin - or that people sin - because just living makes that obvious. There are many who are mean in life - in and outside of permitted social order. Thus, there are many who are "sinners." I can't sin in terms of being separated from God because I can't be separated from something inside of me, but I can sin in terms of being mean to others - even if I am using God as some kind of measure to be mean to others. Lots of people do that. Meanness has many wardrobes, though it has but one intent - to make others suffer.

So, to answer Pat, what should happen to me in life if I am mean? In life, I suppose it might be likely that in some fashion I will be punished for being mean. Some meanness might even get me imprisoned by society. I do believe that is obvious. People are often mean in life for imposing on others; but outside of punishment by another, am I punished in life for being mean?

My answer to that is yes. I think meanness is punished as virtue is rewarded simply by way of attitude and continuing an attitude. I do not believe there is any punishment for meanness more severe than simply continuing to be mean. Continuation of meanness, in my opinion, is the worst punishment of all for meanness - as continuation of kindness is the greatest reward for kindness.

Given that I am mean, however, what would be my worst punishment for being mean? To continue to be mean. Now, you can flog me or imprison me for my being mean, and that would not be pleasant, but once your flogging is done, your punishment is done too; but my self punishment would not be done until I change course in life. Would it? Until I change my attitude, my punishment would continue. Would it not?

Now, take that a step further. Say I die with an attitude of meanness. Oh, woe is me! As I lived a life of despair - or meanness - maybe nothing will change when I die. Maybe I won't be able to change my attitude of meanness because it will follow me wherever I might go. If so, my own "self punishment" would continue - even after death.

Of course, I do not know that is the case. No one does; but given my experience in life, attitude continues - until changed; and it is really attitude that is the biggest issue of life. Attitude says it all; and thus, if attitude is not likely to change in my soul after my soul will have departed from a body, then it behooves me to make sure my attitude is right in life to assure that it will be right in death. Makes sense. Right?

There is a lot of meanness in this old world; and much of it could just be stemming from previously mean people just returning to life in another incarnation. It is unlikely, I think, that if I was a mean soul last time that I won't find a way to be mean a next time too. If you wonder where some meanness came from - even amidst otherwise kind souls - the answer could well be that it simply continued from a previous life.

I am guessing, of course, but I think it is a pretty good guess. Why? Because it is based on experience within life. I think we have all witnessed people who have steadfastly maintained a certain perspective - even after that perspective has been demonstrated as false; and, if we are honest, we will include ourselves in that number. They - or we - are always right - even if they - or we - are proved wrong; and that is certain proof that souls simply continue as they are. Thus, one can be almost certain that each of us will wake up tomorrow and be the same person that we were today - regardless of any different opinion about us.

If life demonstrates continuation of attitude of soul, why should we believe that death can change that? And if a soul is reborn into another body or vessel once one body has been discharged, so to speak, it is completely likely it will maintain its last attitude. Life teaches us that people do not change their attitudes - for the most part - and that says to me that souls probably do not change attitude upon "charging" into another body. If souls have some sort of soulful attitude that pervades their human existence - once they enter human bodies and become human - then I think it is likely that attitude will attach itself to a next life.

That doesn't sound very appealing, however, to lots of minds. Some people think that a mean person ought to be punished by God or some other person or agent when they die - and some people think that it is unfair that a mean person can't begin with a whole clean slate - once they pass from a given life.

Well, I somewhat sympathize with both sentiments, but I do not see that it is likely that anyone is punished by another as a soul once they pass from a body simply because they no longer have a body to punish; and I don't think any soul can begin with a "clean slate" upon passing from life because it is likely a soul will have to continue as it is - that is at least in terms of "attitude" or "disposition."

That is not to say, however, that a mean soul can't change. It is only to say that having to retain an attitude would probably make it hard for a mean person to change - or a kind person to become mean. Change happens all the time, however. People do "see the light" and change to become something other than they were. There is no reason to say people - even super mean people - can't change. In that light, "redemption" - if you want to call it that - is always possible.

I think we all know mean people who think they are not mean, however. They think they are somehow "just." They are not mean in demanding punishment for others. They are simply "just minded." Well, whatever they are, they will continue with that attitude - and that will be just as much a "punishment" for them as they chose to punish others.

In soulful reality, one gets back what one gives out. Call it soulful trickery, if you wish, but if you insist on punishing another, your act turns back on yourself - and you become what you do to another. If you think you are being just and you are punishing me for something by slapping me in the face, you are also slapping yourself in the face - even if it is for a lack of compassion. You pay in some way - if you punish. So, why spend anytime in life at all seeking to punish when it all comes back to you - in some way?

Meanness comes in all sorts of packages. Doesn't it? In the end, it does not matter what any law might define as meanness, if one is mean, one is mean - and it is meanness itself that is the greatest punishment for meanness - just as it is kindness itself that is the greatest reward for kindness. It is my attitude - and it makes no difference if that attitude is shared by others or not. Whatever is my attitude, logic says it will continue - until I change it.

But what a world we could have if people did not deal out meanness for meanness - and call it justice. If you are miserable because you think someone else did you a terrible wrong, you are mostly miserable because of a failure to forgive. You are not mostly miserable because of something another did. Each of us has it within ourselves, I think, to treat others as we want to be treated - and that is irrespective of the way we may have been treated by someone else.

There is an old saying that goes: *Except for the Grace of God, there go I.* Well, I do not believe the "Grace of God" has anything to do with it because I think all are equally blessed and imbued of God, but the sentiment is correct. Except for my having a fortunate upbringing, there go I. It only makes sense to realize that others might not have been so blessed as I was - and realize that if I had been in "their shoes," I might have done the same thing.

As it was said in a play I recently was privileged to participate in, *Forgiveness Is The Answer.* And it is in forgiving that I can stop being mean. We all know some who absolutely refuse to forgive - with some legal judges and prosecutors and prison guards being right there in front - but legal judge or prosecutor or prison guard or otherwise, we have to pay for our lack of forgiveness - simply because our attitudes are our punishment. At least, I think so.

I am reminded of a current court case in Denver, Colorado. Last year, a young man planned and executed a horrible crime in that he assaulted and killed many in a theatre in the area. No, I do not think the lad, James Holmes, should be let go and not reprimanded for what he did, but I think it serves no one any good to act like we might not have done what he did - given walking in his shoes. I feel very sorry for all who bear horrible grudges because it is their bearing their grudges that will make them suffer the most.

I am told that James Holmes recently agreed to plead guilty without possibility of parole if he would be spared the death penalty. Many of his victims - and survivors of his victims - would have preferred such a course so they could get on with their lives - perhaps with some proper forgiveness attached - but many others - including the main prosecutor

- believe Mr. Holmes deserves no less than death and will not accept his guilty plea on condition he be spared the death penalty. No, they want him tried and proved guilty so they can kill the poor man as he killed others - even though that course of trial may take a year to complete and cost millions of dollars and untold human misery to pursue. Mr. Holmes is willing to admit guilt, but that is not enough. Some think they must punish Mr. Holmes to the so called "fullest extent of the law."

What absolute stupidity in my opinion! Little do they realize that they are the ones who will suffer the most - not James Holmes - because they will have to live their hatred - not only until James Holmes is rendered guilty or innocent by insanity - but perhaps forever - even after death in this life.

But let's get back to what I think happens to a soul when it dies - or when the body of a soul dies? I do not think many people really think about the issue when they offer that a soul is likely to be punished if it "deserves" punishment - that is, by another. The main reason for that is that punishment by another is probably strictly body oriented. Thus, if my soul no longer has a body, then how can it be punished? No body - no punishment. That is how I see that it probably is.

Many will object, of course. They want another who was mean to them to "burn in Hell" forever - or the like; but once again, no body, no pain. How can I "burn in Hell" if I have no body with which to be burned? Tell me that.

In a way, then, since I can't get to a body of yours to punish you after death since you will have no body, then it is true you can "begin again." In that way, your soul can start again with a "clean slate"; and I am grateful for that because I do not want anyone to suffer for any reason. That is just me. I am glad that upon death of your body that you will have a clean slate in that no one is likely to be able to pursue you, but I think having to continue a next life - if one chooses to incarnate again - with the same attitude of a previous life, it should behoove all of us to live this life like we will have to live it all over again - in the same way.

With that, let me offer that personally I think a soul needs a body to maneuver itself. That is probably why souls choose to incarnate in bodies in the first place. I mean, it makes sense, doesn't it? Why would

I now be in a body if I did not think there is some advantage in having a body - or being in a body? Maybe a soul by itself can do nothing. Maybe it needs a body with which to act as it might act. If so, If I can't do anything to express myself as a soul without a body, then when I get a body again, it is likely "full speed ahead" - starting out with the same attitude with which I ended my last life.

We have all heard the argument - BORN THAT WAY. Well, I think it is likely true. I was "born that way" in terms of having to inherit myself from a previous life. Why do some seem to have an "inherent" talent when they are born - to become a master musician or a master painter or a master anything? Well, I would suspect it has a lot to do with how they lived their last life. In some way if one was a musician in a last life, then they might be born again with "music in their soul." That would explain why we all seem to be born with different talents.

But like one could have spent a last life appealing to the music inside of them, another could have spent it as a rapist or murderer. Sad to say, murder can be in my person's soul too - if that is what one was in a last life. If I spent my last life looking for a way to murder you and kill you and divest you of peace, then it is likely if I return, I will be on the lookout for one like you all over again - to murder anew. In that way, one can be BORN THAT WAY too.

But, Pat, what this is all to say is that whatever I am, I will likely inherit that self - even beyond the grave; and that is my greatest form of punishment or reward - to have to inherit me to do me all over again - until I might change course, of course.

To put it in a personal frame, I was born delighted with life. I do not know how I was as a baby, but I would not doubt that my parents could not keep clothes on me. Why? Because in inheriting the me of a last life, I had no need for clothes. I wanted to explore the life I had been given; and my guess is that even as a baby, I began that way. I began that way because in all likelihood, I ended that way in a last life.

And if I was not that way as a baby, I was that way as a child. Every chance I got - when I knew I could get away with it - off went my clothes. If I was walking in a field on the family farm, off went my clothes. If I was wading in a canal that passed through the farm, off went my clothes. If I was hiking in the hills beyond the family farm, off went my clothes. Why? Because I was simply practicing what I had learned in a past life - that real virtue is embracing the gift of life - not denouncing it for some ulterior purpose of being able to control it - or more likely, control others by denouncing their most precious possession - their bodies.

So, as a child I was free to be me - even though I lived with two parents who did not sympathize with me and seven siblings who may have thought me outrageous if they had known what I was doing. I do admit I kept most of my love of life a secret because, having been raised a Catholic, I knew such activity would not be applauded. So, for the most part, I "hid out in nakedness" in secret. But I was *BORN THAT WAY* - and the likely reason I was "born that way" and practiced even differently from my own family is that I had simply inherited the me of the past. Probably!

And I am still that way today. Even though I live in a world that frowns upon accepting nakedness - except for sex - I still throw off my clothes every chance I get in order to embrace the real gift of life I have. It is not at all a matter of sex for me. It is simply doing what is right - being unashamed of the gift of life. For what it's worth, I strongly encourage it. I am not so much enthralled with me - by embracing the naked me - as I am enthralled with Nature in general. I go naked not to be different, but to know I am the same as all others and to experience bonding with Nature and being part of it. I have no shame because it makes no sense to be ashamed of a gift. Does it?

Many are born with shame, however. Aren't they? Why? I think it is largely because that is the way they lived in a past life - and past lives perhaps. Those many are simply continuing their attitude of the past - just like I am continuing my attitude - as perhaps current rapists and killers and executioners are continuing their attitudes. We are all probably *BORN THAT WAY*; and if we are perceptive, we will learn from our experiences and either continue living some way - or change to be able to inherit another way and another perceptive.

But maybe I can help another wayward soul who was not born the way I was born too, having inherited a very different self than that which I inherited. Maybe I can make contact with another soul who entered this world as a "lost soul" and maybe I can show him that rage and anger - and justice over forgiveness - is not very healthy for a soul. Maybe he can reach out to another life and another attitude - simply because I offered him an alternative by my example. That is always possible. Isn't it?

Personally, I think that is why souls like Jesus were born, Pat - and probably continue to be born - to declare their own personal peace and hope it runs off them to others who may need it. I don't think Jesus was a Jewish or Christian Messiah intent on saving a world from sin because I don't think Jesus even believed in sin in the traditional sense of "being separated from God" - but I do believe that Jesus probably lived - not only to experience life himself - but to show others the way - by example, mostly by forgiving to avoid being driven by grudge; and, perhaps, I am like that too - as everyone of us can be.

Perhaps there is a *little Jesus* in me, Pat - as I think it would be good if there were a *little Jesus* in everyone. Don't you?

And now a preview of my next article - *THE UNIVERSALITY OF GOD* - to be added as a blog to my website one week from today - April 12th, my departed Mom's 105th birthday. I can't promise satisfying answers to spiritual questions, but as I have responded to a friend's question in this effort, I will be most happy to respond to any question - as I can. OK?

As part of that next essay, I will be including a rather long poem (or song) I just wrote called *EVERY PLACE IS HEAVEN*. Let me end this by offering the first verse of that one.

Every place is Heaven;
it's just a matter of a view.
There is no God outside of life
that's not inside it too.
You cannot divide Infinity
into what's evil and what's good.
So, let everyone realize
All's one great brotherhood.

Thanks! (FWB)

The Universality Of God

By
Francis William Bessler
Laramie, Wyoming
4/12/2013

Note:
I am publishing this on my departed Mom's birthday.
Clara Elizabeth Bessler was born on 4/12/1908
and passed to her next experience on 5/16/2004
at the age of 96.
I will conclude this effort with a 12 verse song entitled
EVERY PLACE IS HEAVEN.
I have included a verse for each of the days
in the 12th of April.
Enjoy my concluding song
and this essay - as you will.
FWB.

Mom's been gone since 20004. She died at the age of 96 in May of 2004; but, realistically, was she a saint when she was born on April 12th, 1908 - 105 years ago from today?

Think about it! Of course, Mom's birth was no different than any other birth - including my own and yours. When each of us emerged from our mother's womb to begin what we call life, what is the likelihood that each of us was possibly missing God? In my mind - and opinion - there is absolutely NO chance that any baby ever born is "missing God" at the time of his or her birth. Amazingly, however, if we are not "missing God" at the time of our birth, realistically we cannot "miss God" any time in our lives either. Sadly, however, we are taught that every one is born somehow "missing God" or "lacking God" - and that life is a journey to "find our missing God."

Of course, those of us who "find God" and plug the hole that lacked God at our birth are believed to go on and "go to Heaven"; and those of us who do not succeed to "find God" in our lives are doomed to "go to Hell." Saints are those who manage to "find God" and end up in Heaven; and Sinners are those who manage to lose out - and have to go to Hell.

But where is there any sense to that? Where is the sense that any baby is born "without God"? And where is the sense that any of us have to live to "find God" - when in all likelihood, we are each born "with God" when we emerge from our mother's womb? Who ever told us we were born "without God" in the first place? And why have we believed it almost since man attained any intelligence in that thing in his head called a brain?

In truth, there is a thing called IGNORANCE; and that is why we have believed all the nonsense of a "missing God" in our lives. Ignorance of what God is begins it; and ignorance of where God is continues it.

So, what is the ignorance of the reality of God? It begins, I think, with our making God a person - like us - perhaps to help us to better relate with God and better to allow some of us to please the "person of God" and some of us to displease the person of God. For God to be either pleased or displeased, God has to be a person - someone with a mind and a heart like ours. Thus, God has very conveniently and strategically been defined as a "person" in order that God can be used to manage our proposed Heaven and Hell. And our IGNORANCE has gone marching on!

In all probability, however, God is not a person in the first place. Why? Because if we had taken the trouble to define where God probably is, we could have never stumbled in our minds and made God a person.

So, where is God and why can't God be a person? If we took a single moment to think about it - which most of us have not taken the time to do in our lives - we would realize that in all probability, EXISTENCE IS INFINITE. By that, I mean that there can be no end to EXISTENCE. If there can be no end to existence, then it stands to reason that there can be no end to God - which must equal Existence if there is God at all. How could you have a finite - or limited God - within Infinity when the very definition of God is "Infinity"? At least, for me, such a concept as a finite God somehow placed within Infinity as if that God is a person that could be one place and not another is a total irrational. It just makes no sense.

If you think otherwise - that existence can have an end - where is that end? If you go out and out and out and out into space and beyond one galaxy after another, where is this end of the world of which you are so sure? In truth, our minds cannot fathom an end to existence - if we think about it; and that is the key - *WE HAVE TO THINK ABOUT IT TO KNOW ABOUT IT.*

But if we do think about it and realize that existence can have no end and that God - if It exists at all - must equal a non-ending existence, then all vision that envisions God here and not there becomes irrational; and all vision that envisions that an existence without end can be divided into potential good & evil regions also becomes irrational. How can you divide something that is endless? Tell me that! Accordingly, how can an endless existence somehow be divided into a proverbial Heaven and Hell where one side is good and the other side is evil?

If you cannot divide something, then there can be no "sides" within that something. If you cannot divide something, then there can be no left or right within that something. Right? Whatever an endless existence is, since it cannot be divided, it must be that something throughout - either all evil or all good.

Evil is normally defined as related to some sense of lack. If I am evil, I am "lacking that which is good"; but if something is endless, it must also be "full" of whatever it is. Accordingly, that which is endless cannot possibly be lacking in anything because, in essence, it contains everything. Another definition of "everything" is "full." Thus, because what is endless must also be full - or lacking in nothing - then the endless must also be GOOD, not evil. If something is *ALL GOOD*, then it cannot be divided into, again, the proverbial good and evil regions representing the traditionally understood Heaven and Hell. If there can be no division, then what is must be *ALL GOOD*. Accordingly, if there can only be GOOD, then there can only be Heaven; and if there can only be Heaven, then there can be NO HELL - defined as "lacking God or Good." See how simple it is - if we only think about it.

It is precisely because God must equal IMMENSE EXISTENCE and must be everywhere, however, that God cannot possibly be a person. Accordingly, *IF THERE CAN BE NO INDIVIDUAL SEPARATE FROM INFINITY THAT IS GOD,* then *NO ONE NEED FEAR AN INDIVIDUAL GOD* - nor any one claiming authority from an Individual God. If an Individual God that is somehow separate from some existence cannot exist, then neither can anyone claim authority based on the existence of an Individual - or Separate - God. Correct?

Did ones like Moses and Peter, however, ever think about a non-ending world - and therefore, Infinite Divinity? Did they ever take a single moment to speculate about the reality of an endless universe, an IMMENSE EXISTENCE that cannot be divided by virtue of its endlessness - or Infinity? I doubt it; but for their times, perhaps, you cannot blame ones like Moses and Peter for bypassing thinking about Infinity. Why would they have thought about Infinity - if they did not take much trouble to think in general?

In truth, I think Moses and Peter - and counterparts - imagined - and imagine - that the world is really finite because only a finite world can allow divisions; and without division, those who would seek authority over others would be left without a base. Accordingly, the world must be finite - to allow division - if any can claim legitimate authority from God.

So, Moses went up a mountain "looking for God in search for authority" - as if God is really a "person" that can be found - and much of the world is still "going up mountains" to "find God" - as if God is still a person that can be found. People are of the mind that God can be "fetched" like any finite thing can be "fetched." Thus, many live their lives trying and insisting that they should be about "fetching God." *Come here, God! Come to me and make me whole! Come here, God, and fill the emptiness that is in my life because there is a hole in it that is missing you!*

Moses looked for God in one he knew as "Jehovah" - and thus imagined that when a voice that called himself Jehovah spoke, it was God that was speaking. Moses did not recognize that God must be in himself because Moses had already separated God from Reality in his mind before he even went searching for God. Accordingly, in expecting God to be a Person - rather than Infinity - Moses found what he thought was God in a person - a real or imagined person he called Jehovah. That is what happens when you begin searching for God not realizing that God is not a "Who," but a "What."

And Peter continued the tradition of Moses by looking for God in another. Where did Peter go to look for God? To a "person" he knew as "Jesus." In looking for a "person of God" rather than an "Infinity of God," Peter found his God in one we know as Jesus. Peter was looking for a person that he could identify as God - in looking for a person of God in the first place. If you go searching for God in a person - rather than in Infinite Reality - then that is what you will find - a "person" that you can imagine just might be the God for whom you are searching.

Did Jesus believe he was the God for whom Peter was searching? I doubt it; but then I see Jesus in a very different way than Peter was wanting to see him. I do not need to be saved from Godlessness as it seemed Peter thought he needed to be saved. I realize that I cannot be "missing God" and therefore, I am not in line to go searching for God in the first place - that is, in a single individual. My God is already in everything and everyone. Accordingly, I do not need to search for God as if God is something "out there" I can attain - if I only put my mind to it.

Ones like Moses and Peter, however, were not of my mind of believing in an Immanent God. They believed that God is something to be accessed, not appreciated for already being within. And people today are still following in the footsteps of Moses and Peter and are still insisting that God is a person - and still looking to find God in a person - like a real or imagined Jehovah or a Jesus.

I will not pursue the matter much here, but there is plenty of evidence in banned gospels - like that of *THE GOSPEL ACCORDING TO THOMAS* and *THE GOSPEL ACCORDING TO MARY MAGDALENE* - that Peter may have not listened to the real Jesus - probably because he was looking for something - or someone - else.

In truth, we see what we "expect" to see. In other words, we see what we "want to see." If we don't want to see Heaven on Earth, for whatever reason, then we will simply not see Heaven on Earth. If we want to see Hell on Earth, then that is exactly what we will see - Hell on Earth - and if there is not a real Hell, we will simply go about making one just so we can believe that we really believed the truth. That is the story of Arrogance in a nutshell; and there are many who are - pardon the pun - "as arrogant as Hell" and thus will insist they cannot be mistaken.

Take it as you wish to take it, but in my defense that Peter may not have seen Jesus as Jesus really was, in the final verse of *THE GOSPEL ACCORDING TO THOMAS*, Verse 114 (of 114), it is found: *Simon Peter said to them: Let Mary go out from among us because women are not worthy of the Life. Jesus said: See, I shall lead her, so that I will make her male, that she too may become a living spirit, resembling you males. For every woman who makes herself male will enter into the Kingdom of Heaven.*

I find in that verse, a man, Peter, who was intent on separating male from female - simply because he was about inequality. He did not want to see women as equal to men; and thus, even though Jesus may have at least hinted otherwise, eventually after the death of Jesus, Peter insisted that he was superior to all others by insisting that Jesus would choose one over another to "lead his church." I think Peter believed he was chosen by Jesus to "lead his church" only because Peter wanted to hear that message. Thus, after Jesus would die, Peter would go forward and declare the very "equality" in which Jesus probably believed to be a "lie of Satan" - in a manner of speaking.

Relating to Verse 114 of *THE GOSPEL ACCORDING TO THOMAS* offered above, why would Jesus offer that he could "make a female into a male"? I must admit that my thinking on that has evolved since first reviewing in 1979 - when I first read the verse; but I think Jesus is only offering that he can "persuade" Mary that she is really equal to Peter and all males. He was only offering that the *Kingdom of Heaven* is only a "kingdom of equals." Thus, anyone who sees him or herself as equal to others, in essence, belongs to the *Kingdom of Heaven*. For what it's worth, that is my current interpretation of that verse.

But why would Peter have argued that *women are not worthy of the Life* if he believed in the true equality of all persons? Why would have Peter argued that anyone is not worthy of the Life? Why? Because that was his vision - that some are more worthy than others; and therein is the story of the Christianity that Peter has, in fact, led - that some are more worthy than others. And what is the destination of those with whom Peter might disagree? In one word - Hell! Thus, if you do not believe in Peter and his vision of Jesus, you will end up in Hell; and therein is the great statement of inequality. Some are more worthy than others; and those who lack being worthy will go to Hell.

But take one moment - if you dare - and TRY ON INFINITY. What does it really say that the world is "probably Infinite"? For one thing, it DECLARES in somewhat astounding terms that if there is a God, that God has to EQUAL INFINITY. Now, how can it be that Infinity can be a Person? How can it be that the endless existence that we know must be "out there" can end at this point or that point? A "person" has to be something that can "end" - something that has limits, something that has a form, something that can be here and not there. That is what a "person" must be.

Infinity can't end, though, can it? That means God can't be a person because a person must end. If any of us took one single moment to think about it, we would know that. We would know that God can't be a person with whom any of us can relate because we would know that God must be a Presence that is WITHOUT END.

Think about it! Can you imagine a "person God" somehow swimming about in an endless pool? How could any individual swim in a pool that's actually equal to itself? I cannot even begin to imagine such. Can you? As far as I can see then, *IF THERE CAN BE NO INDIVIDUAL THAT IS GOD* - as if God is outside of the Infinite - then *GOD MUST EQUAL INFINITY.* How could it be otherwise? If you believe it can be otherwise, be so kind as to tell me how.

To reiterate, there can be no "personal God" outside of Infinity because Infinity includes all that is - and there can be no "outside of

Infinity." Can there? Therefore, if God exists, God must equal Infinity - and thus, BE EVERYWHERE.

And that is why Mom was a saint when she was born. She was a saint because there was no way she could be otherwise. Mom was a saint when she was born of my Grandma Gregory on April 12th, 1908 because there was no way she could have been "missing an Infinite God that must be everywhere." And I was a saint when I was born of my Mom, Clara Elizabeth Bessler, on December 3rd, 1941 because there is no way that Mom's womb could have been "missing an Infinite God."

So, in all probability, Clara was - and is - Saint Clara; and I am - in all probability - Saint Francis - and will be when I die too; and you are Saint Harry or Saint Harriet or Saint Jay or Saint Jane - or whatever your name is. But what good is it be a saint - unless you are aware of it? And therein, I think, is why there is so much tragedy and murder and rape and war and conflict in the world - because almost none of us know the truth that we are really saints. We are told we are sinners; and thus, we act like it.

A "saint" is one who has "found God" or who "has God" in his or her life. Well, what do you think? Can anyone really be "lacking an Infinite God"? Can there be any place that God can be missing? If so, can there be any place that is not Heaven - or any place that is Hell - with Hell being defined as "a place with a missing God"?

Infinity - and the notion thereof - KILLS IGNORANCE - if we let it. The question is - do we really want to kill ignorance? Do we want to admit to the truth and give up hanging on to stupidities we call wisdoms? Do we want to give up hoping to find a better life some-where else - and use God as an excuse - as if another place can be better because God must be there and not here? Do we want to take off the notions of the past that were based on the Earth being flat and God being UP IN THE SKY - or ON TOP OF A MOUNTAIN - or IN A PROPHET or IN A SPECIAL SON OF GOD? Do we want to FIND HEAVEN HERE ON EARTH? Or do we want to continue the "Mosaic" and "Peteraic" Traditions of Ignorance and insist that every baby is born in sin - meaning that every baby is born "separated from God"?

Sorry! I cannot believe it! Little baby, Clara Elizabeth Gregory, was not "missing God" when she emerged from the womb of Grandma Gregory on April 12th, 1908; and neither was she "missing God" when she passed at age of 96 on May 16th, 2004. Never in any moment of her life did Clara Elizabeth Gregory Bessler "miss God"; and that, in all probability, is the REAL TRUTH! In reality, no one can miss God because God can't be missed - being Infinity.

Now, wouldn't it be a whole lot wiser to know we are actually in the Paradise right now that we would seek later? WHY PUT PARADISE OFF? I suspect that if we do - keep putting Paradise off - we will never find it because in our continued ignorance, we will always search for God somewhere else - and never find it. Wouldn't it be so much better if we realized that EVERY PLACE IS HEAVEN - because there is no place where God cannot be? Let me leave it to you in a bit of verse. OK?

Thanks! (FWB)

Every Place Is Heaven

By
Francis William Bessler
3/1/2013 - 3/5/2013

Every place is Heaven;
it's just a matter of a view.
There is no God outside of life
that's not inside it too.
You cannot divide Infinity
into what's evil and what's good.
So, let everyone realize
All's one great brotherhood.

Every place is Heaven
because God is everywhere.
What makes a place a Heaven
is the Divinity that is there.
So, it stands to reason, My Friend,
if all existence is of God,
all existence must be Heaven
and where I stand I should applaud.

Every place is Heaven.
It's so very clear to me.
Every place that I do look
all I see is Divinity.
No flower can exist on its own.
Every tree needs sunlight.
No matter where I might look
there are only miracles in sight.

Every place is Heaven
as every dog does know.
Take your doggie for a walk;
let it follow its terrific nose.
And as you walk, be so gracious
as to let your doggie lead.
See the world as it does;
you'll see it filled with Divinity.

Every place is Heaven,
but God's neither Queen nor King.
God's not a person of sex,
rather only a Presence in everything.
Everyone belongs to God
and God belongs to everyone.
If we all really believed that,
there could be no wrong.

Every place is Heaven,
be you of generosity or of greed.
Heaven is not defined by conduct,
but by the Presence of God, indeed.
God is simply the source of life,
but not what life may do.
It is up to each of us in life
to believe and follow through.

Every place is Heaven,
but most do not see it that way.
Most see Nature as wonderful,
but do not see themselves in play.
No one is separate from Nature
no matter how much we hope it's so.
To know you are part of it all
is to be engulfed in the flow.

If Heaven is every place,
where does Hell fit in?
Hell is not a place - like Heaven.
It's when Heavenly creatures sin.
To sin is to believe in less worth
or to claim that of another.
Hell is only insisting
on a right to plunder.

If Heaven is every place,
what will happen when I die?
I suppose that if I found Heaven here,
I'll find it again next time.
But if I insisted on making life hard
for others in this life,
then it is likely I will continue
to live another life of strife.

Heaven is every place,
but it's up to each to choose.
If you insist that God is missing,
more than likely, you will lose.
Why waste life looking for Hell
when Paradise is at hand?
Open your mind and soul
and know you're in command.

Heaven is every place.
It cannot be otherwise.
How can it possibly be
that God is missing in this life?
Everyone is a Heavenly creature -
like an angel in disguise.
So, let's join in Heavenly song
and praise God for our lives.

Every place is Heaven;
it's just a matter of a view.
There is no God outside of life
that's not inside it too.
You cannot divide Infinity
into what's evil and what's good.
So, let everyone realize
All's one great brotherhood.

When
Bad Things Happen

By
Francis William Bessler
Laramie, Wyoming
4/22/2013

So, why did bad things happen in Boston last week? Why did two apparently somewhat "normal" young men decide to commit to a little terror and kill and maim fellow humans - with a couple of dastardly home made bombs? I suppose one could detail all sort of "reasons," but in the end, there was only one "reason" - as far as I can see; and that one reason is a little thing called *SHAME*.

Of course, many will disagree, but in my opinion, killing and hurting others *ALWAYS* stems from a sense of shame - not of others, but of oneself. No matter why one kills or hurts another, it can always be reduced to shame - again, self-shame. *Shame is the foundation of all evil,* in my opinion, because without it, no one would have any reason to either loathe themselves or loathe others. Shame is the great BLINDNESS that allows any individual to fail to see his or her own wonder - and then to take that emptiness into the world and just flail about - often intentionally murdering others in the process.

Show me any case of abuse - and I will show you "shame." That is, I can prove to you in every case that every single abuser lacked a sense of self-esteem. Amazingly, there is NO WAY I can abuse you unless I am not pleased with myself. If I am full of self-esteem and full of a sense of self-worth, there is no way I can abuse you. Why? Because in being so full of myself and my own worth, I would have no need of you to either enhance me or complete me. In "not needing you" to complete me, in terms of worth, then you need not fear that I will take something from you to complete me - including your life - as if in taking your life, I would be adding your life to my own.

And yet, shame is precisely what our human race - and the many factions within it - are born to believe. When we pop out of our mother's womb, it starts - and it never ends. We are constantly told we "must be ashamed" of this or that - about ourselves. What is that tale except to drum into our little minds that there is such a thing as good and bad - again, about each of us? We "must be ashamed" of ourselves because we are inherently a "bad lot." We are bad, bad, bad - unless somehow we turn things around and start to be good. Then good can come into the picture, but it can only happen if we first realize that we were bad in the first place. We must "admit" to being bad before we can turn around and achieve some semblance of good.

And as it begins, it continues. *Good is seldom emphasized in our lives. For the most part, Bad gets all the press.* Why, then, should we be surprised when one of us "bad guys" really acts bad? After all, bad "has to happen" for anyone to decide against it. Good cannot exist all by itself. Right? It MUST be preceded by evil somehow being overridden. Or so, many, if not most, believe - though not I!

I see ONLY GOOD in life because nothing in a Creation from God can be bad. If you see bad where there is only good - and thus make bad out of good - I would say you are a fool. I would say you are "wasting" the good of life to find bad. In my opinion, Good should always stand by Itself - and should never be contingent upon bad - or upon having to overcome some perceived bad or sin - in any way.

Ah, but we are so quick as to punish the bad ones because without such punishment, once again, good cannot triumph. Thus, as we DEMAND bad things to happen - and must preserve Shame for and to that end - we also DEMAND that some must be punished for being bad if others of us can hold our heads high and pound our chests and bellow - *Look at me! Am I not grand for not doing all those bad things that other jerk just did!*

WHEN BAD THINGS HAPPEN like that which happened in Boston last week, I shake my head and say - why? But my why is not why those bad things happened, but rather why we let them happen? I know full well why those bad things happened. They happened because participants on both sides of the proverbial "good and evil" sides decided in favor of them happening. That is "why" they happened. They happened because the two young men in the current episode were probably taught that they "must be ashamed" of themselves from the day they were born. *They were only acting according to character.*

Well, it is truly sad because that beginning is a humongous lie. No one should ever be told he or she "must be ashamed" of themselves. Why? Because it is not true. In truth, none of us are born in shame *BECAUSE ALL OF US ARE BORN IN GOD* and there is nothing about us that should be considered shameful; but if that is what we are told, then that is what we will tend to believe.

What fools we humans are! We put on clothes & masks and we cover up the good - and yet we don't believe we are covering anything that is good. We are really covering up the bad, the "shameful" - and that is why shame is so good. Good ole - *Saint Shame!* Without it, we would not have any reason to cover up the bad. So, it is *God Bless Shame!* - and God bless the sinner who knows he is a shameful specimen of existence.

But all that shame - it does exactly what we should expect. It makes us do all sort of "shameful" things. Little shame just grows into big shame; and before you know it, "little shameful beings" turn into "much bigger shameful beings." It is only a matter of growth. Shame starts little and then grows and grows and grows - until it begins to eclipse the shame of a subject and overflows into the world of others. Now, society thinks it really has something to resolve; but just imagine if society had never watered the seed of shame in the first place. JUST IMAGINE!

Imagine popping into the world as a baby - and being told from the start that you are such an angel. Imagine never being told that you must be ashamed of yourself for any reason. On the contrary, Imagine being told that you should be proud of yourself as a Wonderful Creature of God. Imagine being hugged and kissed because you are deserving of such on account of your being really "inherently good." Imagine being indoctrinated that there is no such place as Hell - and you have no need to fear such a place because it can only exist in the minds of those who believe in it; and a mind is not a place. Imagine hearing that there is only Heaven because Heaven is only being in the Presence of God and that since there is no place that God can be absent, Heaven must be present Everywhere. JUST IMAGINE!

I was listening to Fox TV commentator, Bill O'Reilly, last Friday night on the matter of the Boston bombings. One of the young perpetrators was dead and the other was wounded, in custody of police. Bill said, WITH GREAT CONTEMPT AND ANGER: *One of the brothers is already in Hell - and the other is soon to follow!* That may not be his exact words, but it is close. And I was under the impression that a fellow Christian should not judge. Very Interesting!

Hell! You can bet that Bill was taught "you must be ashamed of yourself" as a kid and you can be sure he was taught that if he is not ashamed of himself, he will go to Hell. You can be sure that he was taught that there is such a place called Hell - for bad ones to be discarded there in time. You can be sure, too, that Bill does not think he will follow those "other bad people" into Hell because he will have learned to be ashamed of himself and will not have done any evil things to grant him admission to Hell.

And what would the dead brother think of that? In all likelihood, that dead brother probably thought he was being one of the "good guys" and was only doing his part to "wipe out those shameful ones." That dead brother probably thought his action to "wipe out evil" would grant him some wonderful honor in his own Heaven. That dead brother probably believed in Hell too - and he probably believed that the likes of Bill O'Reilly must go there.

So, there it is! Chaos on parade - all due in the end to a sense of SELF-SHAME! One of one Hell doing bad to one of another Hell - and neither one believing that they are ones in Hell. Amazing! Isn't it?

To each, his or her own, but I have long ago given up any belief in Hell - as a place. I don't have to deal with it because I just don't believe in it - or that it can exist - let alone does exist. Where is this Hell for which the dead brother and Bill O'Reilly have such fondness? Where is it? If you tell me I am going to go to Hell, hey where is it? And if you cannot provide me a map to this wonderful place - for someone else, of course - then do not waste your time telling me about it. OK?

But Heaven! Hey, I think it does exist - and I can provide you a map right to it - to your own front door and back door and kitchen and living room and bath room and your yard and swimming pool - and your garden - and to the neighbors to the left and right of you and across the street. *There "ain't" no Hell because God cannot be dismissed from any place, but there is Heaven - simply because there is no such place as Hell.*

Now, ask Bill O'Reilly and the young dead brother if they agree. Where is Hell for them? One has gone on to find it probably doesn't exist - AS A PLACE - but he has probably found that the other place - Heaven - doesn't exist either. At least, not in the way of expectation. Given the young dead brother was somewhat of a radical Islamist, he probably expected he would be greeted by his Allah and then given over to 700 young virgins - or is it 70 - or 17 - or 7? It is unlikely, of course, that his Allah was there waiting for him and it is unlikely that even 1 virgin was there to say - *Welcome, Brother! Here I am! Take me for your own - and give me children!*

And when Mr. Bill passes on, it is totally unlikely that his God will be there waiting for him - nor his Jesus. Bill will probably be on his own, just like the current dead brother.

I am on my own too. I just didn't have to die to find that out. *I have Heaven Here.* I do not need to find it in any number of virgins or even in a Jesus. Jesus does not need to save me because I have never needed to be saved - being full of God as we all are. How can one "full of God" need salvation? How can one who is "full of God" have any need for "more of God"? And how can I not be "full of God" if God - being truly Infinite - is everywhere and in everything?

Did the young dead brother believe he is "full of God" just like me, however? Of course not. Does Bill O'Reilly believe he is "full of God" just like me? Of course not. *I can do no evil because I see no need for evil.* It may be as simple as that; but how long and how many lives must the dead brother and Mr. Bill live to realize that truth?

I wonder!

Thanks! (FWB)

The Sands Of Yucatan

A free style song or poem
by
Francis William Bessler
Laramie, Wyoming
Composed at
Hotel Riu Palace resort hotel
in
Cancun, Mexico
4/30/2013;
modified slightly at home in
Laramie, Wyoming
5/5/2013

I'm standing here in the sands of Yucatan
in dear ole Mexico.
I'm wondering if man will ever come to understand
how easy Life is to know.
It's not complicated - just don't overrate
a sense of community in the flow.
It's not a matter of three or four - or more -
to set your life aglow.
It's only one. Start there for your fun.
Look at yourself - and from there, Go.

I'm standing here in the sands of Yucatan
in a place they call Cancun.
There's lots of people here, playing about the Square,
but only some are singing a meaningful tune.
There's no meaning to life - unless we're all alike;
that's the key to finding the truth.
There's no strangers about - amidst all the shouts,
regardless of styles and perfumes.
Just be amazed - that we're all the same
as equal children of the Sun and the Moon.

I'm standing here in the sands of Yucatan -
about a hundred miles from Chichen-Ista -
where ancient Mayans thrived, believed that to survive,
they had to sacrifice some of their people.
It's the same ole story - in which many find glory;
it's the way of many temples.
Sadly, each must vow - and to a choice god, bow -
to provide necessary example.
It's said, just do your part - never mind your heart -
lest your nation itself be trampled.

I'm standing here in the sands of Yucatan -
and out there is an ocean.
People are having fun - swimming under the Sun;
it's like a big vacation.
It's the way it should be - that's my belief -
all should belong to that nation.
There's no reason why - we can't survive
as one without commotion.
Just treat each the same - that's the way
of living my Yucatan notion.

I'm standing here in the sands of Yucatan
and my vision is so clear.
Everyone's the same - that's why bright is the day;
there's no need to live in fear.
Just smile and say - Have a Happy Day -
and wipe away all of those tears.
Come along with me - and let's be free
to get drunk without a beer.
Toss away your cares, know life is fair -
and Believe that Heaven is Here.

I'm standing here in the sands of Yucatan -
gentle from head to toe.
My arms stretch wide - as I comprise
the best that man can know.
The sky is bright. In me is no fight
because my soul is all aglow.
The reason, my friend, is I have no sin
because God is in my growth.
There is no way - I should be ashamed
of my Yucatan soul.

I'm standing here in the sands of Yucatan
in dear ole Mexico
as the sands - between my toes commands
to know the worth of my soul.
All I need, for sure, to be free
is to know I'm equal, you know.
It's as simple as that. Never mind the flap.
Just get lost in the flow.
You can be - just as free as me -
and play in the Yucatan Bowl.

Know Thyself!

By
Francis William Bessler
Laramie, Wyoming
5/16/2013

In one of my favorite books - *THE GOSPEL ACCORDING TO THOMAS* (banned by church and state in the 4th Century) - at the end of Verse 3, Jesus said: *If you know yourselves, then you will be known and you will know that you are sons of the Living Father. But if you do not know yourselves, then you are in poverty and you are poverty.*

That is quite a statement. Isn't it? If true, it is to say that the only really important knowledge one needs in life is some "knowledge of oneself" - and of others by virtue of that knowledge. I will continue this little discussion a little later. OK?

To interrupt my main strain of thought, however, let me offer a non-scholarly opinion. When people ask me about so called gospels like *THE GOSPEL ACCORDING TO THOMAS,* mostly they wonder if they are authentic. My answer to that is I DON'T KNOW, but neither do I know that the regular gospels of the *BIBLE* are authentic either. I mean I was not there when any of them were written.

Being a writer myself, however, I am almost 100 % sure that all gospels were written by men - not by God. I am writing this article. God is not writing it. I am a man - not God. Thomas was a man - not God. Matthew was a man - not God. Mark was a man - not God. Luke was a man - not God. John was a man - not God. All gospels were written by men - not God.

As a man - and not God - I can err - or make up things to make a point as if they really happened. Just because I may have written something does not make it true. Does it? In all likelihood, those who wrote about Jesus probably "created events" to better persuade potential converts to follow them.

Did Jesus really heal the sick and dying? Who knows? Some gospels claim he did; but, again, one has to keep in focus why those gospels were written - to convert others of another faith or belief to a faith in Jesus. Could Mark have lied to make a convert? Of course, he could have. If I can lie to make a convert of you, then Mark or John or whoever could have lied to make others converts to their cause.

I think it worthwhile to point out one very likely fabrication; and if one of the gospel writers could have fabricated one event, there is no reason to believe that other events could not have been fabricated too.

Case in point: the story in *THE GOSPEL OF JOHN* that offers that Jesus raised his friend, Lazarus, from the dead after Lazarus had been dead for three days. The reason I believe that was fabricated by John is that John is believed to have written his gospel long after the first three - Mark, Matthew, and Luke (in that order) wrote their gospels. All three of the earlier gospel writers offer various miracles by Jesus to illustrate that Jesus had some extraordinary power. Yet none of the earlier three mention anything about Jesus raising Lazarus from the dead. Just how likely is it that three gospel writers could all either omit or forget a miracle so great that it is considered to be the "greatest miracle of all time"? How likely is it that three gospel writers - who all feature miracles by Jesus - could have possibly bypassed the telling of a story so great as the raising of someone from the dead? How likely is that?

Of course, we should all be left to make our own judgments about that, but I have long ago decided that the chance is almost zilch that three people, writing about the same man, would ignore telling the story of the "greatest miracle of all time." That is to imply that the story by John was fabricated; and therein is one example of one likely fabrication offered in the regular gospels of the *BIBLE;* and if there is one, there may be many more too. Such is as it is.

One thing that is particularly irking to me is an assumption that some writing was written by God - or especially inspired of God where other writings were not and are not. It is really irking to have some one ask me - Do you not believe in *THE WORD OF GOD?* And they ask that as if they are absolutely sure that the writing of reference is really "the word of God" as if no man ever had a part in writing it. Accordingly, in being so sure that a writing is "scriptural" as they say - or written by God - no one should doubt what it says.

Thus, you are given to believe that you are not supposed to challenge the "word of God" - dictated by God but typed or scrawled by the likes of Francis William Bessler or Matthew or Mark or Luke or John - or my favorite, Thomas. You are supposed to believe that God really authored this article, but I was only His instrument in writing it - like being one who simply took notes from a real God who dictated to me what I should write.

But that claim is probably false. God does not write gospels. Men have - and men may continue to do so. I think it is very important to keep that in mind when reviewing any work - be it so called "scriptural" or otherwise. I am a man, not God. All the gospels ever written were by men - not God. The Book of Mormon was written by a man, Joseph Smith - not God. The Book of Islam was written by a man, Mohammed - not God. If we do not approach any writing with that knowledge, then we will likely never attain any true wisdom in life. Why? *Because wisdom is something we know for its intrinsic truth or argument - not for what someone else claimed it to be - or claims it to be.*

Is *THE GOSPEL ACCORDING TO THOMAS* authentic? Did Jesus really say what Thomas claimed he said? I DON'T KNOW, but my own approach to any writing is to ask myself if it makes sense. *Does a writing make sense?* In the end, it may or may not be "authentic" in terms of being a real statement - or something that Jesus really did say; but knowing as I do that Thomas was not God and that Thomas may have not heard what Jesus really did say, I can take all that Thomas says with that proverbial grain of salt. *Let me salt every thing I read and let nothing that I read be taken like it is without possibility of error.*

I do not know the complete history of THE GOSPEL ACCORDING TO THOMAS because whether it is authentic or not, we have no original - just like we have no original from any of the others either. All we have are rewrites of what may have been originals. In the case at point, the Apostle of Jesus named Thomas may have taken some kind of notes during the life of Jesus and jotted them down - and that may be what THE GOSPEL ACCORDING TO THOMAS really represents; but then it may also be true that someone wrote in the name of Thomas and wrote his original a century after the Apostle Thomas died. I DO NOT KNOW - but neither does anyone else in our times.

Some scholars argue that THE GOSPEL ACCORDING TO THOMAS was probably not written by the Apostle, Thomas and was probably written in the 2nd Century. Maybe they are right; and maybe they are wrong too. Maybe the first gospel was that of Apostle, Thomas, but given that an earlier writing had to be rewritten to be recorded safely due to some corruption of an earlier source, maybe the earliest "rewrite" was written in the 2nd Century. Who knows? I DO NOT.

I do know, however, that THE GOSPEL ACCORDING TO THOMAS was hidden away in a cave from the 4th Century or thereabouts to 1945 when a copy of it was found in a cave off the Nile River in Egypt, near a town called Nag Hammadi. The copy found was in a Coptic - or earlier Egyptian - language. In all likelihood, THE GOSPEL OF THOMAS was buried in the 4th Century to keep it from being destroyed because the Christian church of the time had just been recognized as legitimate by Emperor Constantine - and Constantine wanted the church to adopt a canon of only some gospels and ban and destroy all others - in order to make rule within the church and state more commanding - or controlling.

Well, in outlawing all books that did not fit a certain criterion, many were tossed on the scrap heap. But rather than follow an edict to destroy all books, someone probably stashed works like THE GOSPEL ACCORDING TO THOMAS away - and it would be hidden and unknown from that time of its being stashed in the 4th Century to 1945 - when it was discovered by accident by a peasant going through a cave where it was hidden. And the rest is history, as they say. The found Coptic GOSPEL OF THOMAS has been translated into lots of languages, including my English, and thus I (and we) have available for review something that most of post Jesus history has not. Thanks to Fate; and thanks to a peasant stumbling onto a hidden jar in a cave in Egypt in modern times, we now have a somewhat "alternate" view of Jesus.

Is it authentic? Again, that is not for me to either know or say. I DO NOT KNOW, but according to my own approach to any writing, *"if it makes sense, it may be so."*

Personally, I consider two gospels tossed on the scrap heap in the 4th Century to be among my favorite writings - *THE GOSPEL ACCORDING TO THOMAS* and *THE GOSPEL ACCORDING TO MARY MAGDALENE* - both of which I feature as selections in my website - www.una-bella-vita. com. I do not consider either of those gospels completely authentic for no way to prove they are or are not authentic, but I consider both of them as immensely important as "food for thought." Feel welcome to check them out as you wish.

For what it's worth, I have gone through the trouble of formatting each of these gospels so that the pages can be printed and cut into segments. The printed segments can then be inserted like photos into clear sleeves of a standard 4" by 6" twenty-four page photo book for easy reference. My purpose in that is to make it easy to make a handbook of either or both gospels - and then people can either browse them on their own - or perhaps form discussion groups to discuss them. Again, feel welcome to do as you wish. OK?

Also, I reference the Gospels of Thomas and Mary Magdalene considerably in my general writings as found in my *OUT IN THE OPEN* selections of my website. In Volume 7 of that series, I offer a personal interpretation of both gospels as well. That is not to say that my interpretation of various verses is correct, but only that I offer my opinion.

Everything is opinion, as far as I am concerned - and that includes any interpretation of my favorite gospels. I am always learning. I pride myself in that. Accordingly, an interpretation of today may be quite different than an interpretation of yesterday - including the 3rd Verse of *THE GOSPEL ACCORDING TO THOMAS* I am featuring in this article. I may see a meaning tomorrow that I did not see yesterday. Having an open mind always allows for that. Doesn't it?

I consider both of my favorite gospels to be like *LIVING DOCUMENTS* - meaning that each reading can offer a new light. If some verse does not make sense today, read it again tomorrow - and it might make more sense. If not, it's ok to skip a verse too. If a verse does not make sense, it just might be phony for having been added to a version by a party other than the original author, too. That is always a possibility. Isn't it?

For what it's worth, there are 114 verses of *Jesus said* statements in *THE GOSPEL ACCORDING TO THOMAS*. It's not a narrative - like the gospels in the *BIBLE* - but 114 verses is a lot of food for thought - even if a bit of it might be somewhat bitter - or incorrect or misleading. Ah, but most of *THE GOSPEL ACCORDING TO THOMAS*, in my opinion, is as sweet as it could be for its summary tremendous wisdom. I highly recommend it!

Now, let me continue.

Regarding the earlier quote that *IF YOU KNOW YOURSELVES, YOU WILL BE KNOWN*, is it true? I am not sure about the last part of that - the part about my being known if I know myself - but I don't think the last part is very important anyway. I think it is definitely true, though, that you can't know me unless I know myself; and "knowing myself" is the important part of the verse. What does it really matter what you think of me - or think you know about me. It only matters about what I think - and hopefully know - about myself. It is knowledge of myself that is critical - not others perception of me.

But who really knows who they really are? Do you know yourself? Do you know who you really are? Better put from my point of view, however, is - do I know myself? *Do I know who I really am?*

So, who am I really? If I am to gauge an answer to that based on the conclusion of Verse 3 of *THE GOSPEL ACCORDING TO THOMAS*, Jesus would answer that question by telling me that, in effect, *"if I know that I am a son of the Living Father, then I will know who I am."* Right? I mean, if you believe that the Jesus of Thomas is accurate, the end result is that "if I know myself, I will know that I am a son of the Living Father." And since everyone of us is the same - all sons of the Living Father - then if you do not know yourself as a "son of the Living Father," then you do not know yourself.

Makes it pretty simple, doesn't it? All I have to do to really know who I am is to know I am "a son of the Living Father"; and if I do not know myself as such, then what I do know is false - or what I think I know is false. If I think I am something different than a "son of the Living Father," then I really have no handle on who I really am; and it is worthwhile, I think, that "son" in this verse probably does not mean "male progeny," but rather "any progeny" - male, female, or otherwise.

How many do you know, however, who would answer the question about who they are in those terms- about being a "progeny of the Living Father"? If someone were to come up to you and ask you "Who are you?" - what would be your answer? Would you reply - I AM A SON (or progeny) OF THE LIVING FATHER? Or would you go about answering the question with either an "I don't know" or some other answer?

Notice, too, that in Verse 3 of *THE GOSPEL ACCORDING TO THOMAS*, Jesus did not say what one would expect him to say if so many who preach about Jesus were (and are) right. Notice that Jesus did not say that to know myself, I should answer the question about who I am in terms of being a sinner. Did Jesus say such as this: *If you know yourselves, then you will be known and you will know that you are sinners?*

No!

But "being a sinner" and not a "son of the Living Father" is exactly what so many traditional Christians believe. Are we "sinners"? I do believe that the Jesus of Thomas would argue that if you think you are a sinner, then you think wrongly - and consequently, if you think wrongly, then you really do not know yourself. And if you believe you are a sinner, then the last part of Verse 3 is true about you too. *YOU ARE IN POVERTY AND YOU ARE POVERTY.*

Presto! A very succinct explanation of why the world, in general, is so impoverished. In effect, almost no one knows they are *"sons of the Living Father."* Why? At least partly because for all these many hundreds of years, we have had the key to really knowing who we are, but we have buried the lesson.

Why was the lesson buried? Perhaps that is subject to debate, but I believe the answer lies simply in "control." *One cannot control another unless that other is led to believe he or she is inadequate by him or herself.* Thus, the REAL JESUS was probably tossed out and a substitute was put in his place - with what amounts to a totally contrary doctrine. Why? So that some could rule over others - in the name of a Jesus who would have forbid it.

Examine yourself. Do you have need to rule over another? If you answered "yes," then in all likelihood, you do not believe you are a "son of the Living Father." In my opinion, if you do believe you are a son of the Living Father - or son of God - then you will also know that the one upon whom you would impose control is equally another son of the Living Father. I think the evidence of everyday life will tell you that only those who believe they have the right to impose control on others do not believe they are themselves "sons of the Living Father." In essence, they do not know themselves - according to the dictum of the Jesus of Thomas; and I believe the Jesus of Thomas is absolutely right. How about you?

So, where did it go wrong? How come we have been led to believe that we are sinners with that message being preached like it is the ONLY GOSPEL worth believing? Why did the so called Apostle Paul preach otherwise? Why did he preach the opposite message of the likely REAL JESUS? Why did he preach that "all are sinners and all fall short of the glory of God"? Why? Ultimately, I think he preached that lesson because he did not "know himself," as the REAL JESUS would have had him do; but he probably failed to know the real message of Jesus because he probably never heard it. That is being fair to Paul.

Keep in mind that Paul did not know Jesus in his lifetime. He only "came to know" Jesus after Jesus was crucified - crucified probably for arguing that people are not really true sinners - in terms of being "short of the glory of God." In all likelihood, Paul never heard that Jesus ever taught that to know yourself is to know you are a "son of the Living Father." That is probably why Paul carried on as he did - sincerely believing in the Jesus others preached to him; and given the lack of reference to Thomas in the so called "scriptures" after Jesus died, it is likely that Thomas was not one of the "others" that Paul may have heard.

Where was Thomas after Jesus died? What happened to him? Thomas was one of the original twelve apostles of Jesus; and yet after Jesus died, it seems that Thomas just disappeared. What happened to him? Who knows? But reasonably if he was not part of the Israeli segment of Christianity after Jesus died, then it is likely he left Israel - and took his notes about Jesus (or gospel) with him - thereby depriving the likes of Paul from any exposure to an alternate view of Jesus. Paul probably depended entirely upon Israeli Christians like Peter and associates - and since Peter probably did not subscribe to the notion that all are "sons of the Living Father," Paul probably never heard the idea.

Again, what happened to Thomas? No one knows; and it has been my experience that no one wonders either. Some scholars think that Thomas may have been of Greek heritage. If so, maybe Thomas originated from a foreign country like Egypt - and perhaps, from a city like Alexandria, Egypt - known for its Greek oriented culture. Maybe after Jesus died, Thomas returned to Alexandria - or some other foreign establishment. If so, he would have taken his "notes" or "gospel" with him. Makes sense to me.

Some say that Thomas eventually made his way to India and championed a form of Christianity there. I do not know, but whatever happened to him, he probably left Israel and took his version of Jesus with him - thus subjecting Israeli Christianity to a single view of Jesus - that of Peter and his comrades. With Thomas gone, Paul may have never heard that "his" Jesus really preached that all are "sons of the Living Father."

And as it may have happened to Paul, it has happened to lots of us who claim we are Christian - myself included. How was Paul to know that Jesus probably really believed that "knowledge of self is the most important knowledge of all" if no one told him? How are you to believe in that message if all you ever hear is that Jesus preached that all are sinners and that all "fall short of the glory of God"?

Indeed, who would really want to "know himself (or herself)" if one's perception of oneself is that one is "short of the glory of God"? Sadly, Paul probably believed that Jesus taught we are all "short of the glory of God" because that is what he heard from Peter - and associates. If Thomas was right, however, Jesus probably taught that all are "full of the glory of God." That would put a whole different light on "oneself." Wouldn't it?

As a kid growing up, no one told me that Jesus may have preached that I am "a son of the Living Father" because, in all fairness to everyone who ever taught me anything - no one was aware of such an expression. My dear Dad did not know that he was "a son of the Living Father." My dear

Mom - who passed away exactly nine years ago today on May 16th, 2004 - did not know she was "a son of the Living Father." My seven siblings, 4 brothers and 3 sisters, did not know they were "sons of the Living Father." Leastwise, none of us ever addressed ourselves as that. My dear and wonderful priest, Father Carroll, did not know he was "a son of the Living Father." No! No one knew - and that is why I did not know for a long, long time in this wonderful life; but I do know now; and I encourage all to share in that knowledge.

Hey! Time to say "Good Night!" In the end, we all have to make up our own minds; and that is the way it should be. Right? Are you "a son of the Living Father"? I do believe I am because I believe it is impossible to be other than that. No one can escape being a "progeny of the Living Father" - no matter how much they might try - or wish it to be.

Indeed, it's quite a notion - being "a son of the Living Father." I think it is THE KEY to living a good life. *Knowing yourself is important, but knowing yourself as what you truly are - a son of the Living Father - is the most important knowledge of all.* At least I think so.

Let me leave you with the front part of that Verse 3 I quoted up front. If you would, and if you dare, try this one on for size. I offered the last part at the beginning of this article, but the entire verse is below. I leave you to ponder the lines - and maybe come to *KNOW THYSELF* - not in any personal detail - but *JUST GENERALLY* as an equal *"Son of The Living Father"!*

Really, shouldn't that be ENOUGH?

JESUS SAID: IF THOSE WHO LEAD YOU SAY TO YOU: "SEE, THE KINGDOM IS IN HEAVEN," THEN THE BIRDS OF THE HEAVEN WILL PRECEDE YOU. IF THEY SAY TO YOU: "IT IS IN THE SEA," THEN THE FISH WILL PRECEDE YOU. BUT THE KINGDOM IS WITHIN YOU AND IT IS WITHOUT YOU. IF YOU (WILL) KNOW YOURSELVES, THEN YOU WILL BE KNOWN AND YOU WILL KNOW THAT YOU ARE SONS OF THE LIVING FATHER. BUT IF YOU DO NOT KNOW YOURSELVES, THEN YOU ARE IN POVERTY AND YOU ARE POVERTY.

Thanks! (FWB)

Don't Do
What You Hate!

By
Francis William Bessler
Laramie, Wyoming
5/31/2013

DO NOT DO WHAT YOU HATE. Believe it or not, the "*Left Wing" Jesus* supposedly said that some two thousand years ago. A "Right Wing" Jesus, of course, would not agree. Who knows which Jesus really lived? But this is not about that. This is only to pursue an argument that a *Left Wing Jesus* may have made.

What is a "left wing Jesus"? Just the opposite of a "right wing Jesus." What is a "right wing Jesus," then? The "right" of anything, politically and spiritually speaking, seems to be a position that the individual must serve the common good and must not think he or she has the right to step out of bounds from some so called "norm." Right wingers flourish all over the place, prancing about in attempted "dictation." There is some "common good standard" - and all must subject themselves to it. That is the basics of a "right wing" pattern of thought.

Currently, right wing politicians in America are busy trying to impose two specific standards that they believe should be "standard for all" - all abortions should be illegal and homosexuality should be banned. Those are just two of the current examples of right wing thinking. Essentially, a right wing person is one who believes that some common good standards must be demanded - and no exceptions made. The idea there is that an individual should not have the right to decide for him or herself what is right for him or her - but that some standards should be decided by some that all must abide - or obey.

The "left wing" of thought, then, as the opposite of right wing thinking, must stand for the right of an individual to decide for him or herself what is right or wrong. A "lefty" could stand on both sides of an issue - by virtue of an attitude of tolerance. One might choose to oppose abortion - or favor it. One might choose to condone homosexuality - or oppose it; but regardless of decision, a lefty considers it is his or her right to decide an issue - but only for him or herself.

A lefty cannot say it is right for him or her to choose abortion, but it is not right for another to choose for him or herself. A lefty cannot say it is right for him or her to practice homosexuality, but it is wrong for another. A lefty can argue something is wrong or right for all, but a lefty cannot impose that decision on all others. A "righty," however, considers that a given choice or standard should be commanded of all.

If I were a homosexual and took the position that you must follow in my path, then I would be a "right wing homosexual." I must admit that right wing homosexuality is almost an impossibility because homosexuals tend to be very freedom oriented, making it unlikely they would demand their practices for all, but the possibility is there.

What has any of this to do with my initial statement that Jesus may have stated that I should not do what I hate? I think it has everything to do with it.

But before I get into my reasoning about that, let me supply the "proof" that Jesus may have said such a thing at all. Keep in mind that I offer that Jesus "may" have said such a thing - not that he definitely did. As a "left wing Christian," I guess I am open to the possibility that Jesus "may" have said something - and let my reasoning powers decide for myself how likely that "may" may be. OK?

My source is THE GOSPEL ACCORDING TO THOMAS. In previous blogs - as in other writings contained in my OUT IN THE OPEN selection of my website - I offer a little history of THE GOSPEL ACCORDING

TO THOMAS. I will not do that here; but just assuming for argument sake that *THE GOSPEL ACCORDING TO THOMAS* is legitimate and that Jesus may have said what is claimed by that writing, let me cite the verse I am talking about.

In Verse 6 of the referenced work, it is stated: *His disciples asked Him: Wouldst thou that we fast, and how should we pray, (and) should we give alms and what diet should we observe? Jesus said: Do not lie and do not do what you hate, for all things are manifest before Heaven. For there is nothing hidden that shall not be revealed and there is nothing covered that shall remain without being uncovered.*

Imagine, for a moment, a Jesus really saying that. I think you have to imagine the audience as well as the teacher, though. Who was the audience of that teaching? One would expect "all Jews" - or mostly Jews - since the location of both Jesus and his audience was Israel. So, who would have comprised the likely audience of Jews? People who have been taught that what could be called THE LAW is the most important aspect of Jewish life. The Law (of Moses, mostly) was the agenda that all good Jews must obey - lest they be banned by Jewish Law from participating in a society of Jews.

Never mind the details for the moment. The whole idea is that a society had meaning only as a society in general - and that individuals within that society have meaning only related to the society in general. In other words, individuals have no worth by themselves. Their only worth is in respect to some general consensus or general community.

Gaining some extra clarification from the quote at hand, Jews - or good Jews - were expected to "fast, pray, give alms, and observe some restricted diet" to have any meaning. From what I have ever learned about Jewish life and Jewish Law, I expect that to be true. It stands to reason, doesn't it? If I have meaning only related to something outside of myself, then it stands to reason that I would have to "obey" something outside myself to have meaning. My fasting is to "impress" some outside factor. My praying is to "impress" some outside factor. My giving alms is to "impress" some outside factor. My observing some restricted diet is to "impress" some outside factor. Never mind what the "outside factor" is, the whole idea is that there is some "outside factor" that I must "obey" to have any personal meaning.

So, the "Jewish audience" of the above circumstance can be assumed to include Jews who were taught that no individual has meaning unto himself - but has meaning only as part of a general community or a nation - in this case, Israel. In other words, most, if not all, in the audience of Jesus in this case can be assumed to consist of "right wing" members of a community that did not recognize any individual autonomy. You had to abide by THE LAW - whatever that general law was - or perhaps be executed for treason to the community; and if my impression of Jewish Law is correct, many errant Jews leading up to the time of Jesus were "stoned to death" as punishment for disobedience - or non-compliance to "The Law." That is what "right wing" societies do - they "stone to death" or "kill" in some fashion any who disagree with a norm.

One perfect example, perhaps, is the crucifixion of Jesus. Jesus was one to challenge prevailing thought - probably that the individual has no meaning outside of national or religious identity - and for that challenge, he was "killed." Such is the response of many "right wing" fanatics - not all, for sure - but many.

Now, according to the above quote, we have what could be called a "left wing" person addressing a "right wing" mentality of people. That right wing group expected that to have any personal meaning, each had to "fast, pray, give alms, and observe some restricted diet." Thus, someone in the little class of a left wing teacher, Jesus, proposed the expected of a "good Jew." *Hey, Jesus, tell us what we expect. Tell us that we have to fast. Tell us that we have to pray - to an outside God called Jehovah, of course. Tell us that we should give alms. Tell us what diet we should observe. Tell us what we expect is true.*

That is putting into perspective the circumstance of the above speculative statement - Jesus commenting about those things of expected Jewish manners to Jewish persons. But what did Jesus say? He did not say what was expected of a "good Jewish, right wing, person." Did he? No! He actually implied that any of the expected "right wing" manners is foolishness. What did he say when asked if his right wing audience should follow expected Jewish norms?

Well, as a "left wing Christian," he answered like I would have answered. Never mind all your social customs and social laws and social commandments to have any meaning. Let me tell you what I think is important. *Do not lie and do not do what you hate.* Wow! What an answer! Then Jesus added: *For all things are manifest before Heaven. For there is nothing hidden that shall not be revealed and there is nothing covered that shall remain without being uncovered.*

Now, let us assume a different audience. Let us imagine Jesus talking to a group of people who have not been overwhelmed yet with some social agenda. Imagine Jesus talking to some who had never heard of a JEWISH LAW - or some restricted communal standards. Imagine someone in a crowd of open minded people asking Jesus: *Hey, Jesus, what would you recommend as an "ideal way of life"?*

What would a *Left Wing Jesus* say to such a crowd, based on the above quote. I think he would say the same thing as he did to the negative Jews, but in a positive way, expecting his students to be more positive minded. A positive person does not say "do not do this or that." A positive person says "do this or that."

So, what would the "do" be in this case? I think it would likely translate in a manner like this: *TELL THE TRUTH - AND DO ONLY THAT WHICH YOU LOVE.* It's really the same thing as saying *DO NOT LIE AND DO NOT DO WHAT YOU HATE,* but personally I relate much better to the positive than the negative; and thus, I hear: *TELL THE TRUTH AND DO ONLY THAT WHICH YOU LOVE.*

But why would Jesus - or any teacher - offer such a recommendation? Why? Because one's worth is not tied to some social norm. If one's worth is not tied to some social norm - or commandment of outside law - then one is left to fend for oneself, as it were. In that light, for my own sake, I should always "tell the truth" because telling a lie is deceptive - not only to others, but to myself. If I lie, I lie not only to you, but I lie to myself as well. No one who wants to appreciate him or herself will lie to him or herself - and therefore, if I do not lie to myself, then it stands to reason, I would have no reason to lie to you either. But, you see, my commandment to tell myself the truth is for my sake - not for some general norm. I can recommend that the general norm be "telling the truth," but the reason I should tell the truth is not for the sake of community, but for my own sake.

Now, let's address the other "commandment of self worth" - doing only that which you love. Why is that so important? Why? *Because one becomes what one does.* Thus, if I insist on "doing what I hate, *I will become what I hate*" - and, more than likely, I will end up being miserable. No one is happy being miserable. Thus, to avoid hating and being miserable, do only that which you love. It makes sense to a "left wing" person like me. How about you?

The key, though, is to do what you love, not what someone else loves. Let each decide on their own what to love. Anything else is pretense. If I pretend to love in such a way that is intended to impress someone else, I can never impress myself with my pretense because I cannot "get away from myself." I can fool everyone of you, but I can never fool myself - though I guess I can get lost in trying to fool you and lose track of what I really am and what I really love.

In fact, that may be the exact cause of much insanity in the world - people pretending to be something they are not and eventually getting lost in their pretense, as if in a cloud of their own making.

In the above quote - or lesson - however - Jesus said: *For all things are manifest before Heaven. For there is nothing hidden that shall not be revealed and there is nothing covered that shall remain without being uncovered.* But that is only a way of saying: I cannot fool myself. So, why waste any time in life trying to "fool myself" or "lie to myself"? Why waste any time at all in "doing what I hate" if doing what I hate makes me miserable?

Does any of that make any sense to you? It sure does to me; but I must admit that I live in a world that sees the world as wonderful and all things as being Divine - or to emphasize wonderful and Divine - let me say, *Wonderful and Divine.* I do not live in a world that believes there is any separation of existence into so called "good" and "evil"; and I live in a world that does not recognize the usefulness of any sacrifice to some so called "god."

Why is sacrifice of myself to some god - or God - useless? Because it implies that I need to address my source of life further for something other than what I have been initially given. If I am satisfied with the Gift of Life with which I have been endowed, then I would have no need to ask for more. *It is "asking for more" that constitutes the rite and practice of sacrifice.* The Jews of old required sacrifice to their god because they were not satisfied with what they had. They wanted "more" - and thus they deceived themselves into believing they could have "more" - if only they convinced their god they deserved more. Presto - sacrifice became a ritual of The Law of Moses, perhaps best understood as prayer to receive additional benefits.

But I do not need sacrifice because I believe that I should be happy with what I have - or be happy with that which I have been given in terms of the Gift of Life. I live in a world that is "FULLY GOD" and not divided between some assumed "God-less" and some "God-full." Everything is "full of God" to me because I cannot imagine there being a place or a person that lacks "God."

Everything was not God to the Jews, however. They failed to believe that God is in all. In fact, they believed that God can actually be for some and not for others. Witness the exclusion of the Egyptians from being included as "of God" in the time of Moses. It was a perception of the Jews of the time of Moses that God favored - or could favor - one people over another. How could that be?

It is a matter of opinion, of course, but I totally disagree with any notion that claims that God can favor one over another. How could it be that a true God could favor one race called the Jews and disfavor another called the Egyptians if that true God is truly IN everything? In my opinion, it is completely ludicrous to believe that an "omni-present" God can be missing from anyone or anything. Accordingly, the Jewish belief that God could favor them over others has to be sheer fantasy.

Anyway, my world is up to me - and me alone - and I have to decide what to love while allowing others to choose for themselves as well. It is "my soul" that I have to inherit - not someone else's soul. *My God is inside of me and therefore, cannot judge me. I have to "judge myself."* Thus, it is up to me to choose what to love; and I think that is what Jesus was trying to tell the Jews of his time.

You are wonderful as an individual creation - or creature - of all of Creation. Your wonder is tied to being part of Creation, not to a nation within Creation. You are not a Jew. You are a human. Your worth is not tied to some arbitrary law invented by some arbitrary people, but your worth is decided simply by being a member of a *DIVINE CREATION*. Accept that - and you will respect yourself as a holy member of a Holy Creation. Deny that - and you will become lost in some contrived ritual of mankind, hoping for "more" than Life Itself.

So, what do you think? Is the Jesus of *THE GOSPEL ACCORDING TO THOMAS* right? *Does that Jesus make sense?* Well, I believe in the Jesus of Thomas because so much of what that Jesus says makes sense to me. I do understand, however, how it could be that only a few of his audience might have understood him. It's good to keep that in mind, too, as we assess the possibilities of a Jesus gone wrong - or a Jesus being misunderstood - or a Jesus being misused.

In the end, we all hear what we can hear. By the saying - *ALL THINGS ARE MANIFEST BEFORE HEAVEN*, I hear "I cannot fool myself." Others, perhaps like Peter and many of the so called disciples of Jesus, probably heard something entirely different - like - GOD KNOWS ALL AND YOU CAN'T FOOL GOD - as if to use the instruction to pose yourself as God to make others do as you bid.

To a great degree, I think, the "right wing" Christian doctrine of *"The Holy Spirit"* is but an extension of GOD KNOWS ALL AND YOU CAN'T FOOL GOD - in order to use God as an excuse for some authority. I don't think Jesus intended that I should do or not do based upon some judgment of an outside God, but I do think that many within Christianity do believe that Jesus taught a judgmental God. I do believe that to a great extent, the idea of a "Holy Spirit" is but a doctrine to "warn" would be offenders that they cannot get away from God and that God will punish them in the end. It's like the "Holy Spirit" is an ever present "ghost" that is constantly looking over everyone's shoulders and seeing all. Accordingly, you cannot hide from an ever present ghost - who is presented as "recording" every deed you ever do in some kind of scroll that will be referred to on "Judgment Day."

But it's all nonsense, I think. God is not a person to "look over my shoulder" and keep track of what I am and do. God is an Infinite Presence that is IN everything. In short, it is up to me to keep track of my own affairs. God cannot be in the business of doing such because God cannot be separate from anyone in order to judge them. This, I believe; and I suspect the "left wing" Jesus of *THE GOSPEL ACCORDING TO THOMAS* did too.

Be that as it may, if I read *THE GOSPEL ACCORDING TO THOMAS* correctly, I see a very "left wing" Jesus encouraging each of us to make up our own minds and do what each of us loves personally - for the sake of our own souls - but I also know there is another "Jesus world" that attaches to a "right wing" Jesus who commands all to obey some standard doctrine lest they be excluded from the *"Kingdom of God."*

I don't believe I can be excluded from the Kingdom of God because I think the Kingdom of God is Everywhere; and based on the Jesus of *THE GOSPEL ACCORDING TO THOMAS,* it is strongly suggested that Jesus believed likewise. Going back to Verse 3 of *THE GOSPEL OF THOMAS,* Jesus said: *The Kingdom is within you and it is without you* (or outside of you, meaning "everywhere").

Where is your "Kingdom of God"? Mine is inside of me - and in everyone. I do not need to go anywhere to find my Kingdom of God because it resides in me and extends outward. I am "my center" of my Kingdom of God - as you are "your center" of your Kingdom of God. So, why not heed the "left wing" Jesus of *THE GOSPEL ACCORDING TO THOMAS* and always "tell the truth" for your own sake - and "only do what you love" because what you love resides in the center of you?

Love yourself - because you are worthy - being a member of a generally WORTHY WORLD & CREATION. There is no kingdom beyond that is not also here because there is no God elsewhere that is not also here. That has to be true, I believe, because whatever God is, God must be Infinite. Being Infinite means God must be Everywhere. Thus, there is no place you can go where God is missing. That makes Everywhere - including where you are and where I am - Heaven. I think Jesus - my "left wing" Jesus - probably believed that 2,000 years ago; and I believe it Now.

But it is not up to me to command you to believe as I do. You do as you will - and because I am satisfied with my life - I will not interfere. I think only those who do not believe they are complete unto themselves have any reason to object to what others do. Make a case for a given practice, but make it politely, not with arrogance. If it pleases me, I do it. If it pleases you, you should do it. That is what *doing what you love* is all about - as long as "doing what you love" is not imposing on anyone else. That only makes sense, doesn't it? If I am to not be commanded by you, then it stands to reason that you should not be commanded by me. Doing what I love must respect that.

And very importantly, let me respect you for your choice of what to love too. It is only fair. If I am free to be what I am without interference from you, then you should be free to practice your choice of love too. *It should not be for me to protest what you choose to think is right - even as I should be free to "advocate" what I believe.*

"Advocacy" is not "protest"; and advocacy, in my opinion, is light years better than protest. Look, if you do not like something in this world, then advocate for some positive interest - like adoption, if you find fault with abortion - rather than protest what you do not like. Those who oppose abortion because they think a mother should not be entitled to decide she cannot care for a child ought to spend their energy doing something positive rather than protesting what others may consider to be morally right.

If you think that abortion is wrong, care for a needy live child rather than protest the birth of an unwanted child. It makes no sense to cry about someone choosing not to give birth to an unwanted baby - and then ignore the cries of a live child who could use your compassion. There are so many millions of live children in this world who are begging for a parent - or even a meal. If you think abortion is wrong, then do not waste your time protesting the well meaning moral decisions of others. Adopt a needy child instead - or at least, help to feed one.

Well, that is how I see it anyway. For what it's worth, consider it an opinion of a "left wing" Christian. OK?

Thanks! (FWB)

The Politics Of God

By
Francis William Bessler
Laramie, Wyoming
6/16/2013

Note:
Happy Father's Day, Everyone!
Hey, we guys are all fathers on this day -
just like we are all brothers.
I am "your father" and you are mine
in that we all come from one another;
and since we are all the same in our origins,
we are also all brothers - and sisters - and mothers.
A little late on that one, but
Happy Mother's Day too!
Now on with today's "Father's Day article."
Enjoy it as you will.

The Politics of God! I could also call it *"The Excuse of God"* - but essentially, it is the same thing. I think people who want to rule others almost always first decide it is right for them to rule others - and then claim God as their authority - as if God is the *"excuse"* they use to establish and justify their claimed "authority." We all know the argument: *obey me and you will be obeying God; disobey me and you will be disobeying God.* In truth, however, the true entity called God is probably not part of the real picture at all. The real God exists not as an *Outside Person* for the sake of personal appeal, but as an *Inside Presence* for the sake of Creation; and therefore no one can really claim that he or she *"represents God"* - a God that is inside of all and needs no further representation - in some attempted claim for authority.

But how often have we heard it - and how often do we hear it? It is constantly claimed - *AS GOD IS MY WITNESS, I STAND FOR GOD!* And, of course, if anyone should defy my claim, that one is also defying God for whom I stand. Right?

I think most people who claim God as their witness are very sincere in doing so, but I think it is really their "conscience" they are upholding. People sincerely believe something to be right - or wrong - and then they rationalize that God is the reason for their belief. Hey, we all do it - or at least have done it, including me.

As a kid - like many kids - I used to pray for God to assist me in one thing or other. Well, part of belief is that in praying to God and asking for some assistance, one believes that assistance will be delivered; and when some action that can be interpreted as "assistance" is delivered, one naturally concludes that the assistance came as the result of an initial prayer. Thus, even if the REAL GOD was never part of the picture in reality, in *surreality*, God always gets the credit for "answering a prayer." Thus, if part of my prayer is to "ask for authority," then if I get my desired authority, it is God who gave it to me in the first place - just like if I pray to God to let me win over some competition or other - and I win - then it is God who helped me win.

Now, transfer that practice to a "representative of God." I was very guilty of that too - before coming to realize that the person to whom I was praying was not really the "representative of God" I first thought him to be. I am talking about my friend, Jesus. Before I came in life to realize that "God needs no representative" because God is really already in everything, I believed that Jesus represented the Personal God of a former belief. Thus, there was a time when I prayed to Jesus that I actually believed that I needed a "representative of God" who could hear my prayer.

Call my friend, Jesus, "God's substitute," if you like. Hey, if I wanted to "talk to my Personal God," then it stood to reason that if I talked to "God's representative," then God would hear me. In a way, I could "bypass God" by seeking to talk to an "intermediary for God." Know what I mean?

Be honest now, if you are a fellow Christian. Haven't you done that too? Haven't you "appealed to Jesus" for something in the light of also "appealing to God" through Jesus? I would be very surprised if you have not done that very thing. It just comes with the territory of believing in Jesus if you also believe that "God needs a mediary (or intermediary)" in the first place. It is often thought that God really needs a mediary - or substitute - and that substitute is a Jesus - or a Peter (as a "sub" of Jesus) - or a Moses - or a Mohammed - or a whomever.

Earlier in life, I really believed I needed a Jesus or a Peter or a Moses or a Mohammed to represent me before God; and thus, it was easy for me to call on my Jesus to help me out. I needed a Jesus to appeal to my Great and Loving God for favors. Jesus was his *"special son"* - and therefore, it just stood to reason that my Great and Loving God would hear me if I called on his special son. Sure made a lot of sense to me.

But I was not alone, was I? History is full of people looking for favors from God by calling on God's special son to hear them out. Right? Personally, I have come to believe that the REAL JESUS opposed any notion of a "special son" of God - or the need for one (and in other writings of the past, I hope I have made that clear) - but any who think that God could use a "special son" also stand to believe that Jesus could have been a special son. Right? It just goes with the territory of believing in the need of special sons in the first place. If one is needed, then presto, eventually one must come along. Why not Jesus?

In truth, however, why would God have any need for a "special son"? I have asked that question - and in answering that question for myself, I have concluded that the only way God could need a special son is that God can need anything in the first place. My idea of God is now, however, that whatever God is, God must be INFINITE. Infinity declares that which is INFINITE is also FULL. Accordingly, if One is really Full, then that one can have no need for anything at all - including a "special son."

If God does not really need anything - or anyone - what does that do for a "true Christian"? Realistically, a special son status of God must go away. Because God cannot need a "special son" - or anything or anyone at all - then no one should believe in Jesus in that light.

But people see what they want to see. Don't they? - Including such a preposterous notion that Jesus was a "special son of God." Why do they want to see such? *Because their politics requires it.* Their need for authority requires justification; and thus, a Jesus or a Peter or a Moses or a Mohammed become a way - a way of authority. And in the end, it all comes down to God - or how they can "use God." Doesn't it? So, regardless of whether I am calling on a Moses or a Mohammed or a Jesus or a Peter as a "substitute for God," God is listening - and to obey one of them is to obey God and to disobey one of them is to disobey God.

Does your God need a substitute, however? Mine does not. *My God is an INFINITE GOD that resides in all things because of that INFINITY - and my God needs no one or no thing to serve in Its Place.* God is not a "political entity" for me which I can use to establish authority over another. In fact, I have no need for authority because I have no need to rule anyone - anymore that the REAL JESUS had any need for authority.

Realizing it might sound a bit absurd, think about it! Would you need authority over anyone if you feel you are complete unto yourself? If I have need to rule you, it is only because I lack a sense of fulfillment in myself. I will rule you to complete in me what I am not able to complete unto myself - or in or by myself. Thus, if I have a sense of self-fulfillment in terms of believing I am a perfect created being, then I would have no need to rule another. Would I?

But I live in a different time than those of the ancient past. I think it is good to know that and to take all that into perspective in making any judgments about the past. We know so much more today than we knew when Peter and Paul lived. I know that God is Inside of me and therefore I am perfect as a being "full of God." How can I not be "full of God" if God is everywhere; and how can God not be everywhere if God is limitless? It just takes thinking about it to know about it. But it does take thinking about it - and I doubt that Peter and Paul ever took the time to think about it.

For sure, "Brother Paul" had a different vision of God than I do. In one of his epistles, he offered that "all fall short of the glory of God."

I do not agree with that assessment at all because I do not see God in the same light as "Brother Paul." Paul believed in a god that is outside of him - and that is why he saw his god as "unreachable." Of course, for one standing outside of his god, his god would seem to be unreachable. It is simply a matter of perspective. If my god were extending outside of me, I would also "fall short of the glory of my god," but if My God is inside of me - as I believe the REAL GOD is - then there is no way I can fall short of the glory of my God. How can I fall short of something inside of me?

I know, too, that when I stand on the Earth today, there is no below the Earth or above the Earth - looking at the Earth from outer space. There is only an "out from the Earth." I know the Earth is "suspended in space," not some "flat foundation" at the "bottom" of the world. I know that when I stand on the Earth today, the Sun is not going around the Earth - or rising and setting upon the Earth. The Earth is going around the Sun. It is the Earth that is bound to the Sun - not the Sun to the Earth. Peter and Paul certainly did not know that, though, did they?

Occasionally when I bring up a notion like Peter probably was unaware that the Earth is like a round ball suspended in space, someone will say - so what? What does it matter that Peter probably believed he was standing on a ground to be found at what seemed like the "bottom of the world"?

So what? Should it not be relevant that I see myself as standing on a flat Earth looking up - or a round Earth looking out? I think it makes all the difference in the world because it allows me to see me as a created being in a proper picture. Am I one standing on a flat Earth looking "up" to perhaps see some desired Heaven up above - or am I one standing on a round Earth looking out because from the perspective of a round obstacle suspended in space, there can be no "up." Therefore, there can be no Heaven "up there" anymore than there can be a Hell "down here."

If the Earth is a round ball suspended in space, it should become clear that Heaven must be where you find it because it makes no sense that there can be a Heaven "out there" in space some place. That should tell me that those who have believed that Heaven is "up" some place have been wrong all along. If there has never been an "up," how could any of the ancients have been right in believing that when they died, they would "go up to Heaven"? That's to say I should find Heaven Now - right where I am - and to stop looking up as if "up" has anymore Divinity than where I am. So, Yes, it does make a huge difference if the Earth is really flat or round.

I know, too, that it is unlikely that there is an end to the physical universe. I doubt very much that Peter and Paul even gave it any thought at all - let alone considered the ramifications of a limited world perspective.

What is the main consideration of a limitless universe? It says that the universe cannot be divided - with one side good and the other side evil. How can something without ends be divided? A limitless universe cannot allow for division - and therefore, cannot be divided into the proverbial good and evil segments of the past. If there can be no division of reality into good and evil, then only Good can exist. That is the main consideration of a limitless universe; and I doubt very much that either Peter or Paul - or anyone in the time of Jesus - gave it any thought. How about you? Have you given it any thought?

For Peter and Paul, God was here, but not there. For Peter and Paul, God could be summoned to come when He was called. For me, God is not someone to be summoned, but *SOMETHING THAT IS PRESENT EVERYWHERE*. Different views of God are going to translate into different conducts in life. I cannot blame Peter and Paul for not knowing about a *REAL GOD* because they were so much tied to an unreal God - a god they saw as being capable of serving one people and being the enemy of another. That is not *MY GOD*. My God cannot favor Jews over Egyptians - or Egyptians over Jews - or you over me or me over you. My God is not their god; and that is why their god is a "god of politics" whereas My God has no need for politics - or being served at all. How about you?

Thanks! (FWB)

Twinge At My Heart

By
Francis William Bessler
3/1971;
Modified with three additional verses: 7/5/2013

REFRAIN:
There's a twinge at my heart
when I see Old Glory -
waving so proud and so free;
and I wonder how many times
it's told the story
of courage and valor and gallantry.

Several hundred years ago
this nation was founded
on the principle of freedom for all.
Although it's had many trials,
in justice, it still stands tall.
Refrain.

This nation is a land
of believers.
Our lives in the hands of Fortune we entrust.
There is no country greater -
America, the land of the just.
Refrain.

Onward we shall march
as soldiers,
armed with our armor for peace.
Let us march strong -
Americans, united in Freedom's Dream.
Refrain.

Wherever there's a challenge
for tomorrow,
as long as we believe we are right,
we will stand firm -
Americans - united in Freedom's Light.
Refrain.

For sure, there are many
kinds of soldiers.
A soldier is only one who believes.
So, Believe as you will;
and I will Believe as me.
Refrain.

Old Glory is made
of several colors.
It's made of red, white, and blue.
Red's for blood, Blue's for victory;
and White's for the Pursuit of Truth.
Refrain.

Maybe, Friends, someday
Old Glory
will be only White and Blue.
Maybe we can stop shedding blood;
and All will be Free in the Truth.
Refrain (several times).

Dignity!

By
Francis William Bessler
Laramie, Wyoming
7/7/2013

Note:

I wrote this first as one essay, but have decided to divide it into two parts: Act 1 and Act 2, as it were. The reason for that is that my life has taught me that as you act dignified, you can handle more dignity than before. It is like learning to walk before you can run - or learning to flop your wings in a nest before you can fly.

Some us do not want to learn to fly, though. Some of us are content to just "flop our wings" and never progress to our full potential. There will be some who will not want to read any part of my "dissertation on life" as offered in this piece; but some may want to just review Act 1 and be content to just "flop their wings," but others might want to do more than that and get more serious and do more than just flop their wings. Keep in mind, it is all Opinion, though.

Let me begin with a song I wrote in 1983 I called LIKE A BIRD IN THE HEAVENS. I will offer the refrain and 1st verse in Act 1 and the refrain repeated, then a Bridge, and a 2nd verse in Act 2. Enjoy it - and all of my dissertation on Dignity - as you will.

Thanks! Francis William Bessler

Act 1:

Getting Ready to Fly

LIKE A BIRD IN THE HEAVENS

By
Francis William Bessler
1983

Refrain:
Like a bird in the heavens,
I am free to be.
Like a bird in the heavens,
I can fly to thee.
Like a bird in the heavens,
I'm in love, you see;
for love is just being me.

Look at the little birds.
See how they fall.
In seconds, they learn about flight.
There's a lesson so clear;
it should bring a tear.
Man's still at war
with his fears of the night.

My Dad passed quickly from his last known Earthly Experience due to an auto accident on this day in 1966 - at the age of 59. My guess is that his new experience in what might be called the "spirit world" was probably framed within the notion - and spiritual attitude - of *dignity*. I say that because as I see my Dad, I see him as one who believed first and foremost in the *rightful dignity* of all. Even if Dad did not go straight on to a world of dignity in the spirit world, I am sure that would have been his destination. I think that if Dad did not experience *sudden dignity* - or *WORTH* - when he died, I do believe he would have entered that world very soon - simply because that is what he was about in life.

I am currently reading a book by a very highly qualified neurosurgeon by the name of Eben Alexander. His book is called *PROOF OF HEAVEN* and it shares what Eben thinks are his experiences - not as a doctor - but as a patient - lost in a coma for 6 days, due to a mysterious E. coli bacterial meningitis; and on the 7th day he reentered his body and has fully recovered since then - which was November of 2008. Eben wrote his book in 2012.

Not to offer you any details that you should not get yourself by reading his book, but Eben lapsed very suddenly into a coma on a Monday when he was fine on the Sunday before. Let us just say it was quick; and maybe the quickness of it had something to do with his impression of things, but almost immediately within a coma, Eben went through a rather typical "near death" experience. As a "free spirit" no longer attached to his body, Eben first went through a murky atmosphere to eventually burst into a world of complete light. He proceeded to encounter all sort of lovely creatures and spent some significant time with - and among - "spirit people" dressed in various bright colors. One of them told Eben: *you are loved and cherished, you have nothing to fear,* and *there is nothing you can do wrong.*

What does this have to do with Dad - and Dad's passing on July 7th, 1966? I think what happened to Eben - though temporarily - happened to Dad as well. I think the only difference is that Eben chose to "come back" into his body as a spirit soul whereas Dad did not come back. For Dad, it was his time to go on and drink deeply of the same "spirit world" that Eben only tasted.

Well, that is what I believe. I think, though, the notion that both Dad and Eben shared - a notion and attitude of *"dignity"* - is what allowed both to experience the light world they did, assuming, of course, that both Dad and Eben did experience light. I do not believe, however, that everyone who falls into a coma or gets killed instantly all end up in a light world. I think it depends upon the soul as to how the soul will experience - either temporary death as did Eben - or permanent death as did Dad.

Eben says that before his coma experience he was not even sure there is such a thing as a soul, but because of it, he is convinced that it is true that we all have souls which really represent our true consciousness. He says that souls probably produce consciousness and the brain only "filters that consciousness." That fits in very well with what I believe; and it is that "separate consciousness" that determines if we will see light or dark when we enter a coma or experience permanent death.

The reason for that is that we can only experience "in the spirit," so to speak that which we really "know as a soul." But knowledge of the soul is not truth that can be determined as fact - or facts - but truth that is known through attitude. It is attitude that is the true driver of consciousness; but it is consciousness that directs us in what ever life we as souls have.

If my consciousness - or in effect, attitude - is one of seeing the world or existence in dark terms, then that is what I will experience as a soul, whether my soul is in a body or out of it. If Eben had been a different person in life and was really a sour doleful person who saw only the dark and never the light in his current incarnation, then he probably would not have experienced the light world he did in his coma. That is only an opinion, however. I can't prove it one way or the other; but I am sure that Eben will agree that though he may have struggled to find the light in this world, he did find it; and it is that light that he found in this world that drove his experience in a coma - as it was Dad living in the light in his last incarnation that gave definition to his "destination as a disincarnated soul."

This may seem like gibberish to many, but I do not think it is. As I have often declared in other writing, I believe so called *Judgment of the Soul* to be nothing more than a soul having to continue as it is. If I am a soul who is determined that all is dark and there is no good in the world - for whatever reason - then my "judgment" will be that when I die, I will continue in that "spirit world" of darkness.

It really makes sense when you think about it. I can "prove" what I am saying by just looking at everyday life. If I am a depressed soul on Monday, chances are I will continue being a depressed soul on Tuesday - and Wednesday and Thursday and Friday, etc. But if I am an enthusiastic soul on Monday, chances are I will continue being an enthusiastic soul on Tuesday - and Wednesday and Thursday and Friday, etc. By just looking at the "evidence" of everyday life, I can "prove" that my attitude will likely be my judge. Take that to the afterlife - and presto - you have a very good look at the afterlife.

That is why I love to hear about the near death experiences of light minded people. To tell you the truth, I have never read about a near death experience of a usually depressed person, but in my admitted limited reading of coma related soul journeys, all have basically told the same story. They start out in some dark tunnel or murky surrounding, but very quickly, they emerge into a complete world of light - and they know that the light they experience in a coma is like Heaven - or some even believe, is Heaven.

It is good to know! But the biggest reason it is good to know is that I know that my afterlife is entirely up to me - not up to the judgment of anyone else. I am the one who will determine if my afterlife is one of Heaven - or perhaps Hell. If my life was like Heaven before I died, then it is likely it will continue to be like Heaven when I reach that next stage of things. If my life was like Hell before I died, then it is likely it will continue to be like Hell when I reach that next stage of things.

There are so many depressed and sad and lost souls in this world, however, who have no idea that their course as a soul can be so easy. Instead they adopt difficult laws and regulations of others as if those laws and regulations will "save" them. Enter those who use such "light souls" as Jesus - but know neither his light nor his ways.

Jesus was - and is, I think, - a *Soul of the Light.* I think he came to try and teach us that we can be too - but we have to realize we have that wonderful thing called *"dignity"* to join the *"world of the light."* That is all it takes - just dignity, just knowing you have dignity because you have worth as an individual creation of Life & God. If you have that, nothing else matters. If you lack that, nothing else will save you. It is as simple as that; or so, I Believe.

In one of my favorite books - *THE GOSPEL ACCORDING TO THOMAS,* Jesus says it this way. *If you bring forth that within yourselves, that which you have will save you. If you do not have that within yourselves, that which you do not have within you will kill you.*

I call it *dignity, an awareness of true self-worth* - and it is as free as it is astonishing. Know you have worth as an individual simply because you belong to a Worthy Creation. Like Eben, Like Dad, you can live in a world of light and make it your purpose to stay in that light - or you can abandon a world of light and see only darkness and mischievousness and hate. You can strike out at an enemy because you believe that darkness must be obliterated by command - and become one of the darkness yourself - or you can insist that no one will derail you from your way of light - and then wherever you are - you will live in

DIGNITY!

Thanks! (FWB)

Dignity - Continued

By
Francis William Bessler
Laramie, Wyoming
7/7/2013

Act 2:

Beyond The Nest: Flying!

LIKE A BIRD IN THE HEAVENS

- Continued

Refrain:
Like a bird in the heavens,
I am free to be.
Like a bird in the heavens,
I can fly to thee.
Like a bird in the heavens,
I'm in love, you see;
for love is just being me.

BRIDGE:
Oh, how I love all the birds of the air –
no less than I love ole sister Moon.
So, please don't blame me if I follow their lead –
and act like the whole world is my living room.

I don't need a servant
tending my needs.
I don't need the world
feeling sorry for me.
I don't need your glasses
to let me see.
Just set me free
to be little me.

If I were to live only for this life, I might be tempted to disregard my "dignity" and cast it all to the wind; but the likelihood of my being restricted as a soul to just this life is practically nihil. In brief, that is to say that I better pay attention to my dignity in this life in order to know it in a next - and a next - and a next.

Ever since I was a naked kid running around without a care on a farm in northern Wyoming in the '40s and '50s, I have known that I came from some place before I came into this life. I have always sensed that before me, I was - in a sense. I came into this world as a *child of the light* because I was a *child of the light* in my last life. Of course, I am not alone. I am not the only naked kid in the world who has ever realized that Life itself is worthy and that because Life itself is worthy, as a child of Life I am worthy too. There are many who know that - and have known that throughout their lives.

But there are those among us who have not lived as naked kids too. There have been as many who have had no regard for their own dignity as there have been those who have been aware of it; and it is for those who are unaware of their dignity that such persons as Jesus have lived. This, I Believe! You might say that Jesus - like others of like mind and vision - was one of self-worth trying to rescue souls having a sense of worthlessness.

But how does one try to teach others who lack self-esteem that they should have it? To a great degree, it is like trying to tell a drowning man that water is really sacred. I mean if someone is so lost within a mindset that Life itself somehow needs saved or "redeemed," they will see water itself as the enemy because water is part of the Life they want to reject. They will yell out: *Don't tell me that water is sacred when I am drowning in it!*

All too often, however, these who would have drowned manage to escape the water; and then they go forward to preach that anyone can escape drowning who does not go into the water. The water becomes the enemy - and partly because they are so sure that they escaped an evil, which they equate to the water.

Jesus has been used like that in history, I think. He has been portrayed as a singular and solo holy man who has "saved" many who believed they were drowning. How? By obedience to some command or law issued later "in his name" by an assumed "successor of Jesus" - not by imitation of conduct for the sake of imitation itself. The payoff? If you will do this for me now, I will do that for you later. That is how Jesus has been used by so many who have been convinced that Life itself needs redeemed.

But in all likelihood, that is not what Jesus taught. Jesus did not teach that if I come to him, I will be saved. He probably taught that if I recognize my inherent worth - which he has also recognized in himself - I will be saved. Thus, if I was born a "child of the dark" when I entered this world, I can go out of it as a "child of the light." That is the intent and purpose of the Life of Jesus, I Believe.

Welcome, Elaine Pagels!

I would not have known that Jesus may have taught that salvation amounts to recognizing my inherent worth, or *dignity,* though, if a peasant looking for fertilizer in a cave off the Nile River in Egypt had not stumbled onto a wonder jar containing ancient manuscripts written by early believers of a different cloth - that is in the man we call "Jesus." I would not have known that there even existed such beliefs in Jesus had they not been "discovered" in 1945 - when so called Gnostic works and works like *THE GOSPEL ACCORDING TO THOMAS* were "discovered" - strictly by accident. Or was it strictly an accident? (Note:

For those unfamiliar with the story of *THE GOSPEL ACCORDING TO THOMAS,* please refer to my earlier blog: *KNOW THYSELF.*)

I repeat: was it an "accident"? I wonder what my friend, Elaine Pagels, thinks about that. Was 1945 and the discovery of "the other side of Christianity" an accident, Elaine - or was it simply a matter of timing? Has the human race had enough of a so called "Orthodox Jesus" - intent on commanding obedience for the sake of obedience - to finally come to realize that there is nothing wrong with the water - even if I should drown in it?????

Elaine, I hope you do not mind my telling a secret, but Elaine and I are "kindred spirits" - as she wrote in a book of hers - *BEYOND BELIEF* - that I had with me when we met last Saturday in a little church in Greeley, Colorado. You see, I heard from friends in Greeley, Clyde & Rose Edmiston, that someone they knew that I was fond of would be speaking at a church there last Saturday. Elaine has been a scholar and a half on behalf of the long hidden works found in 1945 in a cave off the Nile River - one of which has been my own "savior" in life - *THE GOSPEL ACCORDING TO THOMAS.*

It was there at that local United Church of Christ of Greeley, Colorado that I "officially" met with a dear friend, but in truth, Elaine and I go back "in spirit" to at least 1979. It was 1979 that a relatively young Elaine Pagels (then 35 or so) wrote her book on the finding of *THE GOSPEL ACCORDING TO THOMAS* - and other books that were banned as heretical by the church in the 4th Century. She called her book *THE GNOSTIC GOSPELS* - and it was an early review of the previously hidden works found in that cave off the Nile River.

It was that same year, 1979, however, that Elaine wrote her book on *THE GNOSTIC GOSPELS,* that I became aware of one of the books she reviewed - *THE GOSPEL ACCORDING TO THOMAS.* In 1979, another friend of mine told me about *THE GOSPEL ACCORDING TO THOMAS* - or was it friends? It might have been just Russ Pope who told me about the Gospel of Thomas - or it may have been both Russ Pope and Joe Edgar who told me about it. I do not remember who introduced it to me, but it could have been either Russ or Joe or both of them because the three of us were good friends at the time - and still are.

But Elaine is a "Doctor" of religious studies and even now teaches as such at Princeton University - and I am only a speculator. I have no degrees, but I do have a mind and a brain that has the sense to know that it can not be as "The Church" has been saying since I was a kid. Somehow there has been a part of me that has "chosen" - a "dangerous" word according to Elaine Pagels - to believe that I am already a "child of the light" and do not need to become one.

You see, the word for "choose" in Greek is "heretic" - or so it is claimed by my friend - and if I might claim so - "associate in truth," Elaine Pagels. In the early centuries of Christianity, there were many who believed that it was some so called "faith" that is important for salvation - and that faith must not be encumbered by such a thing as "choice." No one should have the freedom to choose to believe that they are good. We must all believe that no one is good so that some among us can lead others of us to the good.

Well, in my book, Belief is crucial for salvation - but not Belief in another. It is the kind of "belief" that is important - not belief itself. And my friend, Jesus, would agree - though there are many who think they have sole access to Jesus who would claim otherwise. They would argue that "their belief" in Jesus himself is what all must believe; but in my mind, their belief is wrong.

In the "heretical" gospel, chosen to be believed by many in the 4th Century - *THE GOSPEL ACCORDING TO THOMAS*, in Verse 2, Jesus says: *Let him who seeks, not cease seeking until he finds, and when he finds, he will be troubled, and when he has been troubled, he will marvel and he will reign over the all.*

That is to say, I think, think for yourself. Never mind what others think is the truth. In all likelihood, they are as blind as you are - and, as Jesus also offers in multiple gospels, *if the blind follow the blind, both fall into a pit.* The real "heresy" of Jesus was to encourage others to think for themselves and find their own truths because it is only having your own truth that will save you in the end. You don't need a Temple or Church to tell you what to believe. You need to listen to yourself and find your own truth. If you think that another's faith or another's way will save you, then according to the "heretical" Jesus of *THE GOSPEL OF THOMAS*, you will probably stay blind - if blind you were in the beginning.

In another verse, Verse 28, of the branded heretical *GOSPEL OF THOMAS*, Jesus says: *I took my stand in the midst of the world and in flesh*

I appeared to them; I found them all drunk, I found none among them athirst. And my soul was afflicted for the sons of men because they are blind in their heart and do not see that empty they have come into this world (and that) empty they seek to go out of the world again.

That makes sense to me. It says that before I came into the world, I already existed as a soul - just like Jesus and you. That might offer a whole new meaning to what Jesus supposedly claimed: *Before Abraham was, I am.* Maybe before Abraham was, you were too. Suppose? That is not to say that Abraham did not have a previous life, though. It is only to say that before Abraham existed as a person, maybe all of us existed as prior souls as well. Something to think about. Right?

But it also says that as a soul, I will go out of - or leave - this world. It says that I was not wrong in believing as a child running naked when I could that I came from another place - or at least, another time; but it is the same with everyone. *We all existed before we are - so to speak.* We all came into this world as previous souls - and the way we came into it is the way we exited the last time we were here - or anywhere. We did not just start in this life. We came from previous selves; and that is why it is so important to make sure that the self you go forward with out of this life is one you will wish to attend in a next life - or next time.

But why were the men in the Jesus quote above empty? Because they did not believe in their own dignity. They "chose" their own heresy - of believing in their own emptiness and believing that somehow Jesus was supposed to fill that emptiness when he said it plain as could be for those who could listen in Verse 70 of *THE GOSPEL ACCORDING TO THOMAS* - *if you bring forth that within yourselves, that which you have will save you. If you do not have that within yourselves, that which you do not have within you will kill you.*

Some of the major bishops of the 4th Century - when books like *THE GOSPEL ACCORDING TO THOMAS* were banned as heretical - did not want to hear that, though. It did not make any sense to them; and so they "chose" the very heresy that Jesus damned - trusting one's own salvation to another - even if that other was the likes of Jesus.

John - one of the early "real heretics" put salvation in another in very fancy words. He had Jesus saying - *"I am the way and the truth and the life. No one can get to the Father except that he go by me."*

And then blind John went forward to paint Thomas as a doubter in order to dismiss "thinking for yourself." It all sounds so wonderful - that I am going to "get to the Father" - or the Light - by way of another; but it is just not true. You have to know your own dignity in order to "get to the Father." Listening to Jesus is not depending on Jesus. It is only "becoming like Jesus."

It was claimed by some that Thomas was considered a "twin" of Jesus. He was referred to as that in *THE GOSPEL OF JOHN* when John was trying to dispel "thinking for yourself." But as Elaine Pagels pointed out last Saturday, that was probably only to say that Jesus may have considered Thomas a "twin" - or Thomas may have considered Jesus a "twin" - because in believing in the Same Light as Jesus did, Thomas was "like Jesus" - and therefore - the "twin" of Jesus - or a twin of Jesus.

Hello, "Twin"!

Thanks, Elaine, for that idea that Thomas may have been referred to as a "twin" of Jesus for believing "like Jesus." I did not know that before last Saturday. It is always good to realize a new idea; and that is an idea that really seems right to me. Thanks so much for that! Am I a "twin" of Jesus? Is Elaine a "twin" of Jesus? I think so. Do you?

But what is it like to be a "twin" of Jesus? *THE GOSPEL ACCORDING TO THOMAS* tells us about that too - if we will listen. In Verse 37 (of 114), it is found: *His disciples said: When will Thou be revealed to us and when will we see thee? Jesus said: When you take off your clothing without being ashamed, and take your clothes and put them under your feet as the little children and tread on them, then (shall you behold) the Son of the Living (One) and you shall not fear.*

Remember what Eben said he was told in that coma of his - offered earlier in this essay? *You are loved and cherished, you have nothing to fear,* and *there is nothing you can do wrong.*

The naked is only a way of saying that - and showing that you really believe it. *You are loved and cherished!* Why? Because you are really a "child of the light" - but you must believe it to know it. What true "child of the light" is not really loved? What true "child of the light" can be ashamed of him or herself?

You have nothing to fear! You are already saved! The only darkness is the darkness you believe in. Believe, instead, in The Light - and that IT is all around; and you will know you are part of it. How can it possibly be otherwise if God - the Light - is truly everywhere?

There is nothing you can do wrong! As long as you know you are worthy and take off your clothes without shame, you can be "like Jesus." Then you can do nothing wrong. Why? Because you will not want to do anything wrong. Wrong is impeding the search of another and keeping him or her from finding his or her own way - in the light. No one can do that for you. If you are to become a "twin" of Jesus, then you must take charge. When you die, all you can take with you is your attitude. So, why depend on anything else?

But we "twins" of Jesus can go naked because we are not ashamed of Life. It is not "taking off our clothes" that is the important idea to be found here in Verse 37. It is being "unashamed of Life." It is knowing that Life itself is Sacred - and that Life itself is the very treasure of our existence. Life itself is the Miracle we would want to find elsewhere. So why not act like it by going naked now? Yes, I know - Heresy!

Jesus said: I will behold the Son of the Living One if I take off my clothes without shame and I will not fear. Who is that "Son of the Living One"? It is me. I did not take off my clothes to see Jesus. I took off my clothes to see myself. I cannot "fear myself" if I consider myself equal to Holiness Itself. I am "Holiness Itself." *I am what I behold.* It is as simple as that.

Jesus said I have to take off my clothes without shame to see him. I have long known that - though I was not able to put it into the clarity I know now before the now treasured *THE GOSPEL ACCORDING TO THOMAS.* As a kid, I went naked without even knowing that it should be so. I went naked because I wanted to "show" God how much I love what I thought God is doing - giving me the Miracle of Life. But that was probably because I went naked in a last life - and was used to it.

That is not to say that everyone must go naked to express dignity, as it were; but it is to say that you cannot degrade the naked or accuse it of being sordid or sinful. You cannot find the light by denying the blessedness of any of the Creation of The God of Light.

How many have lived their lives in total blindness thinking they could despise themselves and not also despise the God of Light in the process!

My Greatest Friend!

I think I could say that my single greatest friend in this life has been my nakedness. If I am to believe the previous quote of Jesus in *THE GOSPEL ACCORDING TO THOMAS,* Jesus agreed. It makes sense to a "fellow twin." It makes sense to a "fellow child of the light." Of what am I to be ashamed if Life Itself is Grace Itself? That is what I know - and have known all my life. It seems so with Jesus too.

When I die, I probably won't see Jesus or Dad because they will probably be out and about in their next journeys into a next incarnation; but like Eben, I will know I will be as at home there as I am here - and I will be naked! How about you? And when I return? Look for a naked kid running down the road and playing with the butterflies. Hey, you have an invitation to join me! Will you?

I have read about quite a few "near death" experiences - and none of them offer that the "angels" in them are naked. Like Eben's vision, they are all clothed in some really colorful clothes. I think that is so for ones like Eben because they have not yet taken the step to discard their clothes. They are still a little way off from the ideal. They still need clothes to feel safe; and that is why their "angels" are always dressed in "colorful" clothes. But in my dreams and my life as a "holy one," I have gone that extra step. I have "taken off my clothes without shame" - and I have been naked.

My nakedness is singular, though, and it would be singular even if another were to join me. It is "solitary holiness" that I know as a naked one; and I do not need another's nakedness to complete me. I do not need sex. I do not need another to be completed. I need another to have a baby, but I do not need another for any other reason. Why? Because every one of us is perfect as an individual - being wholly of God - and one perfect individual does not need another perfect individual to enhance his or her perfection. I am not saying one who is perfect cannot share in another's perfection. Of course we can;

but one perfect individual does not need another perfect individual because each of us is whole - as perfect - unto ourselves.

I often argue that if I were alone on an island, I could be happy all by myself - simply because I would spend my time admiring the beauty that I have and whatever other beauty that surrounds me. I would be "too busy" with such admiration to notice that I am alone. Therefore, I would not "miss" being with another; and if another were to join me but was distracted with feeling lonely or sad or incomplete, then my focus on the perfect within me might be interrupted - and then it would actually be to my advantage if that person were to leave. I can hear myself saying: *Get off my island and leave me to my peace.*

This world, however, is caught up with "needing one another" - and one of the basic ways people think they need another is sex. Thus, it generally goes with the territory. If I am to go naked, I am also agreeing to "have sex." To each his or her own on that, but I think sex - understood as coitus - confuses things in terms of leading me on a path that makes me dependent on another for my well being. I reject that; and that is why I reject having sex just because I go naked. Naked is not Sex for me. It is only an Admission that All Life is Holy! Non-sexual embracing and exchange is OK, though. At least I have never found it on the side of confusing, but again, to each, his or her own.

And seeing another naked is nice, too. I will admit that. Seeing another naked and/or being with another naked on a non-sexual basis is very confirming that all of us are really "children of the light." We just need to realize it and believe it to allow us to make any life we live also Heaven. That, I Believe!

When I Die

And now the big question: *what happens when I die?* No one knows, including this speculator of life; but what I do know is that anyone who claims they do know is way off base. So many are absolutely sure of themselves when it comes to death; but those same people have no idea what life itself is all about. <u>So, why should I entrust my</u>

soul in death to some who have not satisfied me with answers about life?

The standard answer is that upon death, some will go to Heaven and some will go to Hell - or maybe somewhere in between Heaven and Hell. But where is this Heaven of which they are so sure? Where is this Hell of which they are so sure? Those same people who divide death between Heaven and Hell live to deny that there is any Heaven on Earth. So, why believe them?

What did Jesus say about it? First of all, I think he would tell me to think for myself. Never mind what others claim the afterlife is. They probably don't know. Go with what seems right to you - and ignore all other opinion.

What seems right to me? I have said it before and I will repeat it now: *Judgment of my soul is probably only a continuation of me.* If I lived seeing only light - or concentrating on seeing the light - then I will find myself in the light. If I lived seeing only dark - or concentrating on the dark or sad or cruel or just or whatever - then I will find myself in the dark - or in the same general category of life that I chose before.

Let me seek for an answer to that question, though, from *THE GOSPEL ACCORDING TO THOMAS.* In Verse 24, we find: *His disciples said: Show us the place where Thou art, for it is necessary for us to seek it. He said to them: Whoever has ears, let him hear. Within a man of light, there is light and he lights the whole world. When he does not shine, there is darkness.*

Obviously, Jesus was not talking about the world in general in that message. Jesus was a man of light, yet much of the world of his time lived in the dark. So Jesus did not mean that the "whole world" is light if one of light is there. He could have only meant that one who believes in the light sees only light.

Now take me through death. I have died and what can I expect? If I was a man of light when I lived, then there is no reason to believe that the light of before will not continue. Why? Because the light is me - and wherever I go, my light goes with me. However, contrariwise, if I was a man of dark when I lived and insisted on the doleful and not being happy with my life, then it is likely that the dark in me will continue after death. Why should it be otherwise?

When I Live Again

After some period of time, is it likely that I will live again - in another incarnation? Again, no one knows for sure; but as a realist who is living now and senses that he has lived before, what are the chances that I won't "live again"?

Again, however, there is somewhat of an answer to that question about living again in *THE GOSPEL ACCORDING TO THOMAS*. In Verse 51, we find: *His disciples said to Him: When will the repose of the dead come about and when will the new world come? He said to them: What you expect has come, but you know it not.*

That is to say, I think, that what has happened will happen again - in terms of process. When will those who have died come back again? Jesus would say "they have already come." You may be among your own ancestors. You are the very people that were here before - and you live again. The so called "new world" is only an extension of the "old world."

The biggest "proof," however, that it is likely that I will live again is that I am living now. I came into this life. I am here now. How did I come? I don't know, but I know I am here - and it is realistic to believe that whatever process landed me in this life will be the same process that will rule my return. As I have happened before, I will likely happen again; and that makes it all the more important that whatever I am, I choose the me that will go on.

Let me leave you on this occasion of Dad's Death Anniversary with a poem I wrote in 2001 - all about being a "child of the light." Join me in Believing, if you will!

Thanks! (FWB)

Child Of The Light

By Francis William Bessler
Laramie, Wyoming
5/2001
(A Poem; may also be sung)

Oh, Child of The Light, play as you will.
You have but to live to find your fill.
You can't understand from whence you came
Just embrace it all joyfully as if it's a game.

For a game life is, or should be for all.
Oh, Child of The Light, have yourself a ball.
Look at the Earth and the Sun and the Moon
and know that they are all in tune.

The wonder of all of God's great creation
should fill your mind with jubilation.
Oh, Child of The Light, you fit in well
and you ring as you should as one of the bells.

So, don't fret and worry and live in fear.
As God is your source, It's also your care.
Be not afraid as you go forward in time.
Oh, Child of The Light, you've a life that's Divine.

A Simple Look
At Sex

By
Francis William Bessler
7/11/2013

Note:

I just decided today that this article is going to be the first of three that I am going to write on three different, but perhaps related, topics: SEX, GOD, & JESUS. I will begin with this one on sex and pass it along today and then sometime soon, I will work out the next two on GOD & JESUS. I am not sure what I will offer in the next two articles, though I have almost finished with the one on sex below as I write this note.

In all this, however, be very aware that what I write is only one man's opinion. Do not think that I think that I have an angel on my shoulder or in my head - like so many who have written their own personal visions have done in the past.

I am reminded of one John of Patmos, the author of the famed *BOOK OF REVELATION* of the *BIBLE*. John may have also written *THE GOSPEL OF JOHN*. When I read him earlier in life, I really believed that he was being inspired by God to write what he did; but I have long since outgrown that idea. I think John wrote from his head - like I am writing from my head. God is not inspiring me in any special way; and God did not inspire John in any special way. His writing was based on his vision of life - and my writing is based on my vision of life. That's putting it succinctly - and truthfully.

The problem is that so many have adopted John's vision of life - with all its warfare and battles featuring God and some would be foes; but it's good to keep in mind that John wrote his vision while his people were being thrown to the lions for being fellow Christians. I guess I might have had a bit of a sad tale about life to tell too if I were one to be expecting an ax to come down on me at any moment. So, John wrote about a "new day" where all would be well and all the villains of the world would have been long sent to Hell. That was his moment - and his hope - because that was his experience.

But I am in a different time. I am not one who is expecting an ax to come down on me for what I believe. An ax may well be imposed on me for my beliefs, but, let's face it - it is not likely. Is it? So, it's good to realize that different writers are dealing with different times and because of that, their visions of life have to be different.

I think we humans are mired in a mess in terms of believing this is not Paradise - or shouldn't be - because ones like John of Patmos lived in a mess. I think the ones who gave us that message that life is a mess were too caught up in trouble to realize any peace; and so they "assumed" that sometime their troubles would end and they would find Paradise. The problem with that is that in looking down the road for some peace, they gave up on finding it here; and I think the human race is still doing the same thing today.

Well, I am not John of Patmos - or St. John of *THE GOSPEL OF JOHN*. I am Francis William Bessler of Laramie, Wyoming - and I live in a different time. I do not see the opposition to God of which John was so sure. There are no demons - except that we have them in our minds. There is no foe of God because God can have no foes, being Infinite. Everywhere is Heaven because God is everywhere. This world IS the Paradise that John only dreamed about; but it might as well not be if we insist that John wrote for all time - as if time need not enhance our vision of life.

In that light, let me take you on a trip and let us see three things in a different way from the past: SEX, GOD, & JESUS. Just keep in mind that all of this is only one man's opinion - and vision - and need not be that of anyone else. On the other hand, if it fits, wear it. We are all in this wonderful thing called Life together; and one man's vision may well suit another - or others - too. Just try on these ideas - and see how they fit. OK?

Thanks!

Francis William Bessler - not John of Patmos!

SEX

Let me talk a little about sex. I am 71 as I am talking, but I don't really think it should be any different, regardless of age. As I see it, no matter what age we are, we are essentially *"sensual"* beings - and it is really that aspect of life we are talking about when we talk about sex. Personally, I prefer the term *"sensual" to* "sexual" because it is much more descriptive of most so called "sex."

Thank God, I am a *SENSUAL BEING!* Personally, I am in love with my senses - and I try not to divide myself by thinking I should be sensual here and not there - or restrict myself to talk about one sensual part but not another sensual part - as if the body is divided between the touchable and the untouchable. In reality, it is not divided into good and evil regions or touchable and untouchable parts. In reality, it is ONE - and the one that it is - is wholly wonderful.

I realize the world looks at life in a different way than that, but personally I have long overcome such nonsense that the body should be divided into private and public parts - as if the public can see one part but can't see another part. What nonsense! *One part of me is not any more wholesome or less wholesome than another part.* My hand is not somehow more acceptable than my penis - or should not be. Your arm is not somehow more acceptable than your vagina - or what you can see of it. Or it shouldn't be - in my view.

Mankind has been caught up in divisions since it was able to think, however. We have loved division - and dividing our bodies into touchable and untouchable and seeable and un-seeable is only a product of a penchant for division. *We love division; and our separating our parts is only a product of that.*

Which side of my body is "Godly" and which is "un-Godly"? If we but think about that question for one single moment - not even a minute - we would realize that it is impossible that the left side of me can be Godly and the right side might be un-Godly - but I will get into that *GOD THING* a lot more in my next article. For this article, it should be obvious that the right side of my body cannot be more holy than the left side of my body - and my arm can't be less holy - or more holy - than my penis. Ideally, every part of me should be known as wholesome - and every part of me should be equally touchable - be that I am alone or with another - or others.

I am talking Ideals, though, of course. Knowing what should be "ideal" and acting that ideal out is up to up each of us to do on our own. Many would not see what I am talking about as an "ideal," however, and they might even be convinced that I am speaking as somewhat of a deranged individual. How dare I talk about the penis and the hand as if they are exactly the same! How dare I even use the word "penis" in mixed company - or especially in the presence of a child!

But, in reality, a child should be the start of the new ideal. A child should be taught from the very beginning that he or she is alright - as naked and wholesome - simply because he or she is of God; and, again, we will get into more of that *GOD THING* in my next article.

I am a firm believer, however, that a child should "teach himself" or "herself" - when it comes to what to do with his or her body. It should not be up to an adult to tell a child what to do when it comes to experiencing life. It should only be for an adult to "not tell" a child what to do. I am not saying a father or mother should instruct a child to play with him or herself. I am only saying that an adult should not prevent a child from investigating according to his or her own pace - or curiosity. It is not so much "instruction" - as the "lack of instruction." Let a child know what he or she wants when he or she wants.

But we don't do that, do we? Because of our love of division, we dare to tell our children from the beginning that something is "naughty." That is our way of "instructing" our children to disregard their own curiosity and listen to us older folks who know better. Nonsense! I

108 | Francis William Bessler

think that left alone, a child would normally do what is right because they would not be filled with all sort of ideas about things being wrong.

Then as adults - all we need to do is step forward - and be like the child in our presence. In a way, we should learn from our "free" children. It can be as simple as that. As we let our children be, we adults should be likewise.

But what about mingling? Should "two children" be free to be curious about one another? Of course, but that should depend on the child - or children. Some children will be curious about another; and some might not; but it should be up to the children to decide - just like it should be up to a single child to decide the course of his or her curiosity.

How simple it could be - and should be! Speaking about mingling, however, let me offer my views on that - or one aspect of that - sexual intercourse. Again, I am not saying what others should think about the matter. I am only offering what this "one adult child" has thought about it and still thinks about it.

Many - and maybe most - may disagree with me on this one, but I think coitus should be restricted to making babies. I think we humans have been way out of line from the "natural norm" by having intercourse outside of intended procreation. I mean the "natural norm" is that sexual intercourse is for procreation, not recreation. I think it another one of those "division things" we have come to love. In this case, we love to "divide" or "separate" ourselves from the rest of natural beings and treat sexual intercourse like it is a matter of entertainment rather than procreation. After all, we are "more special" than any other creature. We should be exempt from the rules of all other creation; but as we exempt ourselves from the norm - wow, do we pay a price by complicating the life we live - or lives we live.

My first wife, Dee, and I had sexual intercourse often during the first two years of our ten year marriage (1967-1977) because we both wanted a child. It turned out that Dee could not have a child - but until we knew that, we had intercourse quite often. Once it became clear that Dee could not have a child, we adopted a lovely three month old named Anita Marie; but when Anita Marie (born May 23rd, 1970) came into our lives, the intercourse stopped. Why? Because I did not believe in it for seeing it as a breach or violation of the order of Natural Design.

In a way, there is no such thing as life without some order. Even if we choose to embrace chaos or some assumed "everything goes" type of conduct, it is still a kind of order. It's just "chaotic order" - with order being some kind of guidance on how to conduct life. Even if I conduct life in some haphazard way and see it as without any order at all, it is not true. My order is only chaos.

Others choose some order like some assumed Commandments of God. That becomes their "order." They live - or try to live - according to what they think of as "Commandments of God" - even if in reality, God did not issue the commandments, but someone convinced of the inspiration of God issued them as if he was speaking for God; and again, we will get into that GOD THING much more in the next article.

The point is - everyone needs some kind of "order"; and my order is trying to find guidance according to NATURAL DESIGN. I do not see God outside of life to need any guidance from a God outside of life. So I am only choosing a different kind of "guidance" - and that is guidance to what I think of as "Natural Design."

Of course, it is debatable as to what is "Natural Design." I may see a different order going to it than another. My friend, Nancy Shaw, for instance says that because two people in love want to join together as one in sex that it is an expression of "Natural Design" that they do so. Nature is the one who leads two people in love to have intercourse - and it need not have anything to do with procreation.

Well, that just shows that each of us can interpret Natural Design in different ways. I am sure that many would agree with Nancy - or do agree with Nancy. That's fine, but interpreting Natural Design in that way would not provide any real guidance to two people in love - or two people out of love. If two people want intercourse, then it is OK to have it. That view would not allow usage of "Natural Design" to limit sex. That view would only allow usage of "Natural Design" to permit sex. Well, that is no order at all in my view. It is just order according to the individual - and Natural Design is of no help at all.

But the debate does illustrate that one man's view need not be another man's - or person's - view. In the end, to each, his or her own; but at least, it takes it out of "God's Hands" and puts the responsibility where it really belongs - in our own.

Anyway, later my first wife, Dee, and I divorced and I met Pat a few months after the divorce became final. Pat and I married soon thereafter in July of 1977. Pat wanted intercourse from the start, but I wasn't sure I wanted to have a child. I hesitated because I was of the mind that the world might be ending soon and I didn't think it was wise to bring a child into the world with that idea swimming around in my head.

Soon, however, after about five months of marriage with Pat, the idea did subside and I felt free to have a baby. That one was quick. It might have been so quick as to have needed only one act because once I decided to have a baby, Melissa Dawn was conceived; and then intercourse between Pat and I ended too. Melissa came into the world, however, on Oct. 12th, 1978.

Later, Pat and I would divorce too - a very complicated matter I won't go into - but since my marriage to Pat - which ended in 1978, around the time Melissa Dawn was born, I have had intercourse only a few times - and every time with someone with whom I was engaged - though several engagements were terminated for lack of some major consensus. I did marry a third time in 2000 - but for that one neither Ann nor I wanted another child and neither wanted intercourse either. We divorced in 2001 because it became obvious by living together that Ann's atheism and my Divine Naturism simply do not mix.

The point is that "this one adult child" has adopted a course in life that is almost conservative - in spite of my being a liberal on the matter of life in general. I believe that Natural Design - as I interpret it, of course - is the way to go; and I have tried to commit myself to that. Again, my friend, Nancy Shaw, argues that Natural Design allows for intercourse as a matter of pleasure only and that I am way off base for restricting myself - and perhaps her - from it; but for me, it is very simple. *If an act naturally results in a conception if "left alone," then that act should be practiced for the "left alone" consequence.* Besides being wise, it is also safe; and why should anyone want to be "unsafe"? *Stay with the simple - and stay safe.*

And if one does act in an unsafe manner and gets pregnant without intent, what then should happen? For me, that is an extension of the principle of let each one decide for him or herself. In this case, a pregnant lady should decide what to do. In short, if a pregnant one wants to become a mother, then that should be for her to decide - not for anyone else. Even the fellow who provided the sperm should not have any control over another person's body. It is not his body - and out of respect, he should not interfere.

It is not complicated as I see it. Once I have given away my sperm - regardless of where that sperm ends up, that sperm is no longer mine. I gave it away; and it no longer belongs to me. My lady friend, however, may have it if I gave it to her. If so, then it is for her to own and do what she will with it. I can certainly offer an opinion about what I would like my lady to do, but what she does should be up to her - and her alone. That is how I see that.

The key to living a healthy life, I believe, is to live it in the present as much as possible; and that means to maintain a constant state of curiosity - about the present state of life. I try to do that every day of my life. I love pictures of me and others (especially the naked ones) to assist me in knowing the truth of me. We are all the same except for minor differences; and that is why looking at any other naked person - male or female - is really looking at me. When I see a picture or a movie of a naked one, I see me - the curious me. I am like a little child who is only seeing something for the first time because for me, I am "brand new" every day.

Personally, I think aging is largely caught up with having too many memories of the past and not paying attention to the wonder of the present. A child is caught up with the wonder of the present because she (or he) knows nothing different - and that is mainly what allows her or him to be so healthy. *That wonderful thing we call curiosity should be our constant companion. The more we spend remembering the past is one moment lost on loving the present - and the future.*

Or so I Believe!

Let me finish this by offering a song I wrote several years ago that I called *Kiss Me*. A friend of mine, Amy Parker-Williams, told me - "*Will, that is really erotic!"* Well, I suppose it might be; but I did not intend it to be so. I only intended it to be an expression of what I think is an ideal affectionate relationship. I suppose that could include gay relationships too, though I am not gay. I am for gay relationships, however, for those who are comfortable with them.

But be you gay or heterosexual, enjoy my love song as you will. OK? And stay tuned for my next article. *It will be all about GOD.*

Thanks! (FWB)

Kiss Me

By
Francis William Bessler
4/14/2006

REFRAIN:
Kiss me here and kiss me there.
Kiss me, kiss me – everywhere.
Kiss me where it pleases thee.
Kiss me and enjoy my Divinity.

God said to Adam, go to sleep
and when he awoke, there was Eve.
Eve looked at Adam and winked at him
and said come here, Honey - there is no sin
Refrain.

The way I see it, it's this way.
God's in All, be it night or day.
When you touch me, you touch God.
So come to me – for my applause.
Refrain.

I think many souls have it wrong
who think that God's not in this song.
If God is Infinite, it has to be
that Dear One must be in me.
Refrain.

If it's true, God is in my flesh,
then my soul should be refreshed.
Soul and body are so Divine.
It's just like grapes turning into wine.
Refrain.

So come and sip my wine with me.
Taste, Sweetheart, my Divinity.
Put your lips where you want to go
and you will find what you want to know.
Refrain.

But, gentle, gentle – don't be harsh.
You're not sloggin through some marsh.
There's no need for whips and chains.
Just kiss me, kiss me, and kiss me again.
Refrain (twice).

The Light Of God

By
Francis William Bessler
Laramie, Wyoming
7/18/2013

I look at life and I see only wonder - and very definitely, mystery. I do not believe life is near as complicated as we humans have made it; but there are so many, I think, who have invested their entire lives in insisting it is complicated; and the core of that complication is a belief that life must be lacking. When so many people are so sure that life is not what it should be, it is very difficult to convince them they might be wrong.

One of the reasons I think people see life as lacking is because we have redefined "Good" as "God" and simply left out an "o" in the process. I do not think it is an accident that many can't allow "Good" in their lives because it does not give them some right to impose or supervise; and so they have conveniently redefined the real "Good" that is to make it "God" or "Godly."

But "Godly" does not mean "Goodly" - does it? It means whatever one wants it to mean. *It means mostly "authority" to many.* You can't see authority in Good, can you? So just drop out an "o," make it God and get on with your business of commanding others to do what you want "in the name of God."

As a kid, I was really impressed with the story in the book of *GENESIS* of the *BIBLE* that offered that God created everything and everything was "good" because God can't make anything bad. Just as soon as the author of *GENESIS* told us that story, however, he took it back immediately. Why did he have Adam & Eve whom God made "good" turn around and do something "bad"?

I guess the author of *GENESIS* looked around and saw nothing but evil. So he could not keep with his story that all is really good because for him it wasn't. So he wrote a story to "allow" for how it all went wrong. Sure, God made all "good" in the first place, but something happened to turn it "bad." Very conveniently, he offered that things went sour because "man disobeyed God."

What else could he say? He looked about and saw his fellow man assailing other men and knew he could not call that "good." So he had to find a way to "explain" man's bad behavior. Thus, the story of the fall of Adam and Eve from grace.

Hey, one like me probably wrote that story for looking for the way things are - or seemed to be. If I were to blame that fellow who wrote the story of *GENESIS* for "not knowing the truth," then I would probably be pointing the finger right back at me - or the likes of me.

I am reminded of something my Dad used to say. He said: *If you point one finger at someone else for being mistaken, be careful because at least three fingers are pointing back at you.* So I do not want to dismiss what was told by the story of *GENESIS* as an intended falsehood because I don't think it was, but I do want to argue that it was not true - or probably not true.

With that in mind, let us assume that I was that author of *GENESIS* - and point all those accusing fingers right back at me.

Why Is GENESIS Wrong?

&

Why Has God Been Made Male?

GENESIS suffers mostly for me because it makes God out to be a "person" - thereby setting up the possibility of being judged harshly or rewarded by a "personal God." This God of *GENESIS* made all things, but stood outside of all things to "create" all that "He" created. Now when the author of *GENESIS* told that story, he believed God is a "person" - much like himself - and so it seemed reasonable. God makes this and God makes that, but He is outside of all that He creates. He has to be if He is a "person." If as a person, I create something; then what I create has to be separate from myself.

But God can't be separated from what "He" creates. Therefore, He can't be a person. Let me explain myself more on that in a minute; but why did the author of *GENESIS* identify God as a "male" in the first place. What "male" that you know creates another person? Normally, it takes both male and female to generate a person. So why is it that God generates a person without the partnership of a female?

Let me offer my thoughts on why I believe that God has been assigned "male" status; and that reason is that when ancient man was trying to figure things out, he noticed that a man went into a woman and left his seed. Now what he did not know is that the female also has a seed because ancient man was ignorant of the ovary. Out of sight, out of mind. So it seemed that the "seed of man" was deposited into the female, but the female only nurtured the seed of the man - and did not and does not - supply a seed of her own.

I may be wrong, but I think it was the illusion of man supplying a seed of life without an accompanying female seed that gave the illusion that man alone "creates"; and thus for my ignorance as a long ago writer, I assigned God to be a male. And that is why as the author of *GENESIS,* I called God a "He." Wouldn't you have done the same? Indeed, appearances can be deceiving; and in this case, I think humans were deceived to believe that life comes from the male simply because it "appeared" as such to us before we realized that females have ovaries; and then it was an easy assumption that God is a male because "He" creates.

Infinity versus Personality

Earlier I offered that God can't even be a "person" - male or female. Let me tell you why I believe that.

As I see existence, there is *NO END* to it. I cannot imagine an end to existence. Try as I might, if I apply my mind to thinking about it, I cannot imagine an end. That is probably because since "I" wrote as an ignorant author of *GENESIS*, man has come to find out that in reality there is galaxy after galaxy after galaxy in existence. No matter how far I go out and out and out and out, there is no end. The physical world is actually immense beyond human imagination to comprehend. In other words, the world must be Infinite - as an *Immense Existence* without end.

But "I" did not know that when I wrote the story of *GENESIS*. Did I? As far as I could see back then, hey, the world was not all that big. There was a sky above me, but that sky did not "seem" to go too far. Just beyond where I could see, there was dark; and so I probably assumed that "dark" means "end."

Surprise, surprise, surprise! Dark does not mean end. Does it? But what does the illusion of an end suggest to me? It suggests that whatever God is, God is simply an "overlord" and that leads me to believe that such a God can make all things. God made the seas and God made the mountains and God made forests and all the animals and, of course, Adam & Eve. In my ignorance of seeing no end to existence, I imagined that God could be a man like me because only a man can "create" life - and I imagined that God is a person like me to do all that creating. Was it not argued in *GENESIS* that God made man in His own image? *In truth, however, it is far more likely that man conceived God in his own image.*

But why can't God be a person within the scope of Infinity? Putting it plainly, a person is one who is limited. Infinity means "unlimited" - the exact opposite of "limited." You tell me. *How can there be a "limited person God" somehow swimming about within an Infinity that is boundless?* Good trick if "He" could do it; but it can't be done. Can it? You cannot have Infinity - that is boundless - and also have a God who is really "limited" within it. Can you? *Accordingly, if there is a God at all, that God must equal Infinity - not move as an individual somehow within it.*

And that is why God can't be a person. And that is why as the "virtual author" of *GENESIS*, I had it wrong. God is not a person to make things. God must be that Infinity that I know must exist. How could it be otherwise?

In truth, Infinity is an amazing concept, relating it to God. If you think of God as an "individual" Which Creates all things, it is normal thinking to set God outside of all that It Creates - like a sculptor carving an image out of stone; however an individual God cannot be an individual if it is also Infinite - in terms of "being Immense." Think about it if you dare. How can Immensity Itself also be an Individual within that Immensity? See where I am going on this?

But it is totally unlikely that the author of *GENESIS* knew anything at all of an *Immense Universe.* It is unlikely that he even speculated beyond what he could see; but we all know that there is far more beyond where we can see; and it is that beyond that we know nothing about that can make all the difference in the world.

The Real Story of Creation

What, then, is the real story of Creation? I don't know, but I do not need to know either. Whatever it is, It far exceeds my limited intellectual capacity to understand it. That of which I am certain, however, is that Creation exists. It is obvious it exists. I am in it. Whatever it is, however, cannot be subject to a "personal God." *The wonder of that is that it removes all fear of a personal God.* Anyone who tries to offer that they represent a "personal God" is acting in as much ignorance as "I" was in when I wrote the story of *GENESIS.* "I" was not the only one who has been ignorant, however. All who believe as I did that God is a personal entity are also wrong.

It's ok, though, to know that God is not a person. It (not He) doesn't have to be. Does it? *Ignorance is only terrible when we realize we were ignorant, but choose to ignore our discovery of the truth as if the truth doesn't really matter.* When we find out we were wrong and still act like we were right, then that is stupidity - and no longer just ignorance.

Many do not know what I have just argued, however, and so they may remain only ignorant as they go forward - blind, as it were. But if I were to continue on as if all is the same as I once believed, knowing now that I was ignorant of the truth when I believed it, then I would be *STUPID.* That would not be wise, would it?

God As Light

I mentioned above that I do not know the real story of Creation, but at least I can know about some of it related to our life on Earth. This is not brain science for those of us living today, though it probably did not occur to the fellow who wrote *GENESIS*. It could be argued that the source of life on Earth is the Light of the Sun. I doubt that the fellow of *GENESIS* equated "light" with "life," but I think it is reasonable to do so.

Where would life be without light? If the Sun were to go out, so would life on Earth - and that pretty much proves that all life on Earth is due to the "energy light" from the Sun. So, even if I do not know for sure the story of Creation in general, I can know of it as it relates to life on Earth. *Life on Earth depends on the Light of the Sun.* There is no way around that.

Now, a little step forward, and one can equate Infinity (or Immensity) itself with Light because without Infinity itself, there would be nothing - not even our solar system. Thus, Infinity Itself (or Immensity) can be equated also with Light.

What does that make each of us but "sons of the Light"? Right? At least our bodies are "sons of the Light." And whatever our souls are, if they exist as individual entities, they must also exist as "sons of Infinity (or Immensity)" - and thus, too, our souls can be considered "sons of the Light."

Well, at least that is how I see it. I may not know a lot of details about life - but I can be confident that whatever it is, it is Good; and whatever it is, it owes its source to that Good I call God. There is no sense in believing we can dismiss Good from Life by just omitting an "o" from Good and pretending that will do the trick - in terms of making life evil or lacking Good.

I admit there is evil in the world, but it is not due to a lack of Good. It is due to our believing we lack Good; *but we cannot lack Good if that which is Infinite - and Immense - is necessarily IN us.* Can we? And there is no way that Infinity (or Immensity) can be divided in any way to make one side good and the other side evil because Infinity (or Immensity) can have no sides. As I often argue, how can you divide something that goes on forever and has no ends? You tell me.

The author of *GENESIS* also had God dismissing us via Adam & Eve from the famed Garden of Eden, but keep in mind, that was based on the idea that God is a person - not a Presence. In the first place, God is not a person to relate as an individual to anything or anyone inside of Immensity - Which God Is. Forget that notion that God is "outside" of us at all because being Immense or Infinite, It can't be. Therefore, God can't dismiss us from Its Presence - even by some form of annihilation. Why? Because to "annihilate" us, It would have to be outside of us to do it. Since God can't be outside of us, then we need never fear any judgment of any kind from God or by God.

It might be somewhat misleading to say, however, that "God creates" in the first place. *I know that I am always claiming that God creates, but it is probably much more correct to argue that because of God, Creation happens.* Remember - being Infinity or Immensity, God can't be a person or an individual. God can only be a Presence - or Essence; and I do believe it would be much more correct to argue that because of the Presence - or Essence - that is God, Creation happens. God does not create in the sense that He (or It) fashions individuals. God creates simply by virtue of existing as some kind of Divine and Mystery Presence that allows Creation to develop, as it were. God does not "create me" as much as "God is an Allowance by which I am created."

It is certainly obvious to anyone who observes life that a set of parents - a Mom and Dad - are the ones who "create" the body of a person. God does not create a body. A set of human parents "create" a body; however it is because God exists and because of whatever is God that Mom and Dad can provide the seeds by which a life happens. That is not to take God out of the picture of "individual" creation; it's only to realize that Mom and Dad - and an offspring - could not happen except by virtue of an Infinite Reality we can call "God."

In truth, all are "sons of God" because all are "because of God." God is the "Source" of everything by virtue of being Infinite Reality. I do believe this notion is important because of the idea that many have that God can create in terms of actually generating an individual by a conscious act; but that is probably not true. God is not the "parent" of any individual, but only the Infinite Presence by which all things can be. Whatever we are as individuals, then, we can correctly be called "sons (or daughters or progeny) of God"; but none of us are special in that regard. All are equally "sons (or children) of God" because one of us cannot have more or less of God - or Infinite Presence - than another. Even a fish or a bird or a cat or a dog or a horse - or a grain of sand - is just as much a "son of God" as I am - or you are.

For sure, Creation is a Mystery. We cannot understand it. We need not understand it; but we can Love it and Appreciate it as Holy and Sacred because it must be "of God." And that is surely something to Celebrate! Isn't it?

Let me finish with a poem I wrote several years ago about my belief that All is Divine. Never mind fearing divisions that are not real - for Infinity (or Immensity) cannot be divided - certainly not into good and evil. Infinity (or Immensity) is *ALL GOOD* as I see it; and that is why this "son of the Light" knows only joy - or at least, mostly joy.

Stay tuned for the tale of another "son of the Light" in my next article - Jesus; but consider this poem a bit of an introduction to Jesus too.

Thanks! (FWB)

Song Of My Divine Naturism

(Recitation with Refrain)
By
Francis William Bessler
Laramie, Wyoming
6/28/2004
Verses are to be recited - or sung - as chosen.

REFRAIN:
I'm in love with life and God as if the two are one.
I have no doubt whatever that whatever is – is God's son.
God is the Divine – and Nature is God's Prism.
That's why I call my wondrous belief "Divine Naturism."

As I watch from a window, I see a cloud go by.
I'm amazed at it all and wonder how it can all be so fine.
As I ponder the Sun and its generous sunshine,
I have no doubt in my mind that all that is – is Divine;
but It is not only life that has the spark of Divinity, you see.
Even the sand must contain the wondrous mystery.
For life itself springs from the sand – as if therein is the seed.
God is present in it all – just as It is - in you and me.
Refrain.

People ask me, where is God, and I answer "everywhere."
God is not a person, but rather a Creative Presence of Infinite Care.
There is nothing that can exist that can exist on its own.
God is the wonderful principle by which all that is – is sown.
People have this idea that when they die they go to God.
But if God is in everything, then now should begin the applause.
God is not something that can only come to some of us later.
It must be something that right now every single being can savor.
Refrain.

And God can't be in the business of judging me and you
because a judge has to be outside of that which is viewed;
but God is inside of all that is and therefore cannot be a judge.
That leaves it up to each of us to live without a grudge.
Judgment is only having to continue as I begin.
I am my own judge and it is for me to determine what is sin.
Virtue is only embracing that which sets my soul free.
So I choose to love all that is like all that is – is me.
Refrain.

I am asked many things, but one question is, do I have a soul?
I say I don't know for sure, but it's only smart to act like it is so.
If I do have a soul, then it can only serve as a record of me.
It is then up to me to make sure that I keep that record clean.
Assuming that I have a soul, it only makes sense that I fill that vessel
only with that I'd like to recover – and for me, that's only the gentle.
Surely, it is to each his own, but however we fill our soul,
we will have to inherit later all that we put into our bowl.
Refrain.

I have but one rule that I think Jesus tried to get all to mind.
It's really not very complicated. That single rule is – Be Kind.
Kindness is its own reward because by being kind,
I'm always at peace.
It doesn't matter where I go, what I do, or who or what I meet.
People tell me that you can't be kind to those who are unkind.
They say that justice demands that they must pay the price.
But being unkind to the unkind only makes two who are fools.
No one who is wise would ever attend such a school.
Refrain.

Jesus tried to teach kindness to all two thousand years ago,
but the rulers of the day claimed it to be an impossible way to go.
And anyone who would ask it must be put up on the cross.
Otherwise, society at large would reap tremendous loss.
And so it has continued down through the many, many years.
Justice over kindness has shed a jillion tears.
And today, mankind still loves to go to war and fight
and find in their claimed acts of justice
that which they think is right.
Refrain.

The beat goes on. It cannot stop until mankind
stops punishing the kind
and allows the Heaven they want sometime later to be here in time.
When Jesus said that Heaven is at hand, he did not mean tomorrow.
If you put off until tomorrow, all you'll gain is endless sorrow.
Heaven is something that can be ours once we come to realize
that Heaven is only being aware that everything is Divine.
Life itself can only be a mystery, but the results of it need never be.
As the twig is bent, so it will grow – and the twig that grows is only me.
Refrain (several times)..

God

By
Francis William Bessler
Atlanta, Georgia
2001

Let me offer you some thoughts about God –
One Which I have always found dear.
We all have thoughts – and these are only mine.
Let me make that perfectly clear.

For me, God is not a person in a body like that of man.
It's only a Presence.
God is not a person with heart and head and hands.
It's only an Essence.

For me, God is an Essence, a Being ness,
but not a being that moves from place to place.
God is the Energy in All that gives us each
a chance to have a face.

God is not a judge of that created.
It's only the Force of and within Creation.
God is in All – always has and always will be.
That thought should cause us jubilation.

If man is damned, he damns himself
by thinking he can lose the Divinity he calls God.
If woman is damned, she damns herself
by acting like she is holier than clod.

Clod or dirt has as much of God as any person or beast –
and all are made of sand.
God is in the sand as mysterious energy
that forms that which we call the land.

But be it land or sea, God is there –
and in the air and all about.
There is no place where God is not.
For sure, about that, we should have no doubt.

All should shout and proclaim joy
as life is blessed because God is there.
God is there and here – in you and me –
in all that is; so, let us care.

Let us care about the life we have
and embrace it as a gift for a gift it is.
We know not how it came – or how it will go;
but we can know it's right and show it with a kiss.

Jesus

By
Francis William Bessler
Laramie, Wyoming
7/22/2013

End of a Trilogy

This is the last of three articles that I intend as a sort of "trilogy" - tying together, perhaps, the most important "three" concepts of my life. I am not saying that these three should be the most important of everyone's life. I am only offering they are the most important of my life. If you have been with me, those three ideas are *SEX, GOD, & JESUS*.

I love sex, but I see sex in a rather different way than most do. I see sex as just following the prescriptions of what I think of as *NATURAL DESIGN*. I am free within that scope of things because I do only - or try to do only - that which I think Nature has designed me to do.

For example, looking at Nature as the Master and Teacher, so to speak, I see the general pattern of animals and birds and creatures in general having coitus almost exclusively for procreation. It is easy, then, for me to decide about sexual matters because I see the ideal in sex as staying with the "natural norm" of having coitus for procreation. Believe me, that is a norm that keeps me safe - and anyone with whom I might deal safe too. There will be no "unwanted children" happening through me because I do not believe in taking chances - so to speak.

I guess you could say that I believe in sex - but I believe in SAFE SEX; and "safe sex" is not defined by various drugs that I can take to "avoid" natural consequences, but rather it is sex practiced without inhibition - be that inhibition drug oriented or otherwise. Safe Sex is sex practiced that will not likely damage a human organ by its practice - or alter the human system to be other than it is. Safe sex is not treating an organ of the body - like the anus - like it was "designed" for input when it was actually designed for "output."

An example of "safe sex" is Oral Sex - given that the participants are clean. When people tell me that I am too conservative because I do not practice coitus except for procreation, I tell them that I can please a partner as much by kissing them all over as by "invading them."

I love being sensual and believe that all my senses are "Gifts of Nature & God." I do not see my senses as some kind of "trap" intended to misdirect or mislead my soul - as so many seem to do. My soul is occupying this wonderful sensual body because it is choosing to do so. I am not a "prisoner" in a sensual body. I am a "free soul" in a sensual body.

I offered that I go naked all the time that I can because I do not want to restrict my senses - or if I did not argue that, I am doing so now. I very much enjoy experiencing myself in sensual terms - again within the realistic confines of Natural Design; but as I offered in my article on sex, interpretation of Natural Design should be up to the individual. It should not be for me to determine what Natural Design should be for you, but only for me. I will leave it at that.

My next most important concept that I wrote about was - or is - God. Perhaps I should have written about it first because it is probably the most important for me, but regardless of that, there is nothing more important to me than the idea of God - and what I think a discussion of God brings to the table of understanding life.

In fact, I cannot imagine anything existing without God, but my God is not a personal God. *In my view, a personal God is impossible because that implies that there can be an "individual" we call God that is somehow roaming about that which I think of as Infinity - or Immensity - or, if you wish,*

Eternity. That makes no sense to me whatever. How can there be a "personal God" Which is often dictated as a "Creator" of all things as if that God "personally" crafts all things?

It is obvious to me that Creation Happens because of an Infinite God, but an Infinite God does not make anything that is made. My parents "made me," for instance. God did not "make me." That should be obvious to anyone with a brain to think about it and review life as it is. That is not to say that God is not part of Creation. It is only to say that God is not the "Creator" that many religions claim "He" is. In fact, God cannot be a "He" in the first place because God cannot be a person - be that person a she or a he. In light of the idea of Infinity, a personal God makes no sense; however a Presence God makes all the sense in the world.

God is not a person hanging around me, but God is a Presence enveloping me. That makes me and all things and all existence Holy. In that view, All is Holy and nothing is "profane." In light of God, there can be no "profanity." *If profanity exists, it exists only because people see life - or some part of it - as "profane" - or lacking in the Sacred - and treating it accordingly.*

I must admit that growing up, I "feared" God - perhaps as much I "loved" God - but that was because I was ignorant of the TRUE GOD. I was given to believe that God is outside of me and watching my every move and virtually taking notes; and then at the end of my life on Earth, God would use those notes to judge me.

"Francis, " God would say on "Judgment Day," I approve of what you did at this time, but I do not approve of what you did at that time. Hmmmm - grading on the curve, though, I guess I can approve of you getting into my Heaven."

And therein is the view that most have of God - a personal supervisor who will approve or disapprove of what we do; but I have long passed beyond that notion because of the wonderful Idea and Ideal of Infinity. *Infinity - or the idea of Infinity - frees me like nothing else can.* Knowing now that God cannot be a "person" somehow set outside of me to judge me, I can view God for what God really is - or probably really is - INFINITY ITSELF. I could say more, but I think I said quite enough on that in my previous article on God - THE LIGHT OF GOD. Feel welcome to check out more of my thoughts on God there. OK?

And Now - Jesus!

My view on the one we call "Jesus" is the same as my view on Sex and God. It is "my own." As I have not allowed others to define either sex or God for me, neither is it for me to allow others to define Jesus for me.

Jesus is the last of my trilogy of ideas, however, because it must be - or a discussion of Jesus must follow a discussion of the other two ideas. I could exist without a Jesus, but I cannot exist without sex or God. In that way, Jesus is like a bit of a "postscript" to my understanding of life. If a Jesus did not exist, I would still have been instructed in all I really "need to know." What does it matter that any one individual has existed or not?

Having said that, I know of no one who loves Jesus as much as I do. It's just that my life is not dependent upon Jesus for meaning - and I believe that Jesus would be the first one to applaud that notion. I do not see Jesus as having to be part of my life, but simply being a person I have loved dearly in my life - like a good friend or wife (and in my case, ex-wife and ex-wives), or daughter or sibling - or, of course, parent. Jesus is just one of those people I have loved dearly - and I pride myself on my love of Jesus like I pride myself on any love I have had in life.

In reality, however, my ideas of any person must be consistent with my ideas of God. I cannot claim that God is IN all as I do and then claim that one of us is "more of God" than another. *Accordingly, my Jesus cannot be THE SON OF GOD that many of my fellow Christians believe he is.* For me, everyone is a "son of God" because no one exists independent of God. It means nothing to me to say that Jesus was *THE SON OF GOD* because, for me, there can be no such thing.

Naturally speaking, how could it be? How could an Infinity that is Endless somehow "create" another Endless Being? That is what would have to happen if God could "create" an Only Son. People ought to think about that when they are told that Jesus is "The Only Son" of God. It sounds just fine, but logically, it is IMPOSSIBLE. And why would God want to create an "Only Son"? That is assuming, of course, that God is a person in the first place - which as I have argued, can't be.

In truth, those who have dictated that Jesus is the Only Son of God are among those who use God to threaten the rest of us. John of

Patmos comes to mind - with his unbelievable *BOOK OF REVELATION*. John would have us believe that Jesus - as The Son of God - must be about his "Father's business" - and since the God of John is one who is intent on judging others at some proverbial "end of time," then "The Son of God" must also be about the same thing.

What idiocy! The Jesus I know taught that we inherit what we sow, but that is the extent of judgment. The Jesus I know insisted that he was not into "judging people" and that people judge themselves by how they act and how they conduct their lives. So, why in the world would Jesus change his stripes at some "end of time" and sit at the right hand of God - as John of Patmos did argue - and "judge" us all when, in life, he literally denounced judgment by others?

In a way, I feel sorry for those who see Jesus in the light of how someone else has seen him - or sees him. I think it is truly sad that some have chosen to claim to have known Jesus in some "special way" and then have proceeded to "dictate" their idea of Jesus to everyone else. That is most unfortunate in my opinion.

I think the Gospels of the *BIBLE* are very reflective of the idea that no one really knew Jesus - and that is why there have been so many versions and stories of Jesus written. If Jesus was so clearly understood by his so-called "disciples," then his story would have been clear too; but the very idea that different people wrote different stories proves that no one knew Jesus anymore than I know him now.

Was Jesus a "real lord," for instance? I do not see him now as that, though I must admit I was reared to believe he was - and is. What is a "lord," anyway? Well, when I thought of Jesus as Lord, I saw Jesus as "necessary for my life." I think most traditional Christians believe that they simply could not do "without Jesus" - and that is why they make him Lord. They act like without the "Lord Jesus," they would be lost and without any meaning at all. Well, that is what the "Lord Jesus" folks would have us believe, but I do not believe it because I do not see myself as having to know Jesus to know about life and the wonder and the mystery and the absolute sanctity of it.

What did Jesus think of himself? I suspect he thought of himself pretty much *like I think of myself - as one individual that no one really needs, but one every-one can love.* But I am not "lovable" by virtue of anything special about me - any more than Jesus should be lovable because he is special. *I am lovable - or should be - because of my being a "wonderful creature."* Everyone should love other "wonderful creatures." So, everyone should love me - and I should love everyone else. It is as simple as that.

In one of the many versions of Jesus, *THE GOSPEL OF THOMAS*, Jesus asked three disciples that were about at the time to tell him who they thought he was. He said in Verse 13: *Make a comparison to me and tell me whom I am like. Simon Peter said to Him: Thou art like a righteous angel. Matthew said to Him: Thou art like a wise man of understanding. Thomas said to Him: Master, my mouth will not at all be capable of saying whom Thou art like. Jesus said: I am not thy Master because thou hast drunk from the bubbling spring which I have measured out."*

And that tells it like I believe it. Jesus being a "brother" and not a "messiah" necessary for all to know and love life. In that quote, though many would not agree with it and many have attacked it as "pure heresy," Jesus is saying exactly what I would think he would be saying if he were offering that no one really needs him, though they could use his "wisdom" - or the "bubbling spring" he has measured out.

Simply put yourself in the place of Thomas - since it was Thomas that Jesus was directing mostly in this quote. Jesus did not disagree with Peter who claimed that Jesus is "like a righteous angel" because it was true. Jesus was - and is - like a righteous angel - as one who is worthy of the love of God and Life. Jesus did not disagree with Matthew's impression of Jesus either - "a wise man of understanding" - because Jesus was like a wise man of understanding; however, Jesus did correct Thomas because Thomas was implying something with which Jesus disagreed.

Thomas was at least implying that Jesus was a "master" or a "lord" that Thomas could not do without. Jesus corrected Thomas by saying he was not the "master" of Thomas because Thomas was already believing that wisdom which Jesus was offering. Jesus told Thomas: *I am not thy Master because thou hast drunk (or are drinking) from the bubbling spring which I have measured out.*

In another verse in *THE GOSPEL OF THOMAS*, Verse 108: *Jesus said: Whoever drinks from my mouth shall become as I am and I myself will become he, and the hidden things shall be revealed to him.*

There again is that notion that I love so much - that wisdom about life is the real treasure and wisdom is something that is true for all, not just for Jesus. No one needs the author of a tale - if a tale is worthwhile at all. All one needs is a tale itself. No one needs a teacher of wisdom, but we can all use wisdom itself. *That is what I believe - and I think it is what the Jesus of Thomas is saying as well.*

Note: For those unfamiliar with *THE GOSPEL OF THOMAS* - and a brief commentary about its history - please refer to my article: *KNOW THYSELF.*

Meeting Jesus!

If I were to meet Jesus, I hope that I would be naked. Why? Because I think Jesus would be naked. We would be two naked friends meeting on the path of life! I suspect that if I were not naked when we encountered one another, I would not recognize him - nor would he, me!

In Verse 37 of *THE GOSPEL OF THOMAS*, it is found: *His disciples said: When wilt Thou be revealed to us and when will we see Thee? Jesus said: When you take off all your clothing without being ashamed, and take your clothes and put them under your feet as the little children and tread on them, then you shall behold the Son of the Living One and you shall not fear.*

I think it worthwhile to note that the team of experts who translated my first copy of *THE GOSPEL OF THOMAS* from Coptic to English in 1959 (a team headed by a scholar named A. Guillaumont) chose to put certain words in capitals. Personally, I do not think I would capitalize something like "Son" of "Son of the Living One" because it implies only Jesus - and not the student of Jesus. In this case, it should be "son of the Living One" - not "Son of the Living One" because I think the one who is being revealed is myself - or yourself - as much as Jesus. Of course, it is a "mutual recognition" that takes place, but for the sake of a student, I think the really important recognition is that of oneself. You are "like Jesus" and your going naked together is a testimony of that.

Be that as it may, here is "testimony" of a kind that Jesus would like to meet with another naked individual; and it follows my line of reasoning that shame is the single most unworthy and useless and damaging concept ever dreamed up by man. My Jesus would not be one ashamed of himself - and that is why he would emphasize not needing to cover up - as shyness and fear of nakedness implies.

On the contrary, *nakedness is probably the single most important "way of truth" one can pursue in life because it declares that Life Itself is Shameless. Jesus was not ashamed of Life; and neither should I be and neither should anyone else be.*

I mentioned in my article on sex that "Nakedness has been my best friend" in this world - or the like. That is because Nakedness is Life. It is not shying away from Life - which so many consider to be the great virtue of life. It is embracing it because it is right and holy and wonderful - and I must add, absolutely delightful.

Would Jesus be what we call "gay"? If by that one means two of the same sex having some kind of "genital intercourse," No; but if one means by that two of the same sex being able to embrace one another, Yes, I think Jesus would be "gay." In that light, I am "gay" too; but I am not "gay" in the way that most understand "gay" to be.

And there again is the great "savior" of my life - Natural Design. If I were to meet Jesus naked on a trail, I doubt that Jesus and I would do more than simply embrace one another as brothers and let it go at that, but that is "me and Jesus." I won't define what "you and Jesus" would do. That is for you to decide, not me; and that is as it should be.

In the same light, if Jesus were walking naked with another of the opposite sex, like a Mary Magdalene, I doubt it would be any different. I think Mary and I would embrace too - and do nothing more. The ideal is to treat everyone the same. So if I were to encounter a naked couple rather than just a naked individual, then the ideal would be to embrace them both - given that one of us chose to embrace at all.

Did Jesus fear being killed for his convictions? I do not think so. Why did Jesus surrender to the authorities of his day so quickly - as we are told he did in the Gospels of the *BIBLE?* Why? Because he knew those authorities could not really take away anything that is indispensable. He knew that if he was killed, it would be only his body that was killed. His soul would live on; and that is why he could go forward not fearing death; and that is why all of us should go forward not fearing death.

I do not want to get into an in-depth discussion of the notion of "sacrifice" in this article, but I think I will just say that I do not believe Jesus would have considered himself a "sacrifice" because that would have implied that his death would have had some meaning outside of not fearing death itself. Jesus died on a cross, perhaps, but he did not die to "fulfill the scriptures" or any other such nonsense.

I think it worthwhile to keep in mind that when Jesus lived, he entered into a "personal God" culture - that of the Jews. The Jews believed in a "personal God" they called "Jehovah," but whatever the name of the "God," that God was not really a God at all, but rather just one of the "Pagan gods" of the time.

Who knows how the Pagan god, Jehovah, was born - and what human person fabricated "him" - but it is totally unlikely that the Real God could have acted like Jehovah supposedly did. Jehovah was not a "God In All" but only a "god for some." No Real God could act like Moses claimed that Jehovah did. What Real God would kill the first born of one people - the Egyptians - and "pass over" the first born of another people - the Israelites - simply because he "favored" one race over another - in this case, Israelites over Egyptians? That is some idea of God. Isn't it? My God can't do that because My God must be Present IN all and Jehovah is a perfect example of "a god" that can do only for some and not for all.

Another dead give away that Jehovah was - and perhaps is - a "Pagan god" is the "Pagan" practice of sacrifice. All - or at least many - of the other Pagan gods of the time loved and demanded the rather curious practice of sacrifice. Very interesting! A god of a people demanding that they burn in sacrifice some critter of their culture to "prove" obedience. I must admit that it was this curious practice that seemed to be consistent among all "Pagans" that first alerted me to the idea that Jehovah was probably just one of the many Pagan gods of the time.

Anyway, it was out of that "curious practice" of sacrifice that Jesus was eventually claimed to be a "final sacrifice" - a sacrifice to end the general practice of sacrifice. Even today, Jesus is considered to be a "sacrifice" that was necessary to cleanse man of sin - as if the death of anything could cleanse anything of sin.

But the Jews believed in sacrifice - to Jehovah - and some Jews insisted that Jesus fit into that picture of sacrifice. Thus, they claimed that Jesus was the ultimate sacrifice that would finally appease Jehovah once and for all. After Jesus, no more sacrifice was needed - or so many of the Jews of the time imagined. Eventually, those Jews who believed such emerged to become "Christian"; and many Jews of the time who believed that Jesus was the long sought and promised messiah to come measured Jesus for the very curious rite of "sacrifice." Accordingly, when Jesus died, as all "sacrifices" had to die to please Jehovah, though Jesus was executed for other reasons, his "execution" was turned into a "sacrifice."

What do you think? Do you think that the rite of sacrifice was useful at all? What did it do? What could it do? Would you consider it meritorious in some way to take one of your herd, kill it, and then let it go up in some smoke - as if the rising of the smoke would somehow appease the god to which you were appealing?

Now, put Jesus in that picture. If, in fact, the general practice of sacrifice gained nothing and did nothing for the people who practiced it, why should we think that the "Sacrifice of Jesus" would do anything more?

If I were to be executed for my beliefs as was Jesus, I would not consider myself a "sacrifice" for some cause. I would consider myself a "victim" of a deranged authority; and I suspect the Real Jesus would agree. For sure, I would not want to die for a cause anymore than anyone else would want to die for a cause, but if I did, know that I will not have "feared death" regardless of another taking my life; and that is the real lesson to be had from the crucifixion of Jesus.

Like all other tales about Jesus, I think it is good to keep in mind the authors of those stories and what those authors were attempting to manage with their tales. In the case of Jesus, for whatever reason, so many chose to "use Jesus" to further some cause of their own - and in so doing, "managed" to corrupt the true story of Jesus, making him an authority to fear and obey - rather than the true master of wisdom he was.

Or so, I Believe!

Let me leave you with a song I wrote a few years ago about the way I see Jesus and another about each of us being "Sons of God." Share them as you will - and live them as you will, too. OK? I will add another song too about what I think of as "true mastery." If I might be so bold, I think "mastery - spiritual mastery" is really easy - not hard; and "me and Jesus" could be considered to be "masters" just as everyone in this world can be. *In truth, there is nothing to being a master - except being a grateful son of Life and God.*

Thanks! (FWB)

Jesus Is My Way

By
Francis William Bessler
Laramie, Wyoming
11/27/2008
Note: Phrases in parentheses are spoken.
The rest is sung.

Jesus is my way – but not my lord.
Jesus – for me – represents the word;
but the word is "nothing's evil because everything is pure."
(because, God, as Infinite, must be in everything,
making everything pure)
Jesus is my way – but not my lord.

Jesus is my way – but not my lord.
Jesus – for me – is all I can afford.
All I can afford is to be kind to all that's in this world.
(because kindness is its own reward).
Jesus is my way – but not my lord.

Jesus is my way – but not my lord.
Jesus – for me – is Heaven on this Earth;
but Heaven is only knowing the Divine is in the dirt.
(In the Gospel of Thomas, Jesus says,
The Kingdom of the Father is spread upon the earth –
but men do not see it).
Jesus is my way – but not my lord.

Jesus is my way – but not my lord.
Jesus – for me – is Heaven beyond this birth;
but Heaven beyond this birth is only
extending Heaven here on Earth.
(Assuming, of course, that I know Heaven on Earth).
Jesus is my way – but not my lord.

Repeat all verses, excluding sayings in parentheses.

Son Of God

By
Francis William Bessler
Laramie, Wyoming
10/28/2008

REFRAIN:
I am a son of God – and you are too.
Even if you are a girl – we share the same truth. – for male
Even though I am a girl – I share the same truth. – for female
For God is not a Father – that belongs to only some.
More correctly, God's a Mother – that nourishes everyone.

I don't think God's a moral one.
It's simply the energy for us all.
It's up to each to choose our bonds;
but we'll inherit what we install.
Refrain.

I can be kind or I can be cruel.
It doesn't matter at all to God;
but it matters to me and I'd be a fool
to choose a path of pain to trod.
Refrain.

Some think God's a person like us –
outside – to choose what He might like;
but the God I see and the God I trust
is part of all and in all is inside.
Refrain.

God's not apart as we might believe,
but it's for each of us to realize
that wherever we go and whatever we breathe
is filled with the Divine. *Refrain.*

Some think that there's a Heaven to come.
Well, I'm convinced that is the truth;
but Heaven's only knowing we're all God's sons.
So, I'm in Heaven right now too.
Refrain (2).

A Master's Prayer

(Freedom's Prayer)

By
Francis William Bessler
Laramie, Wyoming
10/29/2007

Our Loving God, My Generous God,
Holy is your name.
I thank you for my life and blessings.
That's why I feel no shame.
Our Father, My Father -
Thy Kingdom's here as well as there.
Thy will is only that I share –
what I am with the world.
Our Father, My Father -
to be forgiven, we must forgive;
that's the only way peace can live.
Our Father, My Father -
I thank you for my daily bread.
My needs are simple – thus I do not dread.
Our Father, My Father -
to see only good is to allow no evil.

I pledge to you a life of no guile.
Our Father, My Father,
I will always be your child.
Our Father, My Father,
I will always be your child.

False Standards - Dire Consequences

By
Francis William Bessler
Laramie, Wyoming
8/18/2013

I have been told a time or two in my life that I am "obsessed with my-self" in that I insist on going natural - and often have my picture taken that way too. That is to say I prefer not to cover the natural as if cloth-ing is somehow more worthy than the natural. For the life of me, I cannot understand why people actually consider clothing more worthy than the natural under it; but for argument sakes, let me agree. By go-ing natural, I am expressing an "obsession with myself." So what? So I am "obsessed with myself" with wanting to have so many pictures taken of me. So what? What does it hurt? And who am I hurting by doing so?

From my point of view, however, I am only trying to take pictures of a "willing" natural person. It just so happens that I am the only "will-ing" person around. Thus, I am somewhat limited to taking pictures of myself - or having pictures taken of me.

Ideally, however, I would like it if more people than can fit into a picture allowed themselves to be taken - au natural. The truth is that almost no one that I know wants to be taken. Ideally, I should not be the only one in my pictures. Ideally, both men and women should appear with me - au natural - because that is the Ideal in life - or what I see as the Ideal in life. *The ideal should be that everyone is comfortable with what they are - not so much with who they are, but rather with "what" they are;* but the truth is that almost no one is - comfortable with "what" they are. Are they? Are we?

But look around! What does all this "discomfort with life" mean? For the most part, it leads to dissatisfaction with life and that leads to all sort of destructive behavior. People who are dissatisfied with life think nothing of destroying it. It means nothing to them. So what does it matter if they destroy it - including themselves? What is war - but a lot of dissatisfied people going about shooting one another - or blowing one another up? For what reason - and for what useful objective?

If I were to be dissatisfied with life and take that dissatisfaction to arm myself with a gun - and then go out and shoot some other dissatisfied person, what have I gained? Tell me! What have I gained by being dissatisfied in the first place - and then taking that dissatisfaction out into the world, combating another dissatisfied person, and blowing him (or her) to "Hell"?

But why are people really dissatisfied with life? I think they are so because they have adopted false standards. What is a "false standard"? It is one that makes no sense. *A false standard is one that is based on something that is not true - but oh, the harsh consequences of false standards!*

False Standard # 1 -
Obedience to an External God

False standard # 1 is a standard that is based on the idea that God is separated from Life. That sense of separation leads to speculation that "maybe" it can happen that some might be able to attain unification with God - and from that "maybe," all sort of variations in "doctrine" occur.

One doctrine offers that to be united with God, one has to "sacrifice" one of his herd to prove to God that one is willing to be obedient.

Another doctrine has it that to be united with God, one has to treat all children of God the same in order to find favor with a God of all. Another doctrine states just the opposite - that only some can find favor with God because all are unequal in the eyes of God. Another doctrine arises that says that men must be willing to kill other human beings who have not recognized the "True God." Another doctrine arises that says that to find God, one must deny all material goods of this world in order to be in alignment with a "Spiritual God." Another doctrine is formulated that says that if one does not say some prescribed prayer in some prescribed way that God will not find that one in "His" favor - and on and on, it goes.

But in all probability, the basis of all this assumed "doctrine" is wrong. In all probability, God is not really separated from anything. Why? Because in all probability, God is really not a "Person" outside of anything, but, in truth, a "Reality in All" because God is probably equal to Infinity - and Infinity is present in All. Thus, no one needs to do anything to be "unified" with God. *Why would anything - or anyone - need to be unified with God if God is already IN all?* All that is required by various doctrines formulated by dissatisfied souls, then, is "probably" for naught.

All of this living life based on someone else's idea of what one must do to find favor with God is just one of the many "false standards" of mankind. It is false because it is not true. No one is really separated from God; and all who are led to believe there is a separation are basing their lives on false standards - or a false standard.

Would a Shiite Moslem be so quick to assassinate a fellow Moslem, a Sunni Moslem, if that Shiite was aware that God is not really separated from Life? Why does the Shiite act to kill a brother if that brother is one of the saved? Why? Because one Moslem is convinced that another Moslem is really a heretic - and thus not really a "true Moslem" at all. Thus, one Moslem is convinced that "his God" will smile down upon him if he "justly" removes all heretics - within the faith and outside of it.

But that standard is based on a false idea in the first place - that God is outside of us to be able to favor one of us over another. Why is it that one Moslem believes another is a heretic? Because one Moslem has been convinced by interpretation of a given "doctrine" that another Moslem is out of order.

From the Moslems to the Jews! At least ancient Jews believed that God can favor their race over another - and that was the entire scope of their religion. Thus, Jews of old believed that they needed to pray to their God in order to find favor with that God. If they did not pray to their God, then even as Jews, they would have been "heretical" and thus deserved to be eliminated from salvation.

In truth, ancient Christianity was no different. It taught that only those who find favor with God can be saved. What is that but an expression of a belief that some can be "outside of God"? But the notion is "probably" false. God is not really outside of anything or anyone; and thus no one needs "saved" from a Godlessness that cannot really exist.

Sadly, though, masses of Christians and masses of Jews and masses of Moslems have chosen to institute doctrines based on a falsehood - that God can favor one over another; and once more, those same doctrines have designated this life as "no good" in comparison to some fantasy existence someplace else. Thus, to find the "good" life someplace else, we must deny the "bad" life that is here and now.

But what are the consequences of believing that this life is bad? Some of us must act bad in order to "prove" that this is really a bad life. From that, we have people acting badly. It goes with the territory of believing that this life is really "bad." We must require a certain amount of bad or else our doctrine that this life is really bad would be suspect.

And if all were really good, then we would have to redefine good to include some bad in it. That is what false standards do. They look to justify themselves; and if need be, some who are really good must be turned bad in order to justify the doctrine of this being a "bad" world.

One of the "bad" acts, then, within a really "good" world is the act of going natural. If going natural were allowed, it would put to pity the doctrine that life is really bad because practice would prove that we are not the monsters without clothes that many insist we are. But we must not be allowed to pity a doctrine that practice would prove is wrong. Thus, going natural is banned - for the sake of the good of the world.

False Standard # 2 -

Everyone is Sinful

I must admit that as a child, I did believe that. I believed that "everyone is sinful" and that "all fall short of the glory of God" because that is what I was taught. Somehow, it made sense to me when I was a child that God could be outside of me. It was that "outside of me" that allowed for me to believe that I "could be sinful."

But those days of that belief have not lasted. I no longer believe I "can be sinful" - related to my relationship with God - because I no longer believe that God "can be outside of me." I guess you could say that I believe in a different God than the God of my youth.

When I was a kid, I saw my little world as just that - little. I saw the Earth as being the "bottom of the world." There was nothing below me but ground. So, within that scope of things, I could imagine a God somehow standing - or flying - above all of that. I was down below. I could imagine a God being above. In fact, I was taught that the Heaven I wanted to reach was up above. God was like a "Super Being" that stood above the Earth and was like someone who would either scowl at those who did not believe in "Him" and sentence them to Hell (always "below") - or as I hoped for myself - like someone who would be there to hand out congratulations and welcomes to that wonderful place called Heaven (always "above"). Nice thoughts - but based on false ideas.

Now I know that it is not likely that the Earth is anything but a spec floating about within an Infinite, Endless Universe of Existence; and I am a spec on a spec. Now I know that the Earth is indeed ground below me, but I know now that there is nothing but sky below the ending of the "bottom of the Earth." In a very real way, there is no such thing as a "bottom of the Earth" because the Earth is a round ball in space. There is no "below the Earth" anymore than there is an "above the Earth." Thus, there can be no "Hell below" as there can be no

"Heaven above." How can there be the proverbial Heaven and Hell if their original definitions are false? Tell me that!

Can God be a "Super Being" that can be imagined to be watching over things, waiting to judge all beings for being good or bad? Well, that is what could be called an "infantile" impression of God. How can God even be a "Being" that is separated from me or anything at all if God has to equal that vast Endless Existence I now know probably exists. How can God be an "Individual" at all if there is no place where God can't be? An individual has to have limits, but God can have no limits being equal to Infinity.

When I was a kid, I did not think much about anything - and I guess that is why my folks and my faith - Catholicism - could lead me to believe things that can't be true. I believed that there is a God outside of me because that is what I was taught - and I am absolutely positive that those folks who taught me that believed it themselves. They really believed that God can exist outside of things, thereby putting God in a position where "He" could judge us for doing good or bad.

But let's be real here! What do you think? Can there be a "Being God" if there can be no real end of existence itself? How could it be? If God is the "Supreme Being" that most folks still believe "He" is, how could it be that a "Supreme Being" could even exist outside of all existence? An Infinite God would have to be separate from all existence if God could be a person. Right? But how can God be separate from all existence if Existence is Endless? How can God be a person that can only thrive "up above" when there really can be no "down below"? Tell me that! Where is this "up above" if there can be no "up" - related to things in space? Where is this "down below" if there can be no "down" - related to things in space? Again, tell me that!

Some folks tell me that I get too heavy thinking such things, but I do not believe it is "heavy thinking" at all to ponder the probable reality of our world. It is not heavy thinking at all. It's only thinking; and I guess that is something I did not do much of when I was a kid - and many (if not, most) don't do much of as adults. We just do not think. I have become convinced of that. And that is why we can be taken by a halter and led this way or that way when it comes to somebody else's perception of God - and right and wrong - and sin.

So, what does it mean that "everyone is sinful" and that "everyone falls short of the glory of God" if, in fact, no one can fall short of God because God has to be everywhere and in everything? How can I be "short of the glory of God" if I cannot even be "short of God"?

The tragedy of false belief, however, is that people act like what they think is true is actually true. They really believe they can be "short of God" and thus they act like it too. If God is "good," then it stands to reason that if everyone falls short of God, then all must be "bad." If I can be bad, then presto, I am given license to act like a fool and to act like the person I really am. What does it matter if I go out and grab some child and rape her? I am only doing what is "expected of a bad person." Right?

Does it matter at all that it cannot be so? Does it matter at all that I cannot be sinful - as in lacking God - because I cannot lack God? Does it matter at all that God can't be a person waiting to rescue me from a "bad life" when, in reality, there can be no such thing as a "bad life" - related to God? Does it matter that because God must be IN all existence and must be equal to All Existence that it is impossible for me to "sin against God"? How can I sin against something that is in me?

Why not accept the "probable truth" that no one can sin against God and nothing can be short of the glory of God? Why not throw all that other nonsense out like a bunch of trash that is no longer of use? Why not take off your clothes and realize that you are "taking off" what man has put on you, not what God has put on you? Why not stand up and tell yourself that you have a new life because of a new vision? Why not realize that all existence is Good because a Good God must be IN all - and that includes you?

For what it's worth, I did so long, long ago; and that is just one example that it can be done.

False Standard # 3 -
Power is Virtuous!

If Pope Francis and Jesus were to meet on the street, would Jesus go to Pope Francis and say "Attaboy!" for all the "power" that Pope Francis thinks Jesus has committed to him? I doubt it - because I don't think

Jesus would applaud any kind of power in the first place - be it in his name or that of any other.

Remember, False Standard # 1? It dealt with man falsely believing that God is really outside of us for any of us to need to be saved. In fact, the traditional Jesus is based on False Standard # 1. In fact, the traditional Jesus is based on the idea that God and man are separated and that for man to be "saved," somehow God and man need to be unified. The traditional Jesus is one who was supposed to unite God with man - or man with God; but what does the notion that God is not really separate from man do to the idea of a "traditional Jesus"? It pretty much nullifies it. Doesn't it?

But power is an aphrodisiac! It gives out another of those many false illusions that man loves so well. If I can't have an orgasm, give me power - or even if I can have an orgasm, give me more of the same by giving me "power." Power is the end of it all. Without power, no one deserves to be alive. Only the "Powerful" are worth anything at all in this life. Thus, the emphasis on Power.

But why is power really an illusion of something beneficial for a lasting soul? It is an illusion because it is so short lived. It is like depositing a penny in the bank when you think you have deposited a million dollars. Why? Because Death Ends It All - that is, all that is "powerful." With death, power ends. So why in the world put any emphasis on it while we are alive?

I think the "real Jesus" was a true advocate of living without power. Was Jesus aware of many of his so called "disciples" - like perhaps, Peter and John - wanting to use him to "achieve power" when he was for having no power at all?

I am reminded of a quote in one my favorite works - *THE GOSPEL ACCORDING TO THOMAS*. Of course those who think power is so wonderful would not agree that Jesus may have said this, but in Verse 21, it is stated: *Mary said to Jesus: Whom are thy disciples like? He said: They are like little children who have installed themselves in a field which is not theirs. When the owners of the field come, they will say: "Release to us our field." They take off their clothes before them to release it (the field) to them.*

What is that to say - even though the words may be somewhat confusing - perhaps due to inconclusive translation from the original Coptic (Egyptian) to English? Still, the gist of it is that many who thought they were following Jesus for the "power" it seemed to invest in them would find upon death that they had no such power. His disciples were like *"little children who have installed themselves in a field which is not theirs."* That is how Thomas says that Jesus defined his disciples; and when, upon death, those disciples - who thought they had power in Jesus - died, they would find themselves stripped of that power as in having no clothes at all.

And that is "probably" the truth too. When we die, we are like naked, with no clothes to protect us or make us seem as we are not. In death, all are naked - and so, in death, so too were the "disciples of Jesus." I wonder if ones like Peter & John were around to hear that description. If they were, it seems they ignored it because it seems they were convinced that Jesus meant - and means - Power.

In another verse in *THE GOSPEL ACCORDING TO THOMAS*, Verse 81: *Jesus said: Let him who has become rich become king, and let him who has power renounce it.* That is perhaps an awkward way of saying that he who is rich is also like a king because there is really no difference between "being rich" and "being a king." Why? Because being rich and being a king are both expressions of power. It is not to say that one who is rich should also become a real king because only one can become a real king - even as there are many who are rich. How can there be "many kings"? So Jesus is not offering that the rich should become kings, but should see themselves as powerful "like kings."

The real instruction follows, however. Be you rich or a king or whatever, *"let him who has power renounce it."* And therein is the "real Jesus," I think. Let him who has power in this life renounce it because upon death, he will lose it anyway. It is only to say that the best preparation for death and the life to come - which may be much longer lasting than the current one - is to have no power at all in this life.

Again, faced with the inevitability of death, no man should think that power is really any advantage in this life. It does nothing for the next life - and being that it is totally contrary to the reality of a bodiless soul in death, it is almost useless. So, why seek it in this life?

But Power is an illusion in this life, isn't it? And one of the ways the so called "powerful" retain their power is to require that all people wear clothes. Regardless of one's reason or claim to power in this life, however, in all probability, upon death, it goes away. It just disappears like a leaf in a wind. *No matter how powerful you think you are in life, you will be without power and impotent in the next Why? Because it is your body that allows you to have power at all in this life; but without a body - no power - until you choose to reincarnate and do the same stupid thing all over again.*

What judge, however, will admit that power is useless - in the long stretch of things? In 1989, I was caught jogging natural on a Friday evening on a beach outside of Savannah, Georgia. I thought I was alone, but some who believed in "power" found me anyway. I was incarcerated for "public indecency" by the power elite of the area and brought before a judge on the following Monday. I was given like the "last rites" before death if I were to ever repeat my daring behavior again. "If you ever do this again," the Judge bellowed, he would "throw the book at me."

Admittedly, I was very timid when I asked the Judge if there is such a law as to really prohibit one from jogging natural on a beach - if that is all he is doing. The Judge literally sneered at me as if I was out of order to ask such a question. "There is such a law," he stated matter of factly, "and if you violate it again, watch out!" Then he fined me $350 for a first offense and let me go.

I have no idea if there is really such a law in Savannah, Georgia that bans jogging natural on a public beach, but if there is, why was it passed? To keep those in power from losing it. It is one of those great illusion things again. Judges think they need power and that the only thing that is worth anything in this world is to have power - and thus laws are passed - legally or illegally - that ban going naturally. Not only would the permission of going natural allow for a judge to be seen as he really is - the same as one brought before him - but there is that horrible thing called "power" that sticks out its rather ugly face.

Let us be reasonable, however. Why is going natural an affront to those who want and need power - or to those who think they need power? Because it is an equalizer. *Going natural tells it like it is; and those in power do not want things to be told like it is - lest they lose their power. So, they rule against going natural to keep them in power.* At least, that is the end of it all. The truth is that if I am allowed to go natural, so would a judge; and if a judge and I were both natural, how could you distinguish between the judge (ordinarily with robe) and myself - in terms of the power that one of us has that the other lacks?

Imagine the little fellow, Kim, who rules North Korea now having to stand in front of his "prisoner citizens" and letting them know that he is no different than they by taking off his clothes and showing all. Would they follow him without resistance then? Hardly! Thus, Mr. North Korea, bans going naturally in public and outfits all his prisoner citizens with "uniforms" - including himself - to offer and sustain the illusion that he is supposed to be more powerful than they.

False Standard # 4 -
The Truth is "Other Oriented"

At the beginning, I admitted that I like to see pictures of the natural me. There is really a good reason for that; and it is not that I am "obsessed with myself." The truth is that I am "obsessed with the truth," but I know that the truth begins with me. That is why I go natural and love to see pictures of me in a natural state. I am looking at the truth when I am looking at me. Now, if I were to go natural for the pleasure of it more than for the truth of it, then, of course, I would not have the same motivation for going natural. Would I?

But why is it so that to find the truth, I must begin with myself. It is because we are all the same and the smallest little atom - as I say in one of my songs - is just as Divine as the biggest star. If that is so, however, and I "know" that, then there is no reason whatever for me to go outside myself to find the truth. If I really believe that all are equally Divine, then that must include me. Right?

But how many preachers believe that? How many would argue that no one can find the truth unless it be told to him - or her? How many preachers are there out there standing in front of millions of people every Sunday telling listeners that they "must believe in Jesus" to be saved - or the like? How many really believe that they are the "center of Divinity" - that is the center of their own Divinity? How about Jesus? Did he even realize that all are equally Divine because all are equally of the Infinite?

My impression of Jesus is that he was very much a "solitary" kind of guy. I get the impression of that by the story that he loved to have children come to him. Why would anyone be "obsessed" with children? Why? Because he realized that every child is the same as every adult - in terms of worth. That is why Jesus would have asked the little children to come to him.

But what does a child know than an adult does not know? All I have to do to learn the answer to that is go back to my own childhood. After all, I was once a child. Wasn't I? What did I know as a seven year old that I should still know today? That is the key to knowing the truth, I think. Look at the world as a child - and treat the world as an adult as you "knew" it as a child.

So, what did I know at the age of seven? In truth, I knew that I did not know much of anything - and that lack of knowledge was far more important to me than the so called knowledge I would later learn in life.

I can "prove" what I am saying by imagining that a seven year old is zapped by lightening and is "taken away" from this world before he - or she - even begins learning much of anything in life. If I had been zapped by lightening when I was seven, would my worth have been impacted by anything at all? If I had been zapped by lightening as a seven year old and had never learned a whit about what people like Moses and Mohammed and Buddha - and even Jesus - might have told me, would I have been lacking in worth?

Any child knows the answer to that. Of course not - that is, of course I would not have been lacking in worth had I died as a child. What does that tell me? What should that tell anyone who has any sense? Knowledge from without is absolutely useless in the long run of things. It is only knowledge gained from within that means any-thing at all.

But the problem is that as we live - and supposedly learn - we actu-ally "dislearn" the most beautiful and wonderful of all truths - that all are equally good and that no one needs another to be saved. Unless you tell a child that he needs some advice from without, he - or she - would never know he - or she - is lacking. It is the process of life, then, that derails most people from really knowing how wonderful they are.

How many great people in the world know that, though? How many kings are aware that they are no more important than the ones who might be serving them? How many servants under kings know that they are as special as the kings they might serve? How many adults know what a child instinctively knows - that life itself is the great treasure of life?

What if the people down below that mountain that Moses supposedly climbed knew they were "as good as children"? What if they had been aware that Israelites could not be more "Godly" than Egyptians? What if they knew they could have no more worth than their children - or anyone's children? What if everyone down below that mountain that Moses climbed were aware of their true worth? Could Moses have come down from a mountain and told them anything that was useful? Of course not; but the truth is those Israelites were totally ignorant of their own worth - and that is why a Moses could come down from a mountain and tell them what they did not need to know - and, in fact, should have never been told.

What were the Israelites told that they should have never been told? They needed to "serve someone else" in order to know meaning themselves. If those Israelites had been aware they were already worthy just being the centers of a Divine Existence, they could have never been misled by a Moses - or a Mohammed - or anyone.

Again, go back to being seven. As a seven year old lost in a little world of worth, would I have had to know anything about what someone else would tell me - like a Moses or a Buddha or a Mohammed - or even a Jesus? NO! One can truly illustrate the worthlessness of some so called item of truth by asking if he - or she - really needed to know that item to have worth. If you need to know something I know - or think I know - and I never tell it to you - would you be less than you are? Of course not!

So, what am I really saying here? I am saying that the truth is really within - and as such - no one need depend on anyone outside of him - or her - to tell him - or her - anything worthwhile. I am saying take off your clothes and go back to being a little child. Imagine yourself being zapped by lightening - and then ask yourself - did I really need to grow up to learn what any so called wise person had to tell me - like a Moses or a Buddha or a Mohammed - or even a Jesus?

In truth, before I knew any of these people existed, I was. That is, before I knew they existed, I was only aware of me; and therein is the key to really knowing the truth.

That is not to say that Moses or Buddha or Mohammed or Jesus may not be filled with wisdom. They might be - or one or two of them might be; but my argument is that whatever wisdom they might have had I do not need to have worth. My worth - or your worth - is not dependent upon someone knowing about it. It just is - by virtue of my life having no dependence whatsoever on any other living being in terms of being dependent upon another living being for personal worth. Again, that can be "proved" by the possibility of my living and dying without any knowledge of any alleged sage that may have lived.

If a child in Iceland, for example, lives and dies without any exposure to any of the great sages of the world, would he - or she - have less worth because he - or she - did not know about a certain sage? Of course not!

Conclusion:

Choose Your Own Standards!

I have often admitted that I love the natural - but not for exhibition reasons. That is, I do not go natural because I think I am some grand tribute to mankind. I am just "one of the gang," so to speak - just one among an "everyone" that just happens to be the same. Sadly, I think, most of the human race has lived and still lives like we are different. In fact, most pride themselves on "being different" - not being the same. From that concentration and insistence on "being different," we have endured and are enduring terrible conflicts and wars because that is what happens when people focus on "being different." Liberty is defined by those who insist on "being different," not by finding common ground, but on standing on uncommon ground and being willing to fight for the right to be different.

I love taking pictures of myself in the buff, so to speak, because I want to see me as I am - not as others might want to see me - which is "different" from them. The natural tells it like it is; and as it is, we are all the same. Most people cannot handle life as it is, however, and insist on making it something different; and they have problems with ones like me trying to do just the opposite - concentrate on how we are the same as if there is nothing more important than "being the same."

Being the same, however, does not mean that we are not different in the details of our anatomies. For ones like me, however, those kinds of details do not matter a whit. Just because I am "different" than you because I have a small penis and you have a large penis does not mean that we are not the same. We are the same in nature - in spite of our differences in anatomy - and pictures once again express how much that is so; and that is another reason I like pictures of natural people so much.

Throw in fashion, though, and the entire picture of our "sameness" becomes obliterated. When we cover up, our sameness disappears. Why? Because our focus then becomes our different clothes and we lose sight completely of our "same nature." Fashion, then, becomes the real King; and we all become servants of that new king - and thereby lose sight of who we really are - wonderful creatures who are being given wonderful bodies and wonderful natures that are all "the same."

In spite of Fashion being the "Real King," however, I have gone natural all my life - when I've considered myself alone or have been expressly invited to do so - to emphasize for myself that I am no different than anyone else; and therein, I think, I have found the *ONLY KNOWLEDGE* that is important - the knowledge of knowing that I am just like everyone else and it is that knowledge that really allows me to live the "liberated life" I have lived - or have tried to live. I have lived outside of the "normal standards" of a man being measured by the size of his penis - or a woman being measured by the size of her breasts. I realize the idea of needing no power significantly aids me in doing as I have done, too. I have also realized that power is an illusion for the soul. That realization, too, has aided me in my own chosen virtue - to love life as it is because it is worthy of being loved.

On occasion, I have spent a few days in jail for stepping outside the normal limits of things. There is that 1989 (or perhaps 1990) Savannah, Georgia incident I mentioned - and then an earlier one in Atlanta, Georgia in 1985 where I was thrown in a cell for riding natural on a bike in an empty parking lot. Then, too, I thought I was alone, but prying eyes found me not alone. In that case, I was detained on a Saturday and released on a following Monday. The Judge in that case was a woman and she actually agreed with me that we should all be allowed to ride our bikes - au natural - but she argued that I had to impress a legislature to pass a law to permit it. She fined me $100 and urged me to appeal to a legislature.

I paid the fine, but I have yet to appeal to any legislature to modify anti-natural laws simply because I know there has been almost no chance of any American legislature doing that. We Americans are much too dependent upon old morality laws to even consider a new morality - or at least we have been. Maybe the time will come, however, when a legislature somewhere - American or foreign - will consider that anti-natural laws are generally harmful - and may cause much of the outrageous behavior - like rape - that it is claimed they should prevent.

Then there was a Virginia incident in 1994 when three truckers trapped me to prove to them that I was driving without clothes down a Virginia highway. Such daring conduct! How could it be allowed? So one trucker kept me from passing another trucker so they could be sure I was without clothes from being able to peer down on me in my smaller car from a lofty seat in a truck.

Normally, if driving without clothes, I do not pass another vehicle unless I can pass it quickly, thus preventing passengers in a vehicle I am passing from seeing me in such an "offensive state"; but in this case, one truck in the right lane just ahead of one I was passing veered to the left while I was passing the truck on the right - thus preventing me from "whizzing by." Apparently the trucker ahead of the one I was trying to pass must have noticed earlier that I was natural - and thus to be sure I was natural - must have communicated with the trucker I was now trying to pass. Then a third trucker pulled over to the left lane behind me and prevented me from falling back.

I may have it wrong, but it sure seemed that way. Call it "entrapment" by a series of truckers. In any case, I was caught driving without clothes when normal practice would have allowed me to pass quickly and give no one a chance to see me from an elevated seat. Before that experience, I had probably traveled at least 40,000 miles driving without cover-up - and had not once had an incident. I am almost certain that I was "trapped intentionally" because later - down I-81 about 20 miles from my entrapment - I was detained by a highway patrolman - even though when the patrolman stopped me, I was dressed. The patrolman asked if I had been driving without clothes about 20 miles back. I said "yes" - and I was told to follow the patrolman as he escorted me to a local jail.

In that jail, a holding cell, I was alone. So, I proceeded to get natural again to focus on the miracle and wonder of life as I often do when I am natural. An officer appeared at a window and commanded me to put on my clothes. For awhile I resisted; but eventually, I agreed to put on my clothes to "keep the peace" in the community. It is truly amazing what we humans consider important. What difference would it have made if I stayed in my cell without clothes? I was the only one there. What did it matter anyway?

On the following Monday, I appeared before a judge and admitted my guilt. I had been driving without clothes on a pubic highway. So, why argue differently? The Judge fined me a whopping $50 and smiled at me as he set me free as if telling me by his fine that he agreed that I had not violated much at all. And so, I really hadn't done anything wrong at all. Had I? Who was hurt by my driving without clothes on a public highway? Why should it have been an issue at all? Amazing!

Some - of both family and friends - have cautioned me that my thoughts - and perhaps, ways - can get me into trouble. Do I ever know that! I have already illustrated that with past troubles that I have encountered by doing what I think is right; and there have been some additional incidents too. Trouble may indeed find me, but given that I am not much of an "exhibitionist," it is not likely I will get into trouble for doing what I do - simply because I do not deal with my beliefs as a public issue, but rather as a private belief.

By that, I mean I have never gone natural in the public when I have known the public is really watching. I realize there are laws against what I consider the Ideal of a Natural Life; and I do not violate them - even as I do pursue my own personal journey to be the best soul I can be. I do not need an audience for that. Like anyone else, the only audience I need - is myself. That may lend to the appearance that I am "obsessed with myself," but the truth is that I am far more "obsessed with the truth" that Life itself is worthy of everyone's respect and that everyone should go without cover-up to prove it.

And again, the reason I am mostly alone in my pictures is that no one else volunteers to join me. How can I take pictures of other natural people if no one agrees to go natural? I have attended a few so call "nudist colonies," however, and I have taken some pictures of other natural people, but for the most part, I have been alone in my love for the natural state. Perhaps someday another or others will join me - and the illusion that I am "obsessed with myself" will go away.

In the end, though, each of us must choose our own standards - or each of us should choose our own standards. If you believe in power, go for it, I guess. You will probably find it rather impotent in the end, but if you believe it is useful, go for it. If you believe that you have to please a God outside yourself, go for that too. If you believe that size really is important, then choose that as one of your standards too. Or, you can take it all off as I try to do - and live your life like there are no judges and no police officers and no dictators and no one to condemn you for doing what is right - to love life because it is worthy - and to do it for that reason alone.

It all works well in the end, though, because in the end, we are all equal. In death, we are all naked - like Jesus argued in the quote I used. In death, we are all without power. In death, size - or color - means nothing at all. So, why act like any of it means anything at all in life? Right? In death, the Kingdom of God in an afterlife will be known to be the same as the Kingdom of God in the life that preceded it.

Where is the "Kingdom of God"? It is right here with you. It is right here with me. It will be there with you; and it will be there with me. The Kingdom of God is a place - but it is a place called "Everywhere." But the Kingdom of God is also a state of mind. Belonging to it virtually requires awareness. I highly recommend that state of mind. OK?

A song about why I go natural follows.
Enjoy it as you will!

Thanks! (FWB)

Why I Go Natural

By
Francis William Bessler
Laramie, Wyoming
8/18/2013

I'm asked why I go natural.
I say it's to be a grateful one.
I don't see how I can say Thanks
by denying what I'm from.
And what I'm from is Nature;
and Nature is Divine.
So I'm so glad to go through life
as a son of Thine.

I'm asked why I go natural.
I say it's to do what is right.
It is not right to accuse life of wrong
as if we have better sight.
I like that I am part of the All
and the All is All Good.
So, let me prance naturally
to find true brotherhood.

I'm asked why I go natural.
I say it's to find Heaven here.
Heaven is only knowing God's all about.
So, that makes Heaven everywhere.
God is really not a person -
rather a Presence in everything.
So, no matter where I go,
Heaven's bells will ring.

I'm asked why I go natural.
I say it is to find I am at home.
When I know that all are the same,
I know that I cannot be alone.
You see, we are all God's children,
whatever it is that God is.
And because we're all of God,
none of us can be of sin.

I'm asked why I go natural.
I say, why not join me?
Look at yourself as a miracle
like the middle of Divinity.
We are all equally worthy
and each of us belongs.
No matter where we might go,
that should be our song.
Yes, no matter where we might go,
Heaven should be our song.

Life Is Beautiful!

By
Francis William Bessler
Laramie, Wyoming
10/12/2013

Misguided Traditions

As I see it, the "truth" is in everything - but if you want the most direct route to it - listen to Nature - not those of us who have been "given" some so called "knowledge" by virtue of inheriting some tradition or other.

In my opinion, because of my experience with life, the greatest obstacle to finding the truth in life has been having to "overcome" some idea that I was given by virtue of a tradition I was handed. People get locked into some tradition - or within some tradition - and it is like they become blind to anything else.

I was born Catholic; and because of my "Catholic upbringing," I was "told" from birth that all life is sinful - and, of course, needs to be redeemed. Is it sinful? NO! But I was taught that it is - and that is just one example of listening to the wrong source for any answers about life.

You may ask how I know that I was told wrong that all life is sinful? Of course, it is but personal opinion, but in thinking about sin as I was taught it is, sin is "separation from God" or the consequences of that. It stands to reason, then, that sin is entirely dependent upon "being separated from

God." Right? But if one cannot be separated from God, then one can't be sinful - given that sin is related to separation from God. I have concluded that since Existence must be Infinite and since God must equal Infinite Existence, then nothing can be separated from God. Accordingly, all that sin that I was taught is my inheritance is not so at all. Is it?

My former tradition is just one example, though. I am not alone, however. Am I? Just look around and observe the world at large. Who among us has been born outside of some tradition or other? No one! We all have to deal with overcoming whatever it is that our various traditions have taught us; but we have to realize that tradition itself is the greatest obstacle for finding the truth.

Just look around - and observe! What Christian kid is free to think about Jesus as a kind of sage, like Socrates, rather than a Jewish Messiah? What Islamic kid is free to think about Mohammed as just one of them? What Jewish kid is really free to think about Moses as potentially only fiction - or at least, partly fiction? What North Korean kid is really free to think about life in a way different than his North Korean kindred? What American kid is really free to think about life in a way different than what "Americanism" is claimed to be about? And it goes on and on and on.

The "truth" is that we are all captive of some tradition; and in the end, that is probably why we fight among ourselves so much. We fight each other because we are upholding our various traditions; and when those traditions are probably nonsense in the end, if we are smart, we would stand up and ask - Why?

In the end, no matter what the kid, the problem with that kid knowing the "real truth" can be reduced to some tradition or other. That is the "plain truth." It could be argued that tradition is the greatest obstacle to finding the truth. If you go to it - regardless of what that tradition is - you will not find truth. You will only find what that given tradition has determined it is - with "it" being "the truth."

Keep in mind, too, that a tradition can be religious or irreligious, political or familial, comprised of one follower or dozen followers or a zillion followers. A tradition is really only at least one following the lead of someone else - and, for the most part, having to answer to that someone else for his or her conduct. It can be harsh or it can be kind to its adherent - or adherents.

I watched a movie recently that featured a wife being unfaithful to her husband. She asked him to forgive her, but she held out a sledge hammer to him if he chose to "punish" her. In this case, he took the sledge hammer and hit her over the head - and, of course, killed her. So much for the possibility of forgiveness; but this was tradition in practice - or a tradition in practice. One person claiming the right to command obedience of another - regardless of what that obedience might be. In this case, I would say it was a very insane tradition - but it is only one example of many absolutely insane traditions.

The Truth - Too Late

Tomorrow I may die; and today is not the time to realize I may have been following a wrong tradition all my life. By "wrong," I mean a tradition based on a "mistaken understanding of life."

It should be clear by virtue of the many various traditions within civilization that in all likelihood, none of those traditions have a correct sense of truth. Why? Because they all have in common needing to listen to - and perhaps obey - some other human source.

Regardless of tradition, if I have to listen to another human being - and again, perhaps obey that other human being - then my tradition is based on being "other oriented"; but in being other oriented, it can only be an interpretation of life by someone else; and who is to say that someone else is any wiser than me - or any wiser than I could be?

In my opinion, every soul should know that it can know what any other soul might know - regarding what could be called "spiritual truth" or truth related to the welfare of a soul. So, let each soul know for itself. That is the safe way to go. If I have to depend on another soul to direct me, that is to imply that I cannot know a truth of myself - or by myself. And if I cannot know a truth by myself, how can I be sure that the claim of someone else is true? If I can't know what is true, how can I know what another claims is true is actually true? Why prance after someone else like he or she can know the truth and I can't if he or she can't really know more than I? If a lead cannot know more than me, why not trust myself to know what I need to know?

It is in that light that I believe relying on a tradition to lead me to the truth is a very dangerous way to go for a soul. Why do it if the truth - if it really is the truth - should be accessible to all by virtue of the same reason that led one person to the truth should also be available in one's mind to lead another to that same truth? And, again, if I cannot know the truth of and by myself, why should I assume that you do? If you are really a fool and do not know the truth, but think you do, in following you, I have followed a fool and have become a fool myself. Why should I choose such a course in life? Why?

I think that the single greatest reason we humans have warped ideas about life is because we insist on listening to the tales of various traditions - and every single one of those traditions pay no mind whatever to the concept of *INFINITY.*

Moses, for example, could not have known about what he was making laws about because he was ignorant of Infinity. I am sure that Moses failed to even speculate about an Infinite Universe - and yet he made all sort of laws that all his kindred were supposed to obey because he was of the mind that Life Is Not Infinite - or Existence Is Not Infinite. He paid no mind to such a concept - and that is why his ideas about life are warped - and that is why all of those who live in his footsteps and act like he was some kind of "prophet from - or for - God" are as blind as Moses was - assuming, of course, that Moses did really live and that the story of Moses is not some fiction tale told in order to establish a tradition.

One's view of the one we call "God" makes all the difference in the world. My view of God is that God is Infinite - and therefore inside of me as well as inside of everyone. Infinity proclaims that; but if I am of the mind that God is not equal to Infinity, then I am led to define God as an individual - and not as an All Present Reality. For Moses, God was an individual - and thus "someone" he could talk with and take direction from - and use to direct others as to what that "God" might be saying to him.

My God and I cannot have a "conversation" because My God is not an individual with whom I can communicate - being simply a presence that is everywhere; but the God of Moses was an individual

- and thus Moses could conceive of one with whom he could converse. Accordingly, Moses "met" his conversational God on a mountain and that conversational God gave him tablets full of commandments which Moses was directed to give to his clan camped below the mountain.

Well, that is what Moses claimed in the *Book of EXODUS* as recorded in the *BIBLE*. But very conveniently Moses destroyed the tablets after coming down from the mountain. He claimed he broke them in anger when he saw his people worshipping some golden calf or such; but the probable truth of the matter is that he had never been given any tablets. For whatever reason, he decided that he needed to claim that his God gave him a bunch of commandments, but for practical reasons he had to destroy the tablets - lest his testimony of tablets be questioned. Without evidence of tablets, no one could review the evidence of his claim; and so Moses simply claimed he was given a bunch of tablets but those tablets were lost. How convenient to not have to "present" evidence. Right?

But apparently the clan of Moses did not question the story of Moses - and Moses went on to "present" all the supposed commandments that his God supposedly gave him - and the rest is history - or should I say, tradition. I am not sure how I would have reacted to Moses if he had claimed that story and not presented any evidence, but I suspect that I would have challenged him and told him that without evidence of tablets, I would not comply. But therein is the problem with hearsay - and believing hearsay without challenging it; it often turns into "tradition."

Now, I don't blame Moses for doing as he did and claiming the authority he did because he was probably only trying to institute order - and he simply used a tale of convenience to do that; but if Moses had not had that idea that God could be an individual with whom he could have communicated, then we probably would not have a tradition called *Judaism* today. In short, Judaism - as all traditions that claim a "conversational God" as their foundation - would not be prevalent today; but Ignorance of Infinity allows so much that would have never been allowed if people only took reality into consideration when forming their traditions.

What did Peter think about life? Was he an "apostle of Moses"? Probably - because he was a faithful Jew. What did John think about life? Was he an "apostle of Moses"? Probably - because he was a faithful Jew. What did Jesus think about life? Was he an "apostle of Moses"? Maybe - and maybe not - but in my opinion, "probably not."

Jesus Versus Moses

My view of Jesus is that he opposed all the laws of the Jews (or at least, many of them) - and since those laws came from Moses - then Jesus had to have "opposed Moses." That would hardly make Jesus an "apostle of Moses." Would it?

Why would I claim that Jesus may have "opposed" Moses - or the ideas of Moses? Because Jesus was strictly an "attitude man" - and Moses was a "membership man." What is the difference? An attitude man is strictly that - one who believes that doing what is right is a matter of attitude and it is the attitude itself that determines if one is "saved" or not. A membership man is one who claims that "salvation" is a matter of membership within some formal group.

The formal group of salvation for Moses was the Jewish Nation. To gain salvation for Moses was to be a Jew - and, of course, comply with all the Jewish Law that went with being a member of that nation. I have no such image of Jesus. Do you? Can you imagine Jesus offering that salvation is a matter of belonging to some nation - as opposed to just "being moral"? I can't imagine any such thing - and that is why I am given to believe that Jesus probably "opposed" Mosaic Ways - and in no way, would he have agreed to be part of such a thing.

Why would have Peter and John - and their likes - have still stayed "apostles of Moses" if, in fact, their "leader" opposed the ideas of Moses? Why? Because they refused to give up their ties to their tradition - which came from Moses, regardless of whether Moses was a real person or fiction character. Jesus was willing to give up those ties, but that does not mean anyone around him was willing to follow his lead.

Did the likes of Peter and John want to risk that their Judaism could be wrong? I doubt it; and so they probably stuck with their ways in spite of hearing their friend, Jesus, tell them his way was better. What was "his way"? Being kind to all! That's all! But could Peter and

John see the light and adopt rule over law? There is NO EVIDENCE they did.

Now, assume that the likes of Peter and John were insistent on claiming to be "believers of Jesus," what would they have likely done - given that they refused to accept that the tradition of Moses was never correct for failure to appreciate a mighty reality like Infinity? Presto - they would have included Jesus within their failed tradition - not excluded him from it.

And therein is the likely tradition of most Christians. In insisting that the tradition of the Jews - founded in part by Moses - was legitimate, they chose to include Jesus within it and make Jesus somehow an "apostle of Moses" when, in fact, Jesus may have opposed everything about Moses. But that just goes to show how absolutely crazy traditions are - or can be.

How many Christians in this world today would even consider that Jesus opposed Moses? How many Christians today are absolutely certain that Jesus followed in the footsteps of Moses - and that no one should deny Moses lest they deny Jesus too? How many? How many? How many?

Let us be honest. What did Peter and John do with what might be called Christianity? They simply extended the concept of a "chosen nation" - or a "favored people" of the Old Jews to the "New Judaism." They did not think they were ceasing to be Jews by believing in what Jesus taught. They simply argued that their "nation" was being extended by allowing a greater "membership." Now, it was no longer necessary to belong to the "nation" of Israel to be saved. Now, it was necessary to belong to a "nation " of Jesus to be saved; and that "nation" was comprised of all who believe in Jesus as a "new Moses" - in general terms, a messiah.

Moses had been their messiah since the time he rescued them from Egypt and led them into a "promised land" called Israel. Now Jesus became their "new messiah" and to reach the new "promised land," they would have to submit to Jesus like they had earlier submitted to Moses. What was the basis of the old Judaism of Moses? It was structured to contain all sort of law and regulation - exactly what Jesus probably opposed, being the "attitude man" that he was. What was the basis - and is the basis - of the new Judaism called Christianity? It is structured to contain all sort of law and regulation. In a way, there is no significant difference between the old Judaism and the new Christianity. Both are "membership" oriented - and not just attitude minded.

As I see it, Jesus taught there is but one thing necessary for salvation - and that is kindness to all for believing in the worth of all. But Peter and John went forward to claim that kindness of itself will gain you nothing. You have to belong to a membership to be saved - not just be kind to all. Am I not right?

What is the so called "Kingdom of God" about for Christians? It is about "belonging to a formal group" - a group of kindred souls who will eventually rule the world. It is about being part of a nation that is above all other nations. It is about having God as the Supreme Head of a "land of salvation" that cannot be opposed and whose members will be forever free. And it is about Power - power to rule others in the name of Jesus.

But Jesus was not about power when he lived; and he will never be about power - no matter how much we may want it so. Why? Because he did not need it to have a sense of worth; and neither does anyone else.

The Dismissal of Jesus

Why was Jesus killed? I think he was killed because he "opposed the laws of Moses"? That is dangerous territory - to be a Jew and oppose the tradition of Jews; but I think that is what Jesus did - and that is why some of his fellow Jews were happy to see him dismissed.

You won't find that in the so called "Christian scriptures," though, because those scriptures were written by Jews - and written by Jews who were intent on holding on to their traditions. So they tell the story that Jesus entered a Jewish temple and overturned the tables of the money changers in anger to suggest that Jesus opposed - not Moses - but an incorrect use of Moses. In the end, Moses is upheld - not dismissed - as I think Jesus was intent on doing.

Of course, that is a personal opinion; but from what I have gathered about Jesus, he "probably" taught that "Heaven is at hand" - meaning here and now. That would have gone completely contrary to the views of the Jewish authorities of the time that depended upon "Heaven being remote" - so they could use the "promise of Heaven" as a way to control their people. And, of course, it goes completely contrary to current views of Jesus that have him being the way to a Heaven someplace else - or at least, to a Heaven not here and now.

But therein is the power of tradition. It is like a huge swamp that can swallow any truth and make whatever truth it wants out of any story - including one like Jesus. Jesus simply became a "substitute for Moses" rather than a "challenger of Moses." Why? Because those who believed that the tradition of Moses was legitimate were the same ones who relayed the story of Jesus; but in making Jesus a part of a tradition he actually opposed - or may have actually opposed - we have lost sight of the "real Jesus." That, I believe.

The reality of the new tradition of most Christians is that in believing that Moses was a true hero of God, they have simply made Jesus a "new Moses." The Jesus I know would never have approved of finding Heaven anywhere but within - simply because "within" is part of "everywhere." How could God not be "within" if God is "everywhere"? The Jesus I know would never have approved of anyone needing to "sacrifice" some animal to please God - and that is exactly what Moses did. His Heaven was not within (or everywhere) - but a present to be for those who obeyed some outside commandment - whatever that commandment might be.

But what did the "new Jews" - the Christians do? They approved of the idea of sacrifice - instituted by Moses - and then turned Jesus into a sacrifice - and turned themselves into sacrifices too because if their leader was a sacrifice, so also must be all the followers. In truth, Jesus probably opposed the idea of sacrifice because it makes no sense to have to "sacrifice" to please a God that is already within, but because his followers were lost within their own tradition, they made Jesus into what he opposed - or may have opposed. Again, that just goes to show the great corruptibility of tradition.

If I may, though many traditional Jews and Christians would pay it no mind, one of the final verses of *THE GOSPEL ACCORDING TO THOMAS* at least implies that Jesus may have taught that Heaven is Imminent - and not remote as many who teach Jesus would have us believe. In Verse 113 (of 114) of that gospel, it is stated: *His disciples said to Him: When will the Kingdom come? Jesus said: It will not come by expectation; they will not say" "See, here" or "See, there." But the Kingdom of the Father is spread upon the earth and men do not see it.*

I offer this only to declare that some who wrote about Jesus would not have made Heaven a "membership" thing as did apostles Peter and John - but rather a "presence" thing; and let that be a little evidence that I might be right that Jesus was not about membership - but attitude. Heaven is already here because God is "spread upon the earth." It is not for us to find Heaven elsewhere, but recognize it is right where we are - because God is where we are.

Did Jesus want to die? No! But he was killed to be an example of what should happen to one who would oppose tradition. He was not killed to be a "sacrifice" to any God because there is no Personal God to be impressed with such an act. But the precursors of Jesus believed there is a Personal God and they believed that such a "Personal God" can be impressed; and so they created temples to do just that.

Again, that is all consequence to an *"IGNORANCE OF INFINITY."* If one is ignorant of Infinity - and an Infinite Existence - then one can lead himself to believe that there is a "Personal God" that can exist here or there within a reality that has an end. A personal God makes sense in such a "creation," but a personal God makes no sense within an Infinite Existence that includes Creation.

If Existence is really Infinite and there is no end to it, how can there be a Personal God marching about somehow within Infinity? How can Infinite Reality - which I now think of as "God" - be also a Personal Reality when the very definition of "person" is something that is limited? *How can God be a "person" when it is impossible that God can be limited?*

Anyway, there it is - an explanation of how tradition itself - or any tradition - can be "misguided." *When reality itself is not taken into consideration, any "truth" can be decided - and so it is with all traditions of which I am aware. Traditions are based on concepts of existence; and if one's concept of existence is wrong, then so also is any tradition based upon that concept. So has gone the world of yesteryear; and so goes the world today.*

A Simple Sunflower

I can know the truth, however, and find truth simply by looking at reality. I said at the outset that I think the truth is in everything - but by "everything" I mean all that is in Nature - that does not see itself as opposed to Nature. That is the condition. "Everything" does not include that which is opposed to Nature - or sees itself as opposed to Nature. From such views of opposition to Nature comes the many traditions that I have already disclaimed as being sources of any worthwhile truth.

A few days ago, I removed the sunflower plants that earlier graced my yard. I removed them because it was time for them to die. I will plant them again - or seeds from them - when it is time for them to live again next Spring. *But in one sunflower is more truth than all the so called truth that mankind has ever claimed to know - or all the traditions of mankind who have chosen to deny the worth of a sunflower - or the worth of anything.*

Look at a sunflower - and therein is the Universe Itself. In every living thing, there is a reflection of all that is. If I want to find the truth of me, then, I should look at a sunflower - and be amazed - not only at the sunflower and its beauty - but at myself for being like a sunflower. Am I not as beautiful as a sunflower?

In one sunflower, I can find that Precious Infinity in which I have to come to believe. It just makes sense. There is no presence in a sunflower of so called "good" and "evil." If so, where would the good end and the evil begin? But as it is in one sunflower, so also is it in the Entire Universe because, at least in my opinion, every entity in Creation reflects Creation itself. You cannot divide a sunflower into good and evil parts; and because a sunflower is a reflection of all existence, then neither can you really divide anything in existence into good and evil parts.

I said that I removed my sunflower plants because it was time for them to die, but what does death really mean for a sunflower? Again, just observe the truth. The seeds of that sunflower will allow the sunflower to "live again" - and so it is with anything that lives - including me - and you. As the sunflower lived in this season, it will live again next season; but it will live again only as a sunflower and not something else. It will not come up out of the ground as a rose or dandelion or a gladiola. Will it?

Why should I take comfort in the truth that a sunflower will again be another sunflower? Because it tells me that I will be the same as I was too. Whatever it was that I chose to be in this life, it is likely I will return as that same thing in the next life - that is, in terms of attitude.

As I have argued in other articles, I don't think I take anything with me when I die, except my attitude. I will have left my brain behind upon death and therefore I will have no memory. I will have left my body behind and therefore I will have no body - to do anything with - be it boss or be bossed. All I will take with me is my attitude; and that is why living in fair attitude is the single most important thing I can do in life. In a way, my attitude is the ONLY THING I can take with me when I die. So, why not emphasize attitude while I live and take that with me?

If I want to be kind in a next life - when I do find myself in another body - then I should be kind in this one. If I want to be a murderer in a next life, then let me plan for that by being that in this life. If I want to be a judge in the next life, hey, let me practice now to be a judge. If I think that outside law should drive the next life, let me be a legislator in this one. Practice makes perfect, as they say. Right? Whatever I choose to be as a soul in this life, however, I will probably repeat it in the next life. That is the likelihood of my existence - if, in fact, there is something about me that lives on.

When people tell me that I won't live on as a soul, I ask them, how, then, as a soul, did I come into this world - assuming I do have a soul, of course? From where did my attitude about life originate? The sunflower did not just begin from nothing in this season. It came from the seeds of a last life. Why, then, should I believe that I did not come from a last life? Did I just poof into existence this time? That is, did my soul just poof into existence? That goes contrary to all that I see in this life. Nothing comes "poof" into any existence. It always comes from something that preceded it. Why should I believe I am any different?

Who knows about the soul? We all speculate about what it is, but the truth is that none of us know for sure what it is and from where it might originate as a soul in the beginning of its life; but for what it's worth, let me say that I have thought a lot about the soul - even as to where it originates or how it originates in the first place. Volume 2 of my *OUT IN THE OPEN* writings selection of my website is dedicated to the soul and ideas about the soul - including an essay composition I call *UNMASKING THE SOUL*. Of course, you are welcome to review that volume - or any of the 10 volumes of my writings from 1963 to 2012 - you wish. *Let me just say, be my guest.* OK?

Anyway, Nature provides many examples that I can imitate; and I can choose to be like anything in that great throng of entities I choose. Not everything in Nature is a sunflower that doesn't eat other sunflowers or other flowers. There are tigers, too, that survive on eating other animals - but they have to kill those other animals first. I can be like a tiger and kill others; but if I choose to be a tiger, then it is likely I will continue to be a tiger - until I choose to change and be more like a lamb, for example.

Personally, I believe that was the basis of the message of Jesus. As we live, we will have to live again. As we reap, we will sow again. It is so plain if we just look at Nature and see how it is all true.

So, I can choose to abide by some tradition or other in this life; and more than likely, I will fall into line in a next life and become one of a tradition once again. Who knows how and where any of us will be "born again" into our next life anymore than how we were born into this life, but I am willing to bet that if I chose to live according to some tradition in this life, I will simply choose a tradition of my birth in a next life too - regardless of what that tradition might be.

Maybe I was born of Christian parents in this life - and was a Christian because of that; but maybe next time I will be born of Islamic parents. What chance will I have of "becoming Christian" in a next life? I will probably be Islamic and maybe even go to war with formerly Christian brothers. That could be the price of adhering to tradition without any effort to challenge it.

In any case, whether there is a next life or not, I think it would be wise of me to act like life is sacred and treat it accordingly. Let me look at a sunflower and know that I am no different - or that likely it is so. There is no evil in me as there is no evil in a sunflower. As a sunflower eagerly takes in life without any

apology or shame for what it is, let me do the same - or be the same. Yes, indeed, a simple sunflower can tell me all I need to know - if I will just listen.
    This, I Believe!

Note:
A song about
"being beautiful"
follows.

Sing It Out!

Thanks! (FWB)

I Am Beautiful

(And So Are You)

a song by
Francis William Bessler
10/12/2013

I am beautiful
and so are you.
That, my friends,
is the wonderful truth.
Life is grand
just as it is.
Because God is in it,
we can have no sin.

I am beautiful
and so are you.
So, let me see
what I can do.
We're all the same,
each and everyone.
Let us all act
like we're all God's sons.

I am beautiful
and so are you.
Let's look around
and enjoy the view.
Everything is a miracle
because it's all Divine.
So, let's not be shy
and see our lives as fine.

I am beautiful
and so are you.
Look at the sunlight
to find a clue.
We are all children
of the light.
Let's not be scared
of the night.

I am beautiful
and so are you.
Like birds in flight,
we're spectacular too.
And like sunflowers
blooming in full array,
let us all have
a happy day.

Indeed, it's time
to open our eyes
and see life
as delightfully fine.
It's time to put away
all of our fears
and finally realize
what we've missed
through all the years.

You are beautiful
and so am I.
We have no reason
to be shy.
We are grand
because we were made
to march proud
in life's grand parade.

You are beautiful
and so am I.
Within us all,
life does abide.
Let's be proud
and each other embrace
and look at each other
face to face.

Yes, let's be proud
and each other embrace
and enjoy one another
face to face.
Don't be shy.
Know of your worth
and let's find Paradise
on this Earth.

Yes, let's find Paradise
on this Earth.
Let's find Paradise
on this Earth.

Life Is Good!

By
Francis William Bessler
10/28/2013

Paradise Valley

The last time I visited "Paradise Valley," it was called "Hidden Valley." I wonder if it has changed since May of 2000, when a dear friend named Koko and I last visited it. Hidden Valley/Paradise Valley is a clothing optional naturalist resort located some 60 miles or so northeast of Atlanta, Georgia, down a Highway 400 and then off a Road 136 a few miles south of a little town called Dawsonville. When I lived in Georgia from 1981 – 2001, I visited Hidden Valley a good bit – being the naturalist I am. In fact, I spent the summer of 1984 as a resident of Hidden Valley as a bit of a caretaker of the yards.

"Hidden Valley" was a good name for this place years ago because it was "hidden" off the road with no signs indicating where it was. You just had to know where it was to get to it. I suppose many of the members preferred that it was "hidden" because it was like a "secret society" in a way – and some (though not all) of the members did not want it to be known that they belonged to such a society. To some degree, it was a kind of hush-hush thing – if you know what I mean; although it was a family oriented, all are welcome, type of organization. As a divorced single at the time when I was a caretaker of the yard, only a few singles were allowed to join – for fear that singles would turn a family oriented venue into a raunchy singles sex club.

After that first year of 1984, however, I have only visited that which was called "Hidden Valley" a number of times without actually keeping up an initial membership. My last visit, as I mentioned, was with a friend named Koko in May of 2000. Koko was in her late '40s as I was in my late '50s. Since moving to Wyoming in early 2002, I have lost contact with friend, Koko, but I will always have memories of our being far more open as naturalists than many who attended Hidden Valley. Koko was about as free a spirit as I have ever known. She danced around on the grounds and wanted me to video her – which I was most willing to do.

When Koko and I visited in May of 2000, however, management was changing. The old management never discouraged me from videoing at all; but the new management warned me that all videoing was discouraged because someone might get caught on video that did not want to be included; but Koko and I were not part of those who were afraid we might be seen – or perhaps afraid of being videoed or pictured as we really are.

In fact, I have long loved going natural as I am for the camera – be that camera my own or belonging to someone else. I have long ago given up any kind of notion that I am not good as I am; and I believe only those can do bad to others who do not accept their own goodness. *I believe that "doing bad" is only an expression of "feeling bad" about oneself and then transferring those "hurt feelings" to being willing to hurt others. Kindness, on the other hand, is only "feeling good" about oneself – and then being willing to share that sense of esteem and comfort with others as if those others are only an extension of oneself.*

Now, don't get me wrong. I am not claiming I think I am any more photogenic than anyone else. I certainly am not. I am only claiming that I believe being photogenic – or attractive in any cultural sense – should not be much of a factor in anyone's embrace of him or herself; and it is really an issue of self-embrace or self-acceptance that should move anyone to join a naturalist community such as Hidden Valley; but as it is with such as Hidden Valley, ideally it should be everywhere on the face of this Earth.

Indeed, if such as Hidden Valley were not treated as "secret societies" and the members of such communities were invited to march proudly down the main streets of the world, that freedom that many of the Hidden Valley types claim only for themselves would be extended to the peoples of the world in general; and then maybe, just maybe, people would realize they should not hide themselves and that this Earth really is a Paradise just waiting to happen.

Paradise Valley – No Longer Hidden

So, Hidden Valley is no longer a "hidden" one. It is now "Paradise Valley." I must say the name change suits me. I am hoping as I write this that during this visit with my daughter, Melissa, I can persuade her to take me to the new Paradise Valley – and maybe roam about there as in the good ole days; but whether that happens or not, I think it is good to know that wherever I am, it should be Paradise. I should not have to "go anywhere" to find Paradise. I should be able to find it wherever I am.

Just think about it for a moment, if you will. What does almost everyone dream about when they ponder Paradise? It is essentially a "place of worth." Right? *Does not everyone who thinks about Paradise agree that it is a place of worth where everyone is equally worthy and no one is left out? OK. Let us make Paradise on Earth.* Why not? If an essential character of it is believing it is a place of worth, then why not recognize the Earth is a place of worth and that everyone and everything on Earth are equally worthy? If it is as simple as that, why not make it happen?

But then there's the issue about "private parts." Isn't there? Many would not visit a Paradise Valley and go about naked because they think their "private parts" would unsettle them and make them uneasy. Alright! Change your perspective and get rid of your "private parts." Consider them "public parts" – and presto, no more concern about having to show your "private parts."

In truth, none of us have any such thing as "private parts" because what we all have is the same – in general. Oh, my "public parts" might vary a bit from yours – but only in size. My hands are a different size than yours too – but are my hands considered to be "private parts"?

The good thing about such places as Paradise Valley – or one of the good things about it – is that they tend to put to rest concern about "private parts." When all go naked, no one has any such thing. We look at each other and see differences, but we don't see "private parts." Only those obsessed with thinking they are different insist that their parts make them different; but thinking so or not, no one is really different – in that which really matters. Are they?

I must admit that it would be a lot easier to live in this world if we all were exactly the same; but that is not the way it is. Is it? We are not all exactly the same. If I were an exact replica of you in terms of man size – if you are a man – then we would not be obsessed with one of us having a "private part" larger (or smaller) than the other. Would we? Sometimes I wish we were all the same in every way because I like easy; and it would be so much easier to live peacefully if we were really all the same in every dimension.

But again, wishing will not make it so. Will it? We are different and we need to deal with our differences and not let those differences be reason for conflict between us. In the end, I am not making me; and you are not making you. *Nature is our parent – not ourselves. So, let no one of us take credit or assume blame for what we are. Just consider our differences as varieties within Nature – and let it go at that; but in spite of our having to deal with differences in size or firmness or color between us, let us strive to attain PARADISE ON EARTH.*

Varieties in Nature

But Thank God we are not the same in every way. I am reminded of a verse in *THE GOSPEL OF MARY MAGDALENE* that has Jesus commenting on that issue. In the first verse of that gospel, we find Jesus saying thus: *Matter gave birth to passion that is without form, because it comes from what is contrary to nature, and then confusion arose in the whole body. That is why I told you, be of good courage. And if you are discouraged, be encouraged in the presence of the diversity of forms in nature.*

It is interesting, I think, that one would offer that passion is somewhat of an "unnatural" expression in terms of it being something "without form"; but it is something to consider. Perhaps we should not allow our "passions" to derail us from seeing the truth in Nature – and our being part of a wondrous Nature. According to this quote, our "passions" tend to confuse us, but we should overlook those passions and *"be of good courage."* But if we are discouraged, what should we do? We should *be encouraged in the presence of the diversity of forms in nature.*

Does that not make sense to you? It does to me – regardless of who may have said it. We should pay attention to the many varieties in Nature to find peace in this world – and one of those "varieties" is ourselves – and each of us within our own Humanity. So, don't look at yourself and moan about being different than another. Look at yourself and "be encouraged" about how you "vary" from another human being. *Love yourself for what you are because what you are reflects a "variety" in Nature. You are the only you in the world. Why not be proud of "your contribution" of your unique self?* It makes sense to me. Does it to you?

Then the author of *THE GOSPEL OF MARY MAGDALENE* continues with the following: *When the blessed one said this, he greeted all of them and said, "Peace be with you. Receive my peace. Be careful that no one leads you astray by saying, 'Look here' or 'Look there.' The child of humanity is within you. Follow that. Those who seek it will find it. Go and preach the good news of the kingdom. Do not lay down any rules other than what I have given you, and do not establish law, as the lawgiver did, or you will be bound by it." When he said this, he left them.*

Child of Humanity

The above quote has been a comfort to me ever since I found *THE GOSPEL OF MARY MAGDALENE* in late 2004. I have commented about *THE GOSPEL OF MARY MAGDALENE* in other of my writings – and I encourage anyone interested to review and research those writings as found in the *OUT IN THE OPEN* writings feature of my website (especially, Volume 7) – as well as my submission of the gospel itself as a feature of my website that I entitle *THOMAS & MARY HANDBOOK.*

Check it out as you will, but I think the notion of "child of humanity" says it all. Jesus says we should follow the "child of humanity" within us and not let others who think our lives should be more complicated than that "lead us astray" with laws about this or that, intended to constrain us or threaten us with going to Hell or some such.

The notion of "child of humanity" is totally positive. It is a declaration of what I am and you are – not what we are "supposed to be" that is other than what we are. There is no "do this and you will become that" in the notion. There is no "don't do this and you won't become that" in the notion. It is a term free of law and regulation from something or someone outside us. Look toward the child of humanity within us, Jesus said, and you will find the Kingdom. The notion of "child of humanity" is what Jesus called *"the good news of the kingdom."*

Personally, when I hear the term "child of humanity," I do not hear "child of civilization." I hear "naked child, natural child" – not "clothed child." I hear innocent child, not child of guilt; and I know that as I see the child of my vision, I should treat myself. I think life should be as simple as that because it makes no sense to me that it should be more complicated than that – simply because if an Infinite God is truly everywhere, everywhere and everything should be equally sacred. That would have to include me – and you. Right?

And so it is with the folks at my former Hidden Valley – and hopefully the "new" Paradise Valley of mention in this article. *Children are precious at Paradise Valley – and none of them have "private parts" to be demonized or commanded by out of control adults.* If you want to see how it should be, in my opinion, go to the likes of Paradise Valley and review for yourself – as long as you go out of a sincere curiosity and not with intent to degrade what you see or what is there.

Thank God, there are Paradise Valleys in this world because they are exhibits of how it should be in the rest of the world; but let us never believe we need a Paradise Valley to find Paradise in our own life – and lives.

Let me leave you with a song about Paradise as I see it that I wrote in March of 2006. I call it *PARADISE, PARADISE.* I hope you like it. I encourage everyone to visit the likes of Georgia's *PARADISE VALLEY* (northeast of Atlanta) or Colorado's *MOUNTAIN AIR RANCH* (southwest of Denver) and *VALLEY VIEW* (in southern Colo.) – three naturalist resort sites I have personally visited. Be encouraged to visit one of these three – or wherever there is a facility like them; but again, *let us all find Paradise right where we are and not go seeking it somewhere outside the "child of humanity" within us all. OK?*

Thanks! (FWB)

Paradise, Paradise!

By
Francis William Bessler
Laramie, Wyoming
3/31/2006

REFRAIN:
Paradise, Paradise – it seems so right to me.
Paradise. Paradise – can you tell me what it would be?
It's easy, My Friend, to comprehend.
It's Innocence, Simplicity, and Integrity.

If God's outside, we must seek to please,
but if inside, we must be pleased.
It depends upon where we place our God
that determines how we will trod.
Refrain.

Innocence means not to impose,
not just to not be imposed upon.
It's treating everyone like they're Divine,
regardless of any wrong.
Refrain.

Simplicity means I should act the same,
regardless of who is around.
It's regarding the Nature of which I am a part,
like no shame in it can be found.
Refrain.

Integrity means I am Part of a Whole
that is Blessed completely throughout.
If the Whole is Holy, so is each Part,
and the Whole is filled with God now.
Refrain.

So, with these three wonderful qualities,
Paradise is given birth.
It shouldn't matter where I am.
So, why can't there be Paradise on Earth?
Refrain (3).

Jesus & Me

By
Francis William Bessler
12/22/2013

Well, Folks, it is Christmas time again as I write this. It is a time for
me to think about the center piece of the season - Jesus. And what a
wonderful center piece to think about. If I had been there when Jesus
lived, I am quite sure I would have been one of his friends - to the cha-
grin, perhaps, of a lot of folks mingling out and about "Jesus and me."

I can see it now. There we would be walking down a path together
and all of us "Jesus people" would be chattering about this or that.
One of us would say one thing about an issue at hand and another
of us would offer a different opinion, but I would have been silent. I
would not have had much to say because I might have been too timid
to say anything. Hey, a lot of us are like that - too timid to say what we
really believe - deep in our hearts. Then Jesus would look at me and
say, *"Francis, what do you think?"*

That is how I see Jesus - encouraging us all to think for ourselves.
"Francis, what do you think?" And that is Jesus in a capsule for me. What
do I think?

Of course, that is not how Jesus has been portrayed. Is it? We have
been given this picture of Jesus as one who would have said: "Francis,
never mind thinking for yourself. Let me tell you what you should
believe - and then if you don't believe it, sorry, you will be among the
lost forever and ever and ever."

I don't think so. I think Jesus would have encouraged us all to think for ourselves; and I think that is what the "real Jesus" was all about.

I am reminded of a verse in *THE GOSPEL ACCORDING TO THOMAS* - Verse 13. *Jesus said to his disciples* (and if I had been there, I would have been one of them): *Make a comparison to me and tell me whom I am like. Simon Peter said to Him: Thou art like a righteous angel. Matthew said to Him: Thou art like a wise man of understanding. Thomas said to Him: Master, my mouth will not at all be capable of saying whom Thou art like. Jesus said: I am not thy Master because thou has drunk, thou has become drunk from the bubbling spring which I have measured out. And he took him, he withdrew, he spoke three words to him. Now when Thomas came to his companions, they asked him: What did Jesus say to thee? Thomas said to them: If I tell you one of the words which He said to me, you will take up stones and throw at me; and the fire will come from the stones and burn you up.*

What would Jesus have said to Thomas that would have angered the others - so that they would have been inclined to throw stones at him? One thing: Thomas: <u>think for yourself.</u> Those would have been the "three" words that would have angered anyone who wants others to think in some strict pattern. Think for yourself! And you will have to admit, those are some "three" words. Right?

What was the "bubbling spring" which Jesus told Thomas that he had measured out for him? That we should think for ourselves. Never mind what others claim is the truth. Think for yourself! Why did not Jesus tell that to Peter and Matthew? Why did he take Thomas aside and tell him that in private? Because Jesus knew that the others would have resented the notion and he did not want to anger his other friends. So he took Thomas aside and confided in Thomas alone.

And as Thomas was, I am - with the blessing of Jesus. Others may paint me as some kind of "doubter" of their words, but what do I care? I am supposed to think for myself. That is what "my Jesus" would have told me - according to this verse from *THE GOSPEL ACCORDING TO THOMAS.*

Do you believe it? What is your version of Jesus? Do you think he would have been one to tell us all that we have to believe some strict message - or do you believe he would have encouraged us all to think for ourselves?

As we celebrate the life of this man, perhaps it is time to ask ourselves what we would have done if we had been there in the company of Jesus and Peter and Matthew and Thomas. How would we have responded to Jesus if he had summoned us to respond to the statement: *Tell me whom I am like.* What would we have said?

I think I would have said: I am not sure, Jesus, but I think you are "like me." I see you, my friend, and I see me - just like I see me and I see you. I see no difference. Perhaps that is because I see all creatures alike in terms of worth. Jesus, I think you and I are of the same worth because we are equally "sons of God." So to answer your question as to whom do I think you are like, I would say "me."

And I think Jesus would have answered: *Francis, you have answered correctly. I agree. We are brothers, born of the same Creation, and participating in the same wonderful mystery of life. Francis, never mind what Peter offers you or what Matthew offers you. Just think for yourself - and you will be free.*

And that is how I think it would have been if I had been there. How about you? Would you have obligated yourself to the likes of another man - like Peter or Matthew - and allowed them to command you to think in one way over another - even if the question was about Jesus himself? Does any one of us have the right to tell others of us who Jesus was and demand that we believe? Sorry, that "demanding that I believe" is not my impression of Jesus. My impression is one who would have encouraged me to simply think for myself and pay no attention to any ritual or set of dogma handed down to me - even if supposedly in the name of Jesus himself.

So, as we celebrate Jesus, let me say what I think Jesus would have said to me: *Francis, think for yourself.* Know that you are as worthy as anyone who has ever lived - or will ever live. Know you are truly a "son of God" and let no one convince you otherwise. You have drunk from the bubbling spring which I have measured out - and that bubbling spring is only a notion that we are all *THE SAME* - *all worthy of the Love of God because we are all one in God.*

Quite a message, huh? Do you believe it? I do!

A song about "being the same" follows.

Thanks! (FWB)

The Same

By
Francis William Bessler
9/15/2008

REFRAIN:
I'm the same – as everyone.
I'm the same – and I'm having fun.
I'm the same as you, my friend;
and I'll be the same – beyond the end.
You're the same – as everyone.
You're the same – you should be having fun.
You're the same as me, my friend;
and you'll be the same – beyond the end.

The rule of life is that you will be
just what you allow within your dreams.
Tomorrow will be like today
in the manner of soulful ways.
If you're kind today, it will be the same
when tomorrow comes, be it night or day;
and if you're cruel now, you'll continue on
just as you are when tomorrow comes. *Refrain.*

People think they need to be different
in order to make life of consequence;
but no matter how much they insist it's so,
underneath, they're the same in Nature's clothes.
If you think you can change the way things are
by finding strength in various wars,
you're only pretending life's not good
and blowing a chance for true brotherhood. *Refrain.*

In the Gospel of Thomas, Jesus said to Salome,
when he was asked of whom he was a son,
he said, I am one who is from the Same
Light as me, thus having no shame.
And it's just like that with each of us
from whom we come should be our trust.
Well, we come from Nature and the Divine
and that is what should be our pride. *Refrain.*

Many people are afraid to die
because they think Nature's a lie.
They think that death should never be
but that is not the way it seems to me.
I look at life and it seems clear
that all things die – so I should have no fear
of anything beyond because the truth
must be the same for me as it is for you. *Refrain.*

What will happen when I die?
Probably more of the same as in life.
There is no reason for me to believe
that my soul will change radically.
As I was before, I will become again,
I will see me as virtuous or filled with sin.
If my soul continues – and the notion's sane,
it will continue on and be the same. *Refrain.*

So, let us all join and celebrate
the wonder of our common state.
We are the same in what's there to find.
Our bodies are alike – as too our minds.
What you really are, I am too –
and that, my friend, is a basic truth.
The way I treat you becomes my refrain
simply because we are the same.
Refrain. (multiple times if wished)

The Garden Of Eden

By
Francis William Bessler
Laramie, Wyoming
1/9/2014

The Garden - Revisited & Revised

Greetings from your *Bella Vita* host!
50 years and maybe a bit more. Last year marked my 50th year of writing. So now it is on to the 50 + marker of my life - in terms of writing.
How long I will go on is anyone's guess. Like anyone else, I may die
tomorrow; and then closure would be automatic. Wouldn't it?

More than likely, however, at some point, I will determine that I
have "written enough" - and simply stop writing. At some later point,
I will die; but when I do die, I will have left all my thoughts & works
behind - at least partially for a "new me" to inherit from the world of
the future when I am born again.

I do believe in being "born again," but that can be taken literally or
metaphorically. Lots of us experience some epiphany - or mind opening - during a given life - and are "born again" within a given lifetime. I
am quite sure that I have experienced a number of those "born again"
experiences in this one life too because I have experienced seeing in a
different way quite often.

At one time, I will look at a tree and see just some trunk and some
branches; and another time I will look at that same tree and take note

197

of a whole new thing - right before my eyes. Those branches are not just lengths of wood; they are sources for wonderful leaves that spring forth in the Spring. It is not that the tree changed. It is only that I will have changed to see it differently. And it might not be that I have changed either. It might be that I have chosen to look at the same thing in a different way. Do I see the branch of a tree in the Fall as just a piece of wood that looks dead - or do I look at a branch of a tree in the Fall as home for wonderful growth in the Spring? It all depends on a little thing called "vision" or "perspective."

I guess that happened to me long ago. I read about the famed "Garden of Eden" as offered in the first book of the *BIBLE - GENESIS*. The author of that book gave me a glimpse at a place he thought could describe "Heaven." I reveled in that story, but I did not like his way of ending that story - with Adam & Eve being banished from "Heaven" because of some act of disobedience; but I was turned on to the possibility of a "Heaven" - even though "that" author decided to banish people from "his Heaven."

In truth, I would have probably written the ending differently - with Adam & Eve being happy and having babies and having a good ole time - and I would have allowed my people to realize how wonderful their life in Eden was - without stopping it like the "other author" of *GENESIS* did; but then that is me. I must admit I am a bit of an idealist and see no reason to write stories that end in bitterness - like the "other author" of *GENESIS* did.

Let's face it, folks! What ending would you have preferred? Look at the ending that the "other author" of *GENESIS* offered to the famed story of The Garden of Eden. Adam & Eve are banished from "Heaven" and they go on to have kids in pain with one of the kids killing the other. What a Beginning! Look at what misery that ending has caused because it ended without hope - except in some vision that one day mankind might return to The Garden of Eden - once he and she got things right and fell down on their knees and worshipped some god or other. But has that happened in 6 million or 6 thousand years - or whatever? *NO!* That ought to tell us a thing or two about waiting to "get things right." Right?

How long must we wait to get back to *The Garden of Eden*? In my opinion, we have had that Garden of Eden thing wrong for all time since that story was written. We have believed what that "other author" offered about it and have been completely oblivious of "another ending." I do not believe we will ever return to where we never were in the first place - as long as we believe we were ever banished in the first place.

The key to living in "a" Garden of Eden, I think, is to realize that the whole world is The Garden of Eden - or every place on this Earth and beyond is "a" Garden of Eden. Why? Because that which makes a true "Garden of Eden" is simply the Presence of a Sacred God; and since God must be everywhere, being Infinite, then everywhere must be "a" Garden of Eden.

When we finally put on some new glasses and see a tree for more than some trunk and branches and look at it for its mysterious and wonderful happening right in front of us, including its dynamic roots below the surface - then we will realize that we are in "a" Garden of Eden - and we will stop believing in what that "other author" of The Garden of Eden offered. We will stop "worshipping gods - or a god"; and we will begin to "Admire Life" that comes not from a "god" that is outside of it, but from a "God" that is completely within it. At that point, my friends, we will have it all - and we will know that no one can take that realization from us.

I have been writing for 50 years, but the gist of my writing has been in the likes of "another author" of *GENESIS*. I have disagreed with the original author for most of my life - seeing what he did not see that a garden is not something that depends on us for its growth and mystery and wonder. A garden is something that is on its own. The key to knowing we can never leave a garden is to know that it is wondrous on its own - and to know we can never change that.

The "other author" of *GENESIS* lacked that vision, I think. He made the existence of his garden dependent upon its occupants - Adam & Eve; and when he made Adam & Eve leave it for some self-serving reason of claiming we have to "earn" our occupation of a garden, he diminished his garden and turned it into an unforgiving desert. And what has that tale done to all of us since he wrote it? It has caused us to be distracted from the real wonder of our lives and has left us a legend of having to "look elsewhere" for our meaning.

Well, I am sorry - or maybe not so sorry! This "author" of *GENESIS* will not do that. I will not write in the next year or month or day - or whatever I have left - anything that derides life and makes its wonder somehow dependent upon my obedience to some law. I live in The Garden of Eden now - at this very moment and in this very place; and I will not allow anyone to take that Garden from me by some idiotic tale that disobedience will make it go away.

In my vision, however, whether I obey or disobey, The Garden of Eden is - and always will be. There is nothing I can do - or not do - to make it go away. I think it is for me to realize that this life is a Garden of Eden and start taking note of the wonder of all its inhabitants - and claiming myself as one of those inhabitants - and knowing what a wonderful life this really is.

Amazingly - or not so amazingly when we realize why "he" wrote it so that Adam & Eve had to be banished from their garden - the "other author" of *GENESIS* made the very existence of The Garden of Eden dependent upon the actions of a single duo; and when they disobeyed (as they had to do for the author to construct the story he was telling), not only were Adam & Eve banished from the garden, but the "Garden" disappeared entirely. Did it not? If you believe otherwise, where is this "Eden"? What happened to the proverbial Garden of Adam & Eve after they were banished from it? It just "disappeared." Right? Where is it if it did not disappear? It's gone. Right? If it is really gone, then its existence depended upon a single duo.

But I have lived with the realization that a "real" Garden of Eden cannot disappear most of my life - beyond my twenties or so - though I have had to negotiate through a great deal of dissent in trying to see things "my way." Others have clung to the original story of The Garden of Eden and have declared that I have had no right to try and change it. After all, "it was written" as it was because that is the way it happened; and it is for me to come to terms with reality and get with the story as it was written and stop all my foolishness in believing otherwise. I have been told a thousand times that I cannot change anything, but still I have tried - and I will keep trying with whatever writing I do from this point on.

What will I write? Ah, for the time being, consider that to be one of those things "blowing in the wind." Whatever the wind blows my way, I guess. That is what I will write about; but I am thinking about beginning with a bit of a discussion about the "birth" of the *BIBLE* - not so much from a scholarly historical standpoint, but from a philosophical standpoint. Perhaps such an article can prove interesting - and I do like to write about interesting subjects. I do believe an investigation of such an idea might prove very "interesting" indeed; and I might just do it. Yes, indeed, I wonder what the "wind" will tell me if I ask it a thing or two! Who knows?

Anyway, to finish this article, in 1963 or so, I began a song called *TWO WAYS*. I say I began it because after writing it a first time, I lost it. Having lost it in time, then, I did not really finish it when I first wrote it. Did I? In 2009, I decided to recall bits of what I had written and try to write it again. I will include it below to finish my "first" article of my 51st year of writing; and I will let that rewritten and finally completed song tell it like it is for me.

As I am writing this, we are beginning a new year! Let me wish us all a fantastic 2014 - and beyond; and may I please encourage everyone to close the book on the "old *GENESIS*" and dare to rewrite it in your own way - and hopefully make for a much better ending - and future for us all.

Thanks! (FWB)

Two Ways

By
Francis William Bessler
Laramie, Wyoming
1/29/09 – 2/4/09

REFRAIN:
There's a road leading downward.
There's another leading up.
These are the two ways.
But the road leading downward
is living like you're lacking luck;
and the road leading up
is knowing it's always a blessed day.

Everyone of us is lucky
because everyone of us has life.
But how many of us know we're lucky
for being caught up in strife?
But what is strife, my friend,
but battling with life –
like taking the day out of time
and leaving only the night? *Refrain.*

So long ago, Jesus said it -
where your treasure is, your heart is there.
That's to say, find your pleasure
in that which does not decay or wear.
For me, that's the Natural
because the Natural goes on and on.
That makes it Infinite
and like the God to which I belong. *Refrain.*

There are two ways of going
through this life we have at hand.
We can love our lives as they are
or listen to some outside command.
Well, I believe life is precious
and a miracle that satisfies
while others see life as a way
to make others cry. *Refrain.*

Repeat first verse – then *Refrain* several times.

Bye for now! Happy Future To Us All! - in a "new" GENESIS!

The Birth Of
The Bible
(Part 1 Of 3)

By
Francis William Bessler
1/31/2014

New Years, 300 A.D.

Where were you on New Years Day, 300 A.D.? Or perhaps better put, what were you doing on New Years Day, 300 A.D.? Whatever it was you were doing, I can assure you that you were not reading *THE BIBLE*. I strongly suspect that most people do not know that they could not have been reading *THE BIBLE* if they were around on New Years Day, 300 A.D. I think most people think that *THE BIBLE* has always been so - that God wrote *THE BIBLE* a long time ago and at least from the time of St. Peter and Jesus, *THE BIBLE* was around to be read and reviewed.

At least, that was my impression when I was first introduced to *THE BIBLE* - sometime after I first learned to read - maybe by the age of eight or so. It was for me that *THE BIBLE* was a book that has always been - and there never was a time when *THE BIBLE* was not. Needless to say, had I known that *THE BIBLE* had not always been around when I was a kid, I would have known that I had been mistaken thinking it had been around for "all time."

So, before *THE BIBLE* came into being, what did folks do - I mean, those of us who think of ourselves as "Christian"? Therein, I think, is perhaps one of the most interesting stories of history. Before *THE BIBLE* came into being, there were a good number of books about Jesus, but the problem was, they all disagreed among themselves - as it were. There were, of course, the now known gospels of Mark and Matthew and Luke and John, but there were also other gospels too - like those of Thomas, one of the accepted Apostles of Jesus, and Mary Magdalene, arguably, another of the "Apostles" of Jesus.

On New Years Day, 300 A.D., for example, there were probably several different Christian "churches" in Alexandria, Egypt. Let's us just imagine that in the northern part of Alexandria, Egypt, there was a parish that taught the story of Jesus according to what was found in *THE GOSPEL OF MARK*. Given that Christian worship was still banned as public offering at the time, Mark's Christians did not meet in a church as such, but probably in the home - or house - of one of the Christians. In 300 A.D., Christianity was banned by Roman edict - that is from worshipping out in the open some place. So, Christians had to meet in one another's home - or maybe out in some woods or other place where Christians could assemble in secret.

Anyway, in southern Alexandria in another home in restricted Alexandria, a few more Christians were meeting and following *THE GOSPEL OF JOHN*. Down the road a bit, other Christians were meeting who paid attention to the Jesus of *THE GOSPEL OF THOMAS*. Across the road, other Christians were meeting who liked *THE GOSPEL OF LUKE*. Across town, there was another band of Christians - who found *THE GOSPEL OF MARY MAGDALENE* to their liking.

Believe it nor not, that is the way it was for what could be called Christianity in 300 A.D. Different Christian sects or assemblies worshipped, as it were, paying attention to different texts - and rather contentiously so. The "bishop" of a given gospel - or the bishop of several communities that attended to the Jesus of Mark - were sometime outraged that another "bishop" over several other communities paid attention to a different Jesus - like that of Thomas; but Christianity was not unified at the time and a dissenting bishop could do absolutely nothing to prevent another "bishop" from supervising several little church groups from using a gospel not of his liking. He could rant and rave that another "bishopric" was following "heresy" in going with another scheme of worship, but he could do nothing about it because Christianity was a hidden religion at the time. Roman Paganism was the accepted religion - and in many places, Christianity was actually banned. Because Christianity was so loosely practiced, then, no one community of Christians could do anything to restrict another community from doing as it saw fit to practice.

Christianity In Conflict

So, what did the various Christian parishes believe that put them in conflict with one another? It is only one man's opinion, of course, but I think the conflict could be summarized as one centering around "authority." Some Christian sects simply had no need for salvation by authority; and other Christian sects depended on salvation by authority. Some saw the individual as front and center in gaining his or her own salvation by listening to him or herself as one might pursue the truth. In other words, in some Christian sects, self-confidence and self-trust to know the truth was the mainstay of a sect. In other Christian sects, it was confidence and trust in some authority that paved the way to what can be called "salvation."

Which way was right - confidence in authority outside oneself - or confidence in oneself? Quite a conflict - I think, huh? Which way was right? In one perspective of Jesus, Jesus came to forgive those of sin who believed in him - and, of course, in those who were "authorized" to represent Jesus in some line of authority - stemming originally from Peter to whomever Peter chose to represent him - down the ages from selection to selection of authority. In the other view, Jesus came to encourage souls to find the truth on their own, listening only to others in terms of guidance by benevolence or kind interest, but not by way of believing that one can gain salvation by way of the authority of someone else - including that of Jesus himself.

Many of the Christian sects of the time believed that Jesus had been a Jewish Messiah - and that offers the notion of authority big time. If Jesus had been a Jewish Messiah, then that would have defined him in a "role of authority." I think that is why some of the gospel writers - like all of those who eventually ended up in *THE BIBLE* - wanted to believe in Jesus as a Jewish Messiah. They wanted the authority that went with such an idea. If Jesus was the Jewish Messiah, then it stood to reason that Jesus would need "lieutenants" to carry out his authority. That paved the way for those who wanted authority; and many chose to believe they were proper "authorities" in the name of Jesus - Jewish Messiah.

Was Jesus really a Jewish Messiah - or the long anticipated Jewish Messiah? Some thought he was; and some thought he wasn't; and therein was the basis of the disagreement that completely enthralled Christianity on New Years Day, 300 A.D.

It would have been hard to know the truth about such a claim when there were so many diverse gospels about Jesus on New Years Day, 300 A.D. Who was to be believed? Those gospels authored by the likes of Mark, Matthew, Luke, and John - or those gospels authored in the names of ones like Thomas and Mary Magdalene?

In *THE GOSPEL OF MATTHEW*, for instance, Matthew claimed that Jesus came to forgive sins - as if he had the power or need to do such a thing. In telling about the supposed conception of Jesus from within one called Mary, Matthew offered in verse 1:20 that Jesus had been conceived by the "Holy Ghost" and not by Joseph, Mary's husband. This was to offer that Jesus was very different from the rest of us - for who is conceived by the "Holy Ghost"?

In the following verse, Matthew instills in us the idea that Mary - who had been the mother of the one "conceived by the Holy Ghost" - was intended to bring forth a son whose name was to be called "Jesus" whose purpose was to "save his people from their sins." Verse 1:21: *And she shall bring forth a son, and thou shall call his name JESUS: for he shall save his people from their sins.*

That, of course, was intended to, number 1: state that the people of Jesus had sin, and number 2: that Jesus could forgive them of that sin. It was all about sin, then, that is "inherited sin."

Did Jesus really believe in sin - or that we all have sin? Who knows? Some believed he did; and some believed he did not. That was the crux of the conflict that was raging at the time of New Years Day, 300

A.D. Some Christian sects did not assume that Jesus had been a Jewish Messiah, intent on saving his people from their sins, and some believed that Jesus could only be appreciated as a Jewish Messiah.

In *THE GOSPEL OF MARY MAGDALENE*, for example, when Peter asked Jesus about sin, Jesus said: there is no such thing as sin, except that you create it, as in adultery. From Verse 1 of *THE GOSPEL OF MARY MAGDALENE*: *Peter said to him, "You have explained everything to us. Tell us also, what is the sin of the world?" The savior replied, "There is no such thing as sin, but you create sin when you mingle as in adultery, and this is called sin."*

And therein was the controversy of the time on New Years Day, 300 A.D. One gospel wrote it that Jesus did not believe in sin, that is "inherited sin"; and another (and others) wrote it that Jesus did believe in sin - or that we all inherit it. Which one was right? Those who wanted to be accepted as "authorities" in the name of Jesus argued one way; and those who had no need for authority argued in another.

But how do you run a church if authority is not needed? That was the compelling question of the time on New Years Day, 300 A.D. Some argued that it is ridiculous to argue that Jesus did not believe in sin and the need for it to be forgiven; and the same ones argued that no church can survive if it does not call for some authority - and the need for authority - to "forgive sins" in the name of Jesus. Some who believed that authority is needed wanted to brand as heretics all those who claimed it was not needed - and burn their books as well. What idiocy, they claimed, to believe that Jesus would not have required authority - and that each of us is free to free ourselves of sin - if we have it at all - by virtue of disposition and conduct alone!

Some gospels, however, like that of the Apostle, Thomas - or at least written in the name of Thomas - claimed that Jesus preached that Heaven is spread about the Earth and implied that it is up to each of us to recognize that Heaven is all about; but some argued that Heaven was a place where the "obedient" go after death. Which idea was right? Which idea was wrong? Is Heaven here already - or do we have to die to get to it? See the controversy swirling about on New Years Day, 300 A.D.

In *THE GOSPEL OF THOMAS,* in talking about where Heaven really is, Jesus said in Verse 3: *If those who lead you say to you: "See, the Kingdom is in heaven," then the birds of the heaven will precede you. If they say to you: "It is in the sea," then the fish will precede you. But the Kingdom is within you and it is without you. If you will know yourselves, then you will be known and you will know that you are sons of the Living Father. But if you do not know yourselves, then you are in poverty and you are poverty.*

And about the place of Heaven in Verse 113 of *THE GOSPEL OF THOMAS,* it is offered. *His disciples said to Him: When will the Kingdom come? Jesus said: It will not come by expectation; they will not say, "See here," or "See there." But the Kingdom of the Father is spread upon the earth and men do not see it.*

Implied in both of those verses is that no one needs authority to gain salvation. Salvation is only recognizing that *"the Kingdom is within you"* and realizing that because it is, you are a *"son of the Living Father."* The "Kingdom" is all about. Just realize it and go forward proud that it is all about and that you are among its citizens.

Where is the need for authority in that message? It is absent. Isn't it? And therein was the basis of the great *Conflict Among Christians* on New Years Day, 300 A.D.

Enter - Constantine

Then fate entered the scene. A man by the name of Constantine, born a Roman Pagan, became emperor of the Roman Empire in 312 A.D. I won't go into details of that story on how Constantine ascended to his position of "Governor of all of the Roman Empire," but suffice it to say, he did; and for whatever reason, he decided that the previously banned religion of Christianity should be recognized as legitimate from that time forward. And not only did he decide to "tolerate" Christianity. He decided to make Christianity a "state religion" equal to the previously dominant paganism of the day.

Having been adopted by the Roman Empire as an acceptable religion, however, that religion faced a huge problem. Which Christianity should be favored - the one that preached the need for authority to gain salvation - or the one that offered that salvation is only recognizing one's own "sacred status" as a "son of the Living Father"?

To answer that question and resolve an ongoing crisis in the church, Constantine assembled all the bishops he could summon to a place called Nicaea in the land of Turkey 25 years after New Years Day, 300 A.D. Constantine directed those bishops to settle on only some of the gospels being used by various Christian sects of the day - and go forward as a united religion - not as a fractured religion. Constantine wanted "one empire" and it stood to reason that to have "one empire," Christianity needed to be "one religion." Jesus had to be either an authority - or Jewish Messiah - or otherwise, but Jesus could not be both Messiah and "mere wise man."

I am quite sure that if I had been there in Nicaea in 325 A.D. I would have witnessed a Constantine arguing that the "authority" side of Christianity must be adopted and the "know yourself as a son of the Living Father" side must be abandoned. Constantine was an emperor with "authority" and I am sure he would have settled for no less than an "authoritative" church.

Anyway, in Nicaea, Turkey in June of 325 A.D. - *THE BIBLE* was born. The bishops assembled at Nicaea decided on certain books that would fit into a canon of books; and the result was *THE BIBLE*. I was not there and do not know how many books were reviewed, but suffice it to say, there were quite a few. In the end, the bishops assembled in Nicaea chose certain books of previous Jewish authorship - prior to the life of Jesus - and certain books written after the life of Jesus.

In my mind, it was an arbitrary way of deciding on which books should be selected, but not terribly so. If a book lent to the need for authority, then it could be included in the *NEW BIBLE*. If a book suggested that salvation should be up to the individual, it had to go by the wayside. It was probably as simple at that. Books included that were written before the life of Jesus became the *OLD TESTAMENT*. Books included that were written after the life of Jesus became the *NEW TESTAMENT*; but sad to say, books that were excluded were not only excluded to be in *THE BIBLE*, but eventually directed to be destroyed - or at least many of them were - if it seemed they were arguing that salvation is not a matter needing authority.

Goodbye, Truth!

Regardless of which side you might take, or might have taken if you had been a bishop in 325 A.D., the result had to be censorship. Remember, before Nicaea, there had been conflict in the church as to which Jesus was to be believed - and often very bitter conflict. With an "authority" in government approving of "authorities" in religion, one could have foretold with accuracy what would probably happen to the dissenting side. It would have been declared as heresy and practice of that heresy would have been banned.

And that is exactly what happened. When bishops of a banned religion had no authority, they could do nothing about those who did not believe in the need for authority, but as soon as authority was granted to those who believed in the need for it, those who did not believe in the need for authority were overridden, to say the least - and declared as "heretics" - sometimes punishable by death.

But what happens when "authorities" choose to "censor" what people can read? What happens if what is censored actually represents "the truth"? The truth becomes a victim. Right? Of course, it is a matter of opinion about whether "the truth" resided in the victorious bishops of the 4th Century. Some - and many, for sure - have no doubt that the "Holy Ghost" was about that day in early June of 325 - and that the bishops only selected those books favored by the "Holy Ghost"; but in retrospect, I am not one of those - though I must admit I may have been had I been a bishop in 325 A.D. Indeed, I may have been one of the "ignorant ones" - for whatever reason.

As it actually happened, though, many of the books excluded by the bishops in Nicaea in 325 A.D. were not only banned, but directed to be destroyed. Authority often does that. It "destroys" that which might challenge its authority. Books like *THE GOSPEL OF THOMAS* and *THE GOSPEL OF MARY MAGDALENE* were directed to be destroyed.

In "truth," however, how would you have liked it if you had been a member of a Christian sect in Alexandria, Egypt in 325 A.D. that had taught from *THE GOSPEL OF THOMAS*? How would you have liked it if your chosen book about Jesus was declared heretical and that you had to abide by a book for which you had had no commitment? How would you have liked it if you could not go to church and hear what you believed was the truth, but now had to listen to a gospel that you found abhorrent?

Very quickly after 325 A.D., the whole world changed. On New Years Day, 300 A.D., Christianity was very diverse and various parishes could believe and teach what they believed is right - though under cover because Christianity was banned. By New Years Day, 400 A.D., Christianity had been set free to worship in the open and had become rather strict and no longer was there allowed an option to see Jesus as only a wise man and not a Jewish Messiah. Those who had wanted authority to rule in the name of Jesus got what they wanted; and once that happened, it was *Goodbye, Jesus of Thomas! Goodbye, Jesus of Mary Magdalene! Goodbye Diversity! And very likely, Goodbye, Truth!*

But fate entered in again. Though many Christian works were destroyed via ecclesiastical command, some monks - or other sources - did not obey the order to burn everything. Some works were hidden away from the authorities - like Coptic translations of *THE GOSPEL OF THOMAS, THE GOSPEL OF MARY MAGDALENE,* and some others.

In one case, many banned books were buried in a cave overlooking the Nile River in Egypt near a town called Nag Hammadi. In 1945, some peasant stumbled on a huge jar containing *THE GOSPEL OF THOMAS* and some other ancient banned works. Was it an accident that the peasant stumbled over such a jar - or was it *"accidental fate"*? I wonder!

In any case, the world can return to Alexandria, Egypt and the year 300 A.D. - if it wants. We can go back and revere some of the ancient texts of the time - if we want - and maybe decide if we want to open those books and look at Jesus in another way.

For what it's worth, I am such a one. I like to have options in life - to read or not to read - to believe or not to believe. I do not like to be told what I should read or what I should believe. Do you? *I do not believe in censorship because I might be censoring the truth; and any who think they have a right to censor me ought to first ask themselves that if the tables were turned, would they like to be commanded to oblige me in what they "have" to believe?*

It is anyone's guess, too, as to what was lost by the burning ecclesiastics of the 4th Century. I mentioned that there was a Coptic version of *THE GOSPEL OF THOMAS* hidden away, but what happened to the original version? Supposedly, Thomas was of Greek origin. That means he probably wrote an original in Greek - if Thomas was the real author of the gospel in his name. Even if the Apostle, Thomas, was not the original author of the gospel in his name, it is likely the original author did not write in Coptic - an Egyptian language. What happened to the original - whatever the language it was written in? Was it burned to destroy the evidence?

As much as I am fond of *THE GOSPEL OF THOMAS* - as has been translated from Coptic to English - I am sure that with each translation, some biased verses were added to an original. That is probably true of gospels found in *THE BIBLE* too. If we do not have access to an original - and we probably have originals of nothing - how can we know that which was written or copied from one language to another represents the original?

Be that as it may, it should be clear that when any "evidence" is intentionally destroyed - as were a lot of Christian works in the 4th Century as part of an ecclesiastical purge - the world is left with a gaping wound. How do you heal a "world body" once you have burned much of it? Sad to say, we will never know just how much was lost, but we can try to make sense of some of what was left, use our brains to fill in the gaps, and still go forward with a wonderful, wonderful world.

Books may have been burned, but the majesty of life continues as it has always been. Perhaps we need to pay more attention to the very evidence of the goodness of life before our very eyes - and march forward as if we have lost little - because, in fact, if we look at life as it is, it should be clear that it has lost none of its original majesty. Of that, this one is sure.

Stay tuned, if you wish, to Part 2 of *THE BIRTH OF THE BIBLE!*

Thanks! (FWB)

The Birth Of
The Bible
(Part 2 Of 3)

By
Francis William Bessler
1/31/2014

BEYOND BELIEF & AGORA

Before I continue, let me take a moment to recommend some reading and some watching - a book and a movie. The book is *BEYOND BELIEF* by a wonderful scholar of Christian history by the name of Elaine Pagels, certainly one of my favorite authors and just a little younger than me. Elaine was born on Feb. 13th, 1943. I was born on Dec. 3rd, 1941. Elaine has helped me to look at history with a different pair of glasses. Unlike me, who is more a speculative philosopher than a scholar, Elaine is what I am not - a scholar.

From the inside flap of her book, *BEYOND BELIEF*, published in 2003: *Elaine Pagels earned a B.A. in history and an M.A. in classical studies at Stanford, and holds a Ph.D. from Harvard University. She is the author of Adam, Eve, and the Serpent; The Origin of Satan; and The Gnostic Gospels, which won the National Book Critics Circle Award and the National Book Award. She is currently the Harrington Spear Paine Professor of Religion at*

Princeton University, and she lives in Princeton, New Jersey, with her husband and children.

Though I am fond of three books I have by Elaine Pagels, namely: *THE GNOSTIC GOSPELS (1979), BEYOND BELIEF (2003),* and *REVELATIONS (2012), - BEYOND BELIEF* is my favorite of hers and is also one of my favorite books of all time. I read it quite often - though each time I read it, it seems like I am reading it for the first time. I think that is because Elaine is a scholar and has an in depth knowledge of what she writes about.

BEYOND BELIEF is a fantastic book that reviews the history of the early Christian Church - including the subject of this essay - *The Birth of the BIBLE.* Elaine reviews that history like no other that I have read - and has helped me considerably in forming my own views about life and truth in general. Elaine still considers herself to be traditionally Christian - in spite of her misgivings about it as offered in her writings. On the other hand, I have long realized that I am not traditionally Christian any more - though, of course, I once was - as I have admitted in many of my writings. *BEYOND BELIEF* also deals with my favorite gospel - *THE GOSPEL OF THOMAS.* Again, I highly recommend it - and am so very proud to do so.

Now, for the movie I want to recommend. It is called *AGORA* - a 2 hr. movie, available on DVD, produced, I believe, in 2008, but only released in 2010. It was produced, I think, in various locations in Europe and Africa by Spanish producers. What a movie! I do not recall it being featured in theatres at all, but if you want to look at what may have happened in Alexandria, Egypt in the 4th Century after *THE BIBLE* was born and Christianity became a "favored" religion, this is a movie to see. It stars Rachel Weisz as a pagan philosopher librarian by the name of Hypatia who is caught up with newly liberated Christians taking over the Alexandrian library known as the *Agora* - and literally destroying any vintage of previous paganism - and literally murdering Jews and Pagans in the process - all in the name of Jesus, of course. It is truly amazing what people do in the name of Jesus, who preached kindness to all, not revenge when it suits one's arrogance.

I realize that the film maker, Alejandro Amenabar, probably took some liberties in making this film, but it seems to fit what I have read about the destruction of a great historical library in Alexandria, Egypt in the 4th Century - after Christians were liberated to join the governing class - or classes - of the Roman Empire. Rather than take any time to detail the movie, I encourage anyone who cares about history and justice to watch it on their own - and take from it what you will.

Brawling Among Pagans

As a kid, I looked at "those pagans" of history as just plain ignorant. Of course, as a traditional Christian in my youth, I believed what I was taught - that we "Christians" and we "Jews" were much better than "those pagans" of the past. I heard about those Romans acting like "their gods" were to be adored; and I thought that I was so much better than they were. I did not worship "many gods." I worshipped One God; and so it was and is with most of my fellow Christians. They do not think they should be classed among "those pagans" of the past because they are of an entirely different cut of humanity.

But when I review what happened in the 4th Century when *THE BIBLE* was born, I see things completely differently now. Now I realize that if I had been around in the 4th Century, I probably would have been one of "those pagans." The main difference would have been that I would have worshipped "one god" and the rest of the Roman Empire would have attended to "many gods." Reduce many to one, however, and you are still left with a "pagan god" - in referencing the "god of the Jews and Christians."

In truth, how are Christians and Jews and Pagans different when all three worship a god outside themselves? How is it any different to worship the Jewish god, Jehovah, than it is to worship any of those other pagan gods? All of the gods of the past have required that their subjects adore them - and sacrifice in their names - including the god, Jehovah. *As I see it now, worshipping a god outside of me is "being pagan."*

In a way, I think the great conflict of the 4th Century was a debate on whether Christianity should continue with paganism - and its practices of idolatry and sacrifice - or branch out to a "more reasonable" belief in truly ONE GOD. Pagans believed in adoring many gods, but those gods were "outside" of them. Jews believed in "one god," but that god was also "outside" of them. In my way of thinking now, the true ONE GOD cannot be subject to being "outside" of anyone. The true ONE GOD is Infinite and Must be present in All.

Looking back at that long forgotten and totally pivotal 4th Century, I think humanity was growing to begin to accept the wrongs of the past - or was growing to realize that the past had been wrong - in terms of belief in an "outside" god; but many within Christianity were not ready for such a realization and they fought to preserve the past. Stalwart books like *THE GOSPEL OF THOMAS* and *THE GOSPEL OF MARY MAGDALENE* were a beginning. I do believe they contained some error simply because they were written by human beings subject to erroneous perception, but there was much that was - and is - wise in them too. Perhaps they were far ahead of their time - and maybe our time too. Why? Because they dared to try and define life as it probably is - an expression of a God Within.

But that was heresy to many Christians of the 4th Century - and even to this day. Many of the bishops of the days of Constantine did not want to accept that maybe they had been wrong - and that maybe they were basically the same as all other pagans.

Why did Pagan Emperor Constantine see Christianity as a religion to be tolerated - and even to be sponsored and supported? Why? Because he was smart enough to see that both his Roman Paganism and Christianity followed the same practices. Both worshipped gods outside of themselves. So, how were they different? It was just that the Christians had this god they named *Jesus Christ* and the Romans had their gods, among which was one called *Caesar*. The main difference between Caesar and Jesus Christ, according to one like Constantine, was that they began at different times. That's all. Both were gods that had once lived as real human beings. The Christians worshipped their god, Jesus Christ, and the Romans worshipped their gods, among which was Caesar - of Julius Caesar fame - who had lived some 50 years or so before Jesus Christ.

The Jews were a bit more difficult, however, because their god, Jehovah, had never lived before as a human being. The Jews demanded that their god not be sculpted and be given a face; but all of the other gods had a face - and many had images sculpted to represent them. I think that at least partly what set the Jews apart from all the other pagans, is that their god - for the lack of a sculpted statue in its image - could not be "torn down" as all the other pagan gods could be. Perhaps the Jews were a league ahead of other pagans in demanding that no image be made of Jehovah. No image - no way to destroy a representation of Jehovah; but what gives Jehovah away as just one of the many "pagan gods" is the practice of sacrifice - *a practice of offering something or someone to a god outside yourself in order to appease that god; and such an offering could very well include oneself.* All the pagan gods required sacrifice. That was an essential aspect of their being worshipped; and in that, the Jews - and subsequent Christians - were no different. Jehovah still "requires" sacrifice; and sacrifice is the mainstay of all pagan religions.

Know What Is In Your Sight!

Gospel wise, what was the heresy - or at least, one heresy - that angered many of the "authoritarian" Christian bishops of the 4th Century? Why were they so opposed to gospels like *THE GOSPEL OF THOMAS?*

As it see it now, it was because *THE GOSPEL OF THOMAS* challenged the notion that we should believe without seeing. In one - or more - of the embraced gospels of *THE BIBLE*, it is stated that Jesus offered that *"Blessed are those who believe, though they have not seen."* In fact, that is probably why John took such pains to call Thomas a "doubting Thomas." He was trying to put down the whole notion - that the Jesus of Thomas embraced - that we should insist on evidence in order to believe what is claimed.

In Elaine Pagels' opinion, *THE GOSPEL OF JOHN* was probably written after *THE GOSPEL OF THOMAS* to try and refute what Thomas had written; and that does make a lot of sense to me. Unlike the previous gospel writers, Mark, Matthew, and Luke - John went through a lot of trouble to specifically denounce Thomas. It is very likely that if Thomas had never written his gospel, John would not have bothered with one of his own.

Personally, I think it goes much deeper than that. I think that all of the gospels embraced in *THE BIBLE* were written after *THE GOSPEL*

OF THOMAS. I get that feeling because *THE GOSPEL OF THOMAS* only offers *"Jesus said"* statements and does not try to offer a narrative about Jesus. In my opinion - though Elaine Pagels may disagree - a "primitive" gospel is more than likely the "first" to be written. Writers tend to expand on what is primitive rather than writers tend to reduce from what is exaggerated. Since *THE GOSPEL OF THOMAS* is by far the most "primitive" of all the gospels, it was probably written first - not last - as so many scholars believe.

From Mark through John, it seems as if they were starting with some statement that is found in *THE GOSPEL OF THOMAS* - and framing and/or refuting that statement the way they wanted - beginning with the notion of faith without knowledge. As I see it now, that is probably the starting point of Thomas - and it is the beginning of it being refuted as well.

"Blessed are those who believe though they have not seen" is the standard of all the gospels but Thomas. *"Know what is in thy sight - and believe accordingly"* is the starting point of *THE GOSPEL OF THOMAS*. Which way was right? Which way is right? What do you think? Which way would you follow?

In June of 325 A.D., almost 1700 years ago, the bishops assembled in Nicaea, Turkey, chose the *"Blessed are those who believe though they have not seen"* gospels - and banned perhaps the most authentic gospel of all - *THE GOSPEL OF THOMAS;* but I think that decision was in alignment with the idea of Jehovah. Being Jews - much more than was Thomas, who was probably more Greek than Jew, if Jew at all, - Jehovah was probably prime in the minds of gospel writers, Mark, Matthew, Luke and John. Accordingly, Thomas may not have had to "fit" Jesus in with Jehovah - whereas the others had to fit Jesus in with Jehovah just to stay faithful with their faith. Thus, to counter Thomas who may not have been concerned with Jewish scripture or prophecy, Mark, Matthew, Luke and John felt they had to write stories about Jesus to fit him in with Jewish scripture. Thus, in Mark, Matthew, Luke and John, stories had to be written - and probably mostly fabricated - "so that scripture could be fulfilled."

For example, Matthew may have had "fulfilling scripture" in mind when he wrote the story of the conception and birth of Jesus. Scripture - Jewish scripture - was likely the main focus of his attention when he wrote his story. It was foretold that the Jewish Messiah would be born of a virgin in a town called Bethlehem. Thus Matthew wrote his story to "fulfill the scripture." I mean it could have happened that way. Since the Jewish Messiah was supposed to be born of a virgin in Bethlehem, so be it. According to the scriptures it was done.

But was Jesus really born of a virgin - and born in Bethlehem? Maybe, maybe not. Who knows? None of us were there. So how can we know? From a philosopher's point of view, however, or at least from "this philosopher's" point of view, one should ask, Why? Why should Jesus have been born of a virgin? What does that really imply?

I think it implies that Matthew saw natural conception and natural birth as somehow not acceptable for a holy one. If Jesus was indeed holy, then he could not have been born in a natural way; but from my point of view, I see natural conception and natural birth as fantastic and miraculous - and from my point of view, I would think that anyone who is truly holy would not want to bypass such a beautiful entrance into the world. If Jesus was "perfect" as Matthew might claim, why in the world would he choose to bypass a natural entrance? Not seeing why he would want to bypass a natural beginning, I would conclude that it is very unlikely that a "perfect one" would choose to be born of a virgin. Accordingly, I would dismiss the story of Jesus being born from a virgin - even if he was born in Bethlehem. Just because something is written does not mean it had to have happened; and if it did not have to happen, it probably didn't.

Now skip to the end of the life of Jesus. Matthew - and the others - claim that Jesus was crucified. Alright, that is reasonable. Lots of people were crucified. So there is no reason to object to that happening to Jesus. It is also claimed that Jesus rose from the dead in full body form after he was crucified. Why would he do that? From "this philosopher's" point of view, death is wonderful as the end of a wonderful natural life. We all die. So why would one of us act like death is not how it is supposed to be and bypass whatever happens with any soul after they die - or after one's body dies?

You see, I see death as a natural wonder and lovely ending; but if I were to see death in some other light, then I might think that "death should be overridden" - and thus I should be able to "triumph over death." If Jesus was perfect, as is claimed, and I should view death as perhaps a consequence of sin, then I would have to have Jesus triumphing over death by being born again - in full body form.

But did Jesus really rise from the dead? From my "philosophical viewpoint," I would say it would prove nothing to do so. So, why do so? Then ponder what they claimed happened after he rose from the dead - and it makes no sense - to a philosopher like me.

Alright, say that Jesus rose from the dead in full body form. If he did that to "prove" he had some kind of "power over death," why would he "ascend into heaven" without walking about the public and testifying that he had "triumphed over death"? I mean it makes no sense that Jesus would have risen from the dead just to appear to a few of his close friends - and then just vanish into the air - in a matter of a few days, not a few years. Why in the world would he do that? Wouldn't it have been much more realistic and sensible to stick around as a risen human being to prove that he had the power he claimed he had? Why go through the trouble of dying just to be resurrected - if no one knew about it?

But someone did know about it - you might argue. Some of his friends were allowed to meet him and talk with him and sup with him before he "ascended into heaven." Again, I would ask why Jesus would not have bothered to appear to some of the main citizens of Jerusalem - like maybe a rabbi in the Jewish temple? That would have been very sensible - in this philosopher's opinion. Why would he have not done that if had really been a "Jewish Messiah"? After all, if he came for the sake of the Jews, why did he not stick around and break bread with some of them - regular Jews, that is?

And if Jesus came to save us all, as traditional Christians claim, why did he not appear to other than his friends? Consider how impressive it would have been to one like Pontius Pilate who had sentenced Jesus to death if Jesus would have paid a call on Pontius Pilate after he rose from the dead? Why not? It really makes no sense that if Jesus really did rise from the dead that he would not have presented proof of his resurrection to the world at large.

But he did not stick around. Did he? I guess the Jews did not need a messiah after all - and Jesus decided to return to where he had come from - heaven. So off he went, waving to Peter and John and some of

222 | Francis William Bessler

the others as he left, telling them to take over his duties as a Jewish Messiah and get on with baptizing all they could in his name. Sorry, but that makes no sense to me. Accordingly, I would have to conclude that it probably did not happen the way Mark through John claimed it did.

What did the Apostles, Thomas and Mary, have to say about the end of Jesus? Thomas did not say anything - probably because he wrote his gospel while Jesus was still alive and would not have had it in mind to comment about his passing. Mary Magdalene commented a little about it, but not much. She said that after Jesus said the last things he said, he "left them." That's all. No mention of where he went or how he went. Just a curt little saying - he "left them."

Personally, I think it is somewhat reasonable to believe that Jesus "appeared" to some of his friends after his death, but probably only in "apparition" form - not in an actual body. There have been reports of people appearing after death in "apparition" form. So it is reasonable to assume that Jesus may have done that; but only temporarily. Temporary seems to be the extent of appearing after death; and anyone who does appear after death can only do so for a little time. Perhaps they have no power as souls to "stick around" for long, but maybe they can "stick around" for a short time - and then have to "disappear" for lack of power to keep appearing.

I am reminded of a story that actually happened - or it is claimed it happened. In the early '70s, a big commercial airliner went down in the Everglades of Florida. A flight engineer, by the name of Dom Comolli - or something close to that - was one of the many fatalities. After his death, he appeared to many - briefly - but he appeared, and even spoke once. The "Ghost of Flight 401" felt responsible for the crash and was volunteering to supervise so that no other flights for that particular airline would suffer the same fate.

By the way, a movie was produced in the '80s called THE GHOST OF FLIGHT 401 that starred Ernest Borgnine as Dom Comolli that somewhat documents this story. If interested, you might try to track it down. More than likely, it is available in DVD format, but that is only a guess.

Be that as it may, though we do not understand how, I think we do survive death - or our souls survive death of body - and now and then, we can manifest ourselves in some paranormal form - or pseudo physi-cal form. Some would call such a phenomenon an "apparition"; and that is quite possibly what happened with Jesus after his death. He may have appeared in an apparition, giving those who saw him an impres-sion that he had "returned from the dead."

In the case of the early '70s, Dom Comolli appeared to others of his airline, warning them of some faulty part that might lead to another crash, but not for long. Perhaps a soul can manifest itself in apparition form only for some limited period of time - and then it can no longer muster the energy to appear. Perhaps that which happened to Dom Comolli also happened to Jesus.

If so, that would explain why some thought they saw Jesus in some "resurrected form"; but only for some brief period of time; but again, appearing in apparition form has its limitations; or so it seems. If Jesus did appear to some of his friends after his death, however, like Dom Comolli appeared to some of his friends after his death, that might explain why Jesus could not stay around any more than Dom Comolli could stay around; and that would also explain why it seemed that when Jesus disappeared, it appeared that he was "disappearing into heaven." It is something to consider, I think.

Anyway, from my philosophical point of view, rising from the dead would only mean something significant if one considers death as some-how unfortunate - that is, death in itself. But if one considers death as only part of a "perfect process of life and death," then one would have no reason to consider it necessary or even useful to overcome death in some superficial way.

Personally I see death as only a transition from one life to another. All die. So why act like death is something that is like a punishment for sin - as many do. *I do not die because I have sinned. I die because that is the natural way.* Sin has nothing at all to do with it. I think it was Paul of Tarsus who proclaimed that "death is the wages of sin" - as if the virtu-ous should not have to die; but from my philosophical point of view, that is a preposterous notion. Even Jesus died. So how can anyone claim with any degree of integrity that we die because we sin? Did Jesus sin? Personally, I don' t think so.

Of course, those who believe that sin is what causes us to have to die argue that Jesus did not sin, but he gave his life for those of us who have sinned. But why would that be? Why would someone who has not sinned have to die anyway because the rest of us have sinned? From a "philosophical point of view" - or my philosophical point of view - that would argue that virtue means nothing at all; and I certainly do not agree with that. Do you?

If we all have to die because some of us have sinned, then it is not sin that leads to death. Is it? But just look around! A squirrel is not guilty of sin. Is it? Why, then, should it have to die if death is the consequence of sin? An eagle is not guilty of sin. Is it? Why, then, should it have to die if death is the consequence of sin? A simple sunflower is not guilty of sin. Is it? Why, then, should it have to die if it has not sinned?

I think people need to think through the claims of others a lot more than they do. If something does not make sense, then admit it makes no sense; and do not follow after those who make no sense in their claims. At least, it makes sense not to do so. Right?

In conclusion, however, in essence, Thomas - or the Jesus of Thomas - was a huge challenge to the idea that some can rule others by virtue of delegated authority from an unseen God - or god. Jehovah did not want to be seen - as those who tried to rule as delegated authorities in his name claimed - and claim. Why? Because if he could not be seen, neither could he be refuted. Thus, the decision by whomever dreamed up Jehovah, keep Jehovah out of sight and without an image. Keep him hidden so that from behind the scenes, he could rule - or more correctly, others could rule in his name. The ultimate strategy: *Keep them in the dark so they cannot see nothing is there.*

Well, that is the way I see it now. Each of us must choose for ourselves in the end, however, and that is as it should be. Which camp of Jesus do you want to believe - and be a part of - if you want to be a part of any camp of Jesus at all?

It is truly a wonderful world in which we live - full of majesty and "without sin" - without separation from an Infinite God. We may not have all the answers about the details of it, but we can "know" that it is good simply by looking at it and being astonished at the mystery and grandeur and gallantry of it all; and then we can and should include ourselves within that mystery - and *KNOW IT ALL.*

And that is the way it works too. *Know What Is In Your Sight - And You Will Know All.* Why? Because everything that is simply continues all that was; and *knowing what is, you will also KNOW WHAT WILL BE.*
Or so I Believe Now!

Let me leave you with Verse 5 of my favorite gospel - *THE GOSPEL OF THOMAS;* but stay tuned, if you wish, for Part 3 of *THE BIRTH OF THE BIBLE.*

Jesus said: Know what is in thy sight, and what is hidden from thee will be revealed to thee. For there is nothing hidden that will not be manifest.

P.S. As mentioned earlier, I believe *THE GOSPEL OF THOMAS* was the first gospel written because it is the most primitive of all gospels - and subsequent gospel writers probably took from *THE GOSPEL OF THOMAS* and used sayings from that gospel while creating worlds of their own. The final statement of the above quote is an example, but I will offer another example in Part 3 of this work.

But take the quote *"For there is nothing hidden that will not be manifest"* from the verse above and compare with other gospels and note how it is used in those gospels. In the verse as offered above, it should be clear that Jesus is offering that "knowing what is in your sight" is a prelim for knowing what is unseen. If you know what is in your sight - in terms of worth - then you will also know what is not in your sight - again, in terms of worth - because what is unknown is only the same as what is known. In other words, that which is hidden is actually "manifested" in or by that which is. So know that which is and you will also know that which is not - or perhaps hidden from you.

Now compare that sense of the statement *"For there is nothing hidden that will not be manifest"* with how it is used in other gospels. In *THE GOSPEL OF LUKE,* Chapter 8, for example, the same statement is used to imply that no one can hide the truth at some judgment time. Luke offers in Chapter 8, Verse 17: *For nothing is secret that will not be made manifest; neither anything hid that shall not be known.* In other words, watch what you do because nothing that you do will be hidden at judgment time. It will all "come out in the end." So, don't pretend you can hide anything you do. At least that is the sense I get from the statement as used in Luke, but that is not how it is used in Thomas. Is it?

Now, let's complete this three part series on *THE BIRTH OF THE BIBLE*.

Thanks! (FWB)

The Birth Of
The Bible
(Part 3 Of 3)

By
Francis William Bessler
1/31/2014

My Bible!

So much more could be said about this drama dealing with *THE BIBLE*, but I think I will leave that to scholars and believers in *THE BIBLE* - neither of which I am. I must admit that I used to think of *THE BIBLE* as the "word of God," but I do not see it that way anymore. I do not even think it is the "word of Jehovah." I see it now as simply a compilation of a lot of stories told as if a Jehovah is a reality; but I do not think Jehovah is a reality. I think Jehovah was invented by some writer who was trying to deal with life. He probably saw other societies as having gods and decided that his society needed one of its own. Thus, he invented Jehovah; and since other "pagans" believed they also needed a "god," they believed in what the original inventor told them - and so it has gone down through history.

As for me, I left Jehovah behind when I left Satan behind. I do not believe there can be any "opposition to God" - as Satan has been claimed to be - and thus I cannot believe in Satan - or that a Satan exists. How can there be opposition to God if, being Infinite, God is Everywhere? God can only be opposed if He (or It or She) can also be "deposed." Right? God cannot be "deposed" because God is Everywhere. Therefore, God cannot be "opposed" - and Satan must be myth.

Perhaps it is because I do not believe a Satan can exist that I cannot believe in Jehovah either - simply because the two go together as if they depend upon one another. Remove Satan - and Jehovah can't exist. So if I have removed Satan from my life, then I have also had to remove a Jehovah.

But what if Satan does exist and Jehovah does exist? What then? Well, my friend, that is the argument of a "non-believer." Those who are sure that Satan and Jehovah exist are the only ones who would ask such a question, perhaps attempting to soothe their souls; but I am a Believer in a God of Infinity. That does not make me incapable of being fooled, but it does provide for myself as much security as what other "Believers" might think they have too.

When I look around and see the wonder of life about me and know that such life is what I think of as miraculous and amazing - including my own - then I have no need for further miracles. I do not have to go somewhere else to find God. I find God wherever I go - and in whomever I meet. *My Bible, I guess, is Life Itself.* Like "my Jesus" of *THE GOSPEL OF THOMAS* said, I *"know what is in my sight"* and what is hidden is really of no concern to me, but if it becomes so, I simply have to remind myself that "what is hidden" is probably only the same as what I can see. So, why waste time looking for a Paradise someplace else when the only Paradise I need is right at hand?

What Will Happen When I Die?

What will happen when I die? I do not know, but I have no reason to suspect that I won't just continue "being me." I don't expect to see God face to face - as some do - because my God does not have a face. My God is not a person with Whom I can walk and talk. My God is an Infinite Presence that makes All Sacred. When I die, I won't see God anymore than I do now, but it is very likely that if I continue to "be me," then I will continue to "see God Everywhere."

I am reminded, however, of a verse in *THE GOSPEL OF THOMAS*, that offers a comment about death and what is beyond. In Verse 4 of that gospel, *Jesus said: The man old in days will not hesitate to ask a little child of seven days about the place of Life, and he will live. For many who are first shall become last and they shall become a single one.*

First of all, let me point out that this is not a "judgmental verse." It is simply commenting about being old, dying, and starting over again as a little child. At least this is what I take from it. The old man in days - any old man (or woman) in days - is close to ending his (or her) life, but what comes after that? That old man (or woman) will simply become a child in a next order, so to speak.

Jesus said: *For many who are first will become last and they shall become a single one.* That is only to say that the old man who is about to die is one with the child who is about to be born. It is a cycle thing - nothing more. An old man - or old woman - will naturally die and then become "new" by becoming a child again in a next incarnation. The old man and the new child, then, are a "single one." Makes sense. Right?

This is but another example, however, of a verse being in *THE GOSPEL OF THOMAS* that seems to be repeated in another gospel, but in that other gospel, the meaning is completely different. In *THE GOSPEL OF LUKE*, for example, Jesus is said to repeat the "first and last" exchange, but in a totally judgmental way. Luke is talking about being "judged" after life - not simply continuing as a child from being an old man. In other words, Luke seems to be taking a verse from *THE GOSPEL OF THOMAS* and changing it to fit some offering of his own; and I think this is another good example of a subsequent gospel writer selecting a verse from *THE GOSPEL OF THOMAS* - and altering the meaning of the original verse.

In Luke, the first will become last and last will become first is offered as a social setting judgmental thing. The "first" become those who think they are "first" in some order of salvation. Those who think they are first are really last. That is the meaning of the verse as offered in Luke, but that is not the meaning of the idea in Thomas. Luke offers his statement in the context of some final judgment. He says, starting from Chapter 13, Verse 24:

Strive to enter in at the strait gate: for many, I say unto you, will seek to enter in, and shall not be able. When once the master of the house is risen up, and hath shut to the door, and ye begin to stand without, and to knock at the door saying, Lord, Lord, open unto us; and he shall answer and say unto you, I know you not whence ye are. Then shall ye begin to say, we have eaten and drunk in thy presence, and thou hast taught in our streets. But he shall say, I tell you, I know you not whence ye are; depart from me, all ye workers of iniquity. There shall be weeping and gnashing of teeth, when ye shall see Abraham and Isaac and Jacob, and all the prophets, in the Kingdom of God, and you yourselves thrust out. And they shall come from the east and from the west, and from the north and from the south, and shall sit down in the Kingdom of God. And behold, there are last which shall be first, and there are first which shall be last.

But did Jesus really say that? I doubt it, but a traditional Jew would have said it because a traditional Jew would have believed it; and that is one of the points of this article. Jesus may well have been taken out of context by fellow Jews and assigned the role of Jewish Messiah. A Jewish Messiah would have offered what Luke offers that Jesus said, but a simple "wise person" commenting about life in general would not have said it. I think it is good to keep all this in mind when making judgments about the real Life of Jesus - as well as about our lives too. I offer this comparison because it exemplifies how an earlier gospel writer could have said one thing - and a subsequent gospel writer could have massaged a same verse and told a completely different tale with the retelling effort. I rest my case.

Let me finish with a bit of a song I wrote a few years ago in December of 2008. This article has been about seeing God in whatever way each of us sees God. So I do believe it is fitting to conclude my thoughts on how I see God. Like I say, I do not see *THE BIBLE* as the "word of God," but rather as a compilation of works by various men and women who pledged their allegiance to a Pagan god named Jehovah; and those men and women see God much different than I do. I see God, not as an outside Lord of life, but as an inside Infinite Presence; but to each, his or her own. I will let my song say the rest.

Thanks! (FWB)

If I Could Talk With God

By
Francis William Bessler
Laramie, Wyoming
12/8/2008

REFRAIN:
If God would speak to me – I think that it would be
that I would hear exactly – what I want to believe.
If I believe that God is just – and will punish those I oppose,
then that's what I will hear – and what I will suppose.
If I believe that God is good – and belongs to everyone,
then that's what I will hear – that everyone's God's son.
If God would speak to me – I think that it would be
that I would hear exactly – what I want to believe.

If I could talk with God, I think that He would say:
My son, I'm within you.
Be aware of that when you pray.
He'd say: My Presence must be mystery
because the Infinite is not for you to understand;
but that Presence is your Divinity;
and that's to say, I'm holding your hand.

If I could talk with God, I think that He would say:
Because everything is equal in My sight,
nothing can be favored in any way.
He'd say: Look at anything, My child
and be impressed with all the majesty
that you see all the while
and know that it's all of My Divinity.

If I could talk with God, I think that He would say:
My son, I am with you
every night and day;
but I am not only with you –
I'm with everyone.
Since I am Infinite, I'm in All –
and everyone (everything) is My son.

If I could talk with God, I think that He would say:
If you doubt that I am Infinite,
just look out into space.
If you can find where it all ends,
then it is for you not to believe;
but if you can't find an end, My friend,
be careful not to be deceived.

If I could talk with God, I think that He would say:
Don't be fooled when others claim
that Heaven is in another place.
He'd say: Heaven is only knowing
that where you are, I am;
and if you can find where I am not,
then Heaven there is not at hand.

If I could talk with God, I think that He would say:
Because I am in you, My child,
you should not be ashamed.
I think He'd say that everything
in that which we call Creation
is blessed of Him because He's there;
and that should cause in us, elation.

If I could talk with God, I think that He would say:
Be not confused, My child.
Just be glad when you pray.
Say thanks for the life you have
because it's generous beyond expression.
I hear Him saying, if you do that,
then you will always be in Heaven.
Repeat *Refrain*.

Heaven!

By
Francis William Bessler
2/14/2014

Where is Heaven?

When I was a child, I was taught that Heaven is up above. If I asked where Heaven was, my parents would point up in the sky and say, *"Up there, Son, Up there!"* So I would look and see only sky - and clouds scattered about. I was told that I had to use my imagination to see Heaven up there. It was there. I just had to imagine it was there.

Well, I am now a much older child of 72 years. I still believe that Heaven is "up there," but I have lived and learned to realize that it is not only "up there." *It is really everywhere because what is "up there" is also "down here."* I can prove that by going "up there" and scanning what is "up there" and comparing what I find - in terms of worth - to what is down below. How is what is "up there" any different from what is "down here"?

Take the test. Compare up with down - and then try to convince me that there is something "up there" that is somehow much worthier than what is down below. Look up into the sky. Focus on one part of it and divide what you see. Be honest, now! Is the left part to your imaginary middle any different than the right part - in terms of worth? Now, expand your vision. Take the whole world into your sight - by imagination, of course - and divide it right down the middle. How is it different than the sky you just looked at? If there was not more worth in the left side of your sky than in the right side of your sky, why in the world would the left side of all existence be any different than the right side of all existence? Tell me that!

Now, expand that all of existence test into an Infinity Test. Of course you cannot divide Infinity anymore than you can divide all of existence; but again, use your imagination and do it anyway. There it is - Infinity - a reality that has no ends or no limits. For the sake of adventure, go ahead and divide that Infinity that has no ends. Whoosh! Right down the middle of everywhere. Now compare the left side of everywhere with the right side of everywhere. What is the chance that the left side is somehow going to be more worthy than the right side - or the right side more worthy than the left side?

But what does all of this attempted division of expressions of reality tell us? In each case, we have determined that it is unlikely that the left side of anything can be more worthy than the right side of anything. That simply translates to everywhere and everything being equally worthy; and that translates into Heaven being everywhere. If Heaven can be defined as a *"place of the worthy,"* then everywhere can be defined as Heaven because everywhere is of equal worth.

Of course, I could be wrong in my thinking, but having taken the above tests long ago in life and having lived the answers I found, I think it is very unlikely I am wrong. Others, however, have not taken the above tests - and so they have not found any of my truths. Others are convinced that one place can be more worthy than another - and on that basis, they have concluded that Heaven cannot be everywhere. They have concluded that there must be a Heaven of seclusion somewhere and they are going to end up in that secluded Heaven - and nothing I can say will alter their thinking. They are going to find that secluded Heaven that must be "out there" - and that is all there is to that. End of story - End of search.

But where is this "secluded Heaven" of which they are so sure? No one can tell you where it is. It just is - because they have said it's so. And how do they know there is a secluded or limited Heaven? Others who never took the division tests above told them so. They are, then, the students of others who have also "been told" by others who supposedly know the truth.

Well, that is a matter of opinion, of course. I like to think of Heaven being somewhere I am not too because I like to think there is somewhere I can go to alleviate all my pain and suffering. *Who doesn't want to believe there is such a place? And maybe there is such a place, too; and maybe I will go there eventually; but if I do go there, it will be because of the way I have lived - not the way I have believed.*

Some think that Heaven is a place where God is. I agree with that. I do believe that is so, but since I do not believe that an Infinite God can be absent from anywhere, once again, everywhere must be Heaven. Not so, Not so! Some are shouting. God is not everywhere. God is only "where the angels are." And, of course, "where the angels are" is where the demons are not.

Demons & Angels

Alright, let us investigate. What are "demons"? What are "angels"? I am somewhat limited in this discussion because I can only define what I can see. So if an angel is beyond what I can see, then I will have to leave a discussion of angels - and demons - to someone else who believes that angels - and demons - cannot be defined by what can be seen - and known. But what is an angel for me?

When I think of an angel, I think of one who is at peace. When I think of a demon - or devil - I think of one who is lacking in peace. My definition of an angel, then, is any spirit or entity that is at peace. Nothing more than that. My definition of a demon, then, is any spirit or entity that is angry and lacks peace.

According to that definition - or those definitions - then, I am an angel or a demon - as is each and every one of us. Are we not all either at peace or lacking in peace? Personally, I think I am a soul at peace with the world. Given Heaven as being defined as a place where angels live, well, folks, once again, where I am is Heaven.

Now, flip it over. If I am one who is angry and lacking peace, I am a demon; and if Hell is defined as a place where demons - or devils - live, then if I am a devil or demon, where I live is Hell. It really matters not about God being there or not being there. If I am a demon or live as a demon, then I am in Hell - if Hell is a place where demons live and Heaven is a place where angels live.

Given that I am an angel and know something about angels, we angels are not only ones who are at peace with the world, but we are also ones who have no need to impose on others. We are satisfied with ourselves, as it were, and in being satisfied with ourselves, we have no need to impose on others or insist that others do as we tell them to do. *An angel is really only a "satisfied entity."*

A devil - or demon - on the other hand, is one who is not satisfied with self. Look about! Who can you see who is not satisfied with self? They are all about, aren't they? In that light of defining a devil as one who is not satisfied with self, the churches have been scattered with demons. That is because the churches - or some churches - thrive on the idea that each of the members need some "outside grace" to be happy with life. That is a dictation for dissatisfaction, not satisfaction - with self.

That is not to say, however, that there are only demons in the churches. Certainly not! From my experience with churches - and especially with churches of the modern era - there are far more angels in the churches than demons. *When and where there is Praise of God for the sake of praise, there are angels; and the churches abound with Praise of God; but to be sure, demons abide in churches as well.* Wherever there is accusation against life, there are demons; and many in churches thrive on accusing others of sin or immorality rather than simply Praising God - or Infinity - or the Source of Life - or Life itself. *Where there is accusation rather than praise, there are demons and not angels.*

Imaginary or real, however, I will admit that I have had to deal with some demons in my life - or at least with "demonic notions" such as the false idea that "life is sinful and needs to be saved from itself." So, I guess I know about demons too - or "demonic notions." Before I came to the realization that everywhere is Heaven because everywhere contains God, as it were, I was vulnerable to seeing life as dividable between worthy and unworthy. Personally, I think that my "demons" have been more of the "notion kind" as opposed to "other person" kind; but they have been about - and I have had to deal with them.

The end of demons - or demonic notions - came for me, though, one night when I was still married to Dee, my first (of three) wives. Lying next to Dee on a night in 1973 or so, around the age of 31, I could not go to sleep for having a very troubled mind. I was not sure that I could be right about life being satisfactory unto itself because so many others around me were so sure that life itself is faulty and needs redeemed. I was scared to death that they might be right and I might be wrong. If I should die in a state of challenging that life is not worthy of itself, I could be whisked off to Hell; or so was my fear - as irrational a fear as it was; but I am not the only one to ever have irrational fears. Am I? Most fears, I think, are probably irrational in that which is feared either doesn't exist or could be overcome by focusing on something more worthwhile.

Anyway, back to my troubled sleepless night in 1973 or so, as it happened, a fluttering curtain in the night eventually rescued me from my struggles. In my fear of being wrong, I imagined a curtain fluttering in the window of a dark night to be a real demon out to take me to his home - because of my "disbelief," of course. Wanting to resolve that a devil was really out to get me for my disbelief - or not - though I was trembling at the prospect of being taken alive, I rose from my bed and investigated the scene.

Grabbing the "mysterious image" in the window, my fears were dispelled. That which I had feared was a demon was only a curtain fluttering in the wind. That curtain in the dark just looked like some foreboding rascal. So I told that "foreboding rascal" in the window to stop bothering me, dismissed forever the "demon" with which I had struggled - imaginary of course - and lay down next to my dear wife, Dee, and slept peacefully that night for the first time in weeks - and I am happy to report that I have slept peacefully ever since. *Goodbye, demon! Goodbye, foreboding rascal! Goodbye, doubt!*

It is hard to know about demons, though. I do believe that some are real - just as mine probably were imaginary. In a way, it stands to reason that if I am one to be dissatisfied with life, then I may also be one who is wanting to *invite* a "prince of peace" into my life to make me worthy; but how can I know that a spirit or entity who might visit me due to my *invitation* is really a "prince of peace" - or a fellow dissatisfied soul wanting to use me to try and satisfy him or her or itself?

It is said that "likes attract likes" - and I do believe that is so. If I am a soul - or entity - who is dissatisfied with life, how likely is it that I would attract anyone to me who is not also dissatisfied with life? Thus, in thinking I am receiving a Jesus into my life by inviting a savior in, I may well be receiving a fellow dissatisfied soul all too eager to pretend he is Jesus. Yes, my friend, it could be so.

Personally, I have never heard voices telling me I should do this or that - mostly to hurt another person because that is what angry and dissatisfied persons do - but I do believe it is possible that those who do hear voices may actually be hearing voices. *If a soul is located somehow in a brain for the time a soul occupies a body, what is to say that "two souls" can't occupy a single brain?* If so, that could account for some people "hearing voices." The voice they may be hearing may be another dissatisfied soul using the same brain to dictate to the original host. It may be so; and I do believe it is something to consider when dealing with someone who seems to be suffering from "mental illness." It may be that mental illness is not due strictly to a brain disorder, but rather to multiple occupancy of a single brain by two different souls. Again, it may be something to consider.

And really, it is not much of a stretch to consider the possibility of two or more souls occupying the same brain - or person. If one soul can dwell in a brain, why not more than one? Multiple occupancy of a single brain could account for all sort of mental illness - like schizophrenia and bi-polar disorder. In a case where one "resident" of a mind (or brain) seems to be "controlled" by an invader, it may be so. That could account for one "hearing a voice" commanding him or her to do something that an initial resident would not do. It's possible.

If so, however, if an initial resident of a mind is controlled by a foreign soul, the key for an initial soul to gain (or regain) control would be to simply not invite another in. For that to happen, an initial soul would simply have to be at peace and attain self-satisfaction - |and not need another outside of him or herself for a sense of worth. Though I suppose it is possible that two souls could reside in a single host where the original host is at peace, I doubt very much that it happens. Satisfaction with self would likely prevent needing to *invite* a "savior" in; and that is why a satisfied soul may not be subject to "hearing voices." Perhaps, Huh, Perhaps!

Unmasking The Soul

For what it's worth, in 1989, I compiled a bit of a book on the soul - after pondering the matter for nearly ten years. If you ponder a matter, it is amazing what you might find. So in 1989, I decided to write down my thoughts about the soul, examining the various theories as to the origin and destiny of the soul, and even offering an idea or two of my own. I called the book *SOULS - ILLUSIONS OR REALITIES?*. In 1990, I sent out manuscripts to a lot of different publishers, but only one was interested - Winston-Derek, located in Nashville, Tenn.; and eventually that one declined to publish my book as well due to a "change of heart" by a managing editor. You see, my book challenged the ideas of most of this publisher's authors - and it was decided that it would be unfair that my book be published and perhaps challenge all the other authors. So my work on the soul went unpublished.

Then in 2005, I rewrote the initial manuscript and called the rewrite - *UNMASKING THE SOUL*. When I decided to start my own original writings website in late 2012, my "new" book on the soul was added to Volume 2 of my *OUT IN THE OPEN* feature of my website. Accordingly, if you wish, you can review my ideas about the soul in that location - starting from page 90 of that volume. OK?

Be An Angel

It's pretty simple, then, if an angel can be defined as one who is at peace with him or herself and the world at large, well - *be an angel!* Being an angel is nothing more than seeing the world as one - and failing to divide the world into so called "good" and "evil" camps. Yes, some of us are good in that we act good - and some of us are bad in that we act bad, or badly - but if you take the division test offered above, it is unlikely that there can be good and evil sections or territories in the universe - or existence. *The key to being an angel, then, is to see only good because, in fact, only good exists.* Even an evil person is a good reality in terms of being a Divinely inspired - or filled - entity. So just treat every person - good or evil acting - like they are good - and presto, one is an angel.

And when I die, whatever it is that comes afterwards, hey, I will just continue "being an angel" - or a devil, if that was my choice in the life that preceded my death. None of us really know for sure what the soul is - and some of us are convinced that the soul is as imaginary as a dream - but I think that it is probably safe to believe that if the soul does exist, it will continue as it is. So the key to assuring a wonderful next life is to live this life as wonderful and then just continue on with wonder in the next life. *If, in fact, souls do exist to incarnate bodies, then by being an angel, one's future is secured - as well as one's present.* If, in fact, however, souls do not exist to incarnate bodies and are just mirages of happening, well, being an angel in this life is still the best way to go because it is the only way of peace; and who wants to live in anger and despair?

As I see it - and believe it - I came into this life and this incarnation with a certain consciousness - which could be supposed as equal to "attitude." Otherwise I could not have even challenged an idea that was prevalent - like Heaven can only be some place and not every place. I would have fallen in step with all my family who believe in a territorial Heaven and Hell if I had not entered with my own consciousness that told me otherwise.

Well, it stands to reason. If I entered this world with a certain consciousness, then I will probably leave it with the same consciousness - unless I alter that consciousness during life. If I exit this life with a certain consciousness, then it is likely I will enter another incarnation with the same consciousness. *If I want to assure myself of a good life in the next realm of things, then, I better lead a good life now in order to inherit a "good me" afterwards.* Makes sense. Right?

Old & New

Let me finish with a couple of songs - one old and one new. I wrote the "old" one in the early '80s for a four volume audio cassette album of original commentary and music I produced about life as I see it - *Naturally Divine*. Each volume is about 90 minutes long. What a joy that was! With the help of a lot of fine technicians and musicians - including singers - in Atlanta, Georgia, where I lived, *MASTER OF*

YOUR OWN FATE, the name of the album, was produced. That project took me from 1983-1992 to accomplish because I could only afford to record one song at a time. I would work as much overtime as I could to earn money to pay for studio and musicians; and then I would record a bit on my program. It took a long time to complete a rather simple program; but eventually I finished it - with the help of a lot of very talented musicians and singers.

After finishing *MASTER OF YOUR OWN FATE* in 1992, I tried to find a sponsor who could help me promote it, but to no avail. Since then, audio cassette format has become obsolete. Perhaps some day I will convert the program to CD format - and try again; however, in order to be able to share *MASTER OF YOUR OWN FATE* with any who wish to review it now, I just produced a DVD series that I call *THE STORY OF LOVE* that features my *MASTER OF YOUR OWN FATE* dubbed onto a friends and family pictorial of photos I have taken from 2009 through 2013.

THE STORY OF LOVE is comprised of 3 DVD 3 hr. volumes - with Volumes 1 & 2 of *MASTER OF YOUR OWN FATE* dubbed onto Volume 1 of *THE STORY OF LOVE*. Volumes 3 & 4 of *MASTER OF YOUR OWN FATE* are dubbed onto Volume 2 of *THE STORY OF LOVE;* and Volume 3 of *THE STORY OF LOVE* features all the songs and music found in *MASTER OF YOUR OWN FATE*.

As you should know if you have been with me in this writing, I believe that life is good as it is and all should embrace the naked because of that. Volumes 1 & 2 of *THE STORY OF LOVE* contain only minimal asexual nudity, but Volume 3 of *THE STORY OF LOVE* features considerable personal asexual nudity mixed with clothed subjects photos. That was done to allow for the ideal of nakedness to be featured, but only in a special volume. That special volume is intended to be an optional only volume. Some may find nudity objectionable; and thus if so, one can audit *MASTER OF YOUR OWN FATE* on DVD without any nudity at all - except for one photo of me standing in a stream with back to camera and one photo of me sitting in a chair with legs crossed. Then if nudity is acceptable, a special volume allows for it.

THE STORY OF LOVE is so titled by virtue of one of the songs of *MASTER OF YOUR OWN FATE* called *"The Story of Love."* I did this series just to make *MASTER OF YOUR OWN FATE* available, using somewhat low-tech mediums, however, anyone who wants to produce their own dubbed series featuring *MASTER OF YOUR OWN FATE* should consider themselves welcome to do so.

Hey, I think *THE STORY OF LOVE* is worthwhile, but I believe someone else could do a different - and probably better - production. My production is VHS based and is somewhat less quality than other mediums. In addition, my dubbing equipment is probably less quality too. Another could use my copy of *MASTER OF YOUR OWN FATE* and produce a more quality program. I would be open to another - or others - doing just that. Dub my *MASTER OF YOUR OWN FATE* onto some Naturalist based program of your choice and call your production what you will - and then be my guest on sharing your production with the world as you choose. Alright? If interested, simply let me know by email via my website - www.una-bella-vita.com - and I will be glad to make needed arrangements. OK?

In the meantime, if you would like a copy of *THE STORY OF LOVE,* as long as I can do so, I will be glad to make a copy for you. Simply request the volumes you wish, given my description of volumes above, and I will be glad to make a copy for you. Again, feel welcome to contact me via my website.

Anyway, the song I am featuring below that I wrote for *MASTER OF YOUR OWN FATE* is called *Be An Angel* - just one of 30 songs I wrote for the project. *Be An Angel* is the first song I will feature below.

The "new" song featured below, however, is really new. I wrote it now, I guess you could say, for this essay on *HEAVEN.* I call the song by the same name as this essay - *Heaven.*

Both songs are about *Heaven,* of course - and how I see Heaven. One can describe Heaven in terms of place - which is really everywhere - and one can describe Heaven in terms of conduct - which is what being an angel is all about. *Take your pick - Heaven as a place - or Heaven as a conduct.* In any case, I think it's good to know what Heaven is about if we are ever to experience it - wherever it is.

I will leave you to my songs. Please enjoy them as you can and will. OK?

Thanks! (FWB)

Be An Angel

By
Francis William Bessler
Atlanta, Georgia
1983

Be an angel, be an angel, let me be me.
Be an angel, be an angel, don't make me see.
Be an angel, be an angel, it's really easy.
Be an angel, be an angel, go Naturally.

Be an angel, be an angel, don't tell me lies.
Be an angel, be an angel, lies are not wise.
Be an angel, be an angel, to lie is to die.
Be an angel, be an angel, don't compromise life.

Be an angel, be an angel, don't scream at me.
Be an angel, be an angel, it's you that can't see.
Be an angel, be an angel, don't imitate God.
Be an angel, be an angel, for God's not a rod.

Be an angel, be an angel, it's simple you know.
Be an angel, be an angel, take off your clothes.
Be an angel, be an angel, don't live for dough.
Be an angel, be an angel, I love you so.

BRIDGE:
There's no such thing as a bad angel.
There's no such thing as a good devil.
There's no such thing as a bad angel.
There's no such thing as a good devil.
Angels are those who care for us all,
but who know it's our way or no way at all.
Devils are those who would capture us all,
make us go their way or no way at all.

Be an angel, be an angel, obey no one else.
Be an angel, be an angel, live for yourself.
Be an angel, be an angel, don't live in Hell.
Be an angel, be an angel, for Hell's someone else.

Be an angel, be an angel, don't step in my way.
Be an angel, be an angel, don't ask me to pay.
Be an angel, be an angel, light up my day.
Be an angel, be an angel, go your own way.

Be an angel, be an angel, don't be a leach.
Be an angel, be an angel, never deceive.
Be an angel, be an angel, don't hang on me.
Be an angel, be an angel, let me be me.

Repeat *BRIDGE.* Then repeat last verse, duplicating last line.

Heaven

By
Francis William Bessler
Laramie, Wyoming
2/2014

REFRAIN:
Let me tell you about a place called Heaven,
a place called Heaven, a place called Heaven
where you can reside.
All you have to do to live in Heaven,
to live in Heaven, to live in Heaven,
is to know that - you are God's child.

Where is Heaven, my friend?
It's where you are.
Look up in the sky
and find a star.
Imagine you're there
and you can know
there's no more God there
than on the Earth below. *Refrain.*

What is Heaven, my friend?
It's knowing you belong.
Be proud of what you are
and sing your song.
There is no room in Heaven
for a thing called shame.
If you're ashamed of yourself,
you've got yourself to blame. *Refrain.*

Where is Heaven, my friend?
It's in your dreams.
It's up in the mountains
and down in the streams.
It's in the fish that swim
and in the squirrels that lurch;
and, yes, it's even in all
who praise in a church. *Refrain.*

What is Heaven, my friend?
It's having an open mind.
It's knowing all are worthy
and it's being kind.
It's believing Life is a miracle
that's full of majesty.
Each is part of that miracle
and is a king or a queen. *Refrain.*

Where is Heaven, my friend?
It's in yourself.
It's in all that you see,
all that you feel and smell.
It's in all the sounds you hear,
all that you love to taste.
It's knowing that all of this
is what makes Life great. *Refrain (2).*

Ending:

All you have to do to live in Heaven,
to live in Heaven, to live in Heaven,
is to know that - you are God's child -
is to know that - you are God's child -
to know that - you are God's child.

Sainthood!

By
Francis William Bessler
Laramie, Wyoming
4/27/2014

I used to believe that I had to be a "member" of an organization or community of saints to be a saint myself; but I have long ago given up such a belief because, upon analysis, it makes no sense to me - mostly because of the scenario of "Infinity." Infinity translates as "endless" - and endless does not allow one place to be more "Heavenly" than another. If every place is equally worthy because it contains the same Infinity - or Divinity - then every place must be Heaven. It is only a matter of being aware that all is "Divine" and acting accordingly. That, for me, is what "Heaven" is all about; and since "Heaven" is the "abode" of the "saints," then everyone is a saint as well. It is only a matter of knowing it, being aware of it, and loving who and what you are that amounts to "Sainthood."

Today is a very special day, however, for those who believe that sainthood is a matter of belonging to a community - or nation of believers. Today, two who believed that "membership" is required for sainthood are being "canonized" as being dignified members of a "community of Heaven." I think it is wonderful that Pope John XXIII and Pope John Paul II are being canonized as saints because, as you know, I am a very committed believer in sainthood, but I wonder why these two and so many others have not realized that sainthood cannot be a "membership" oriented matter.

I am not alone in my thinking either. Am I? I am reminded of the 4th Century when a debate raged within Christian communities about that very thing. Some believed that Jesus taught that Heaven is an "awareness" (of worth) thing; and others taught that Jesus taught that Heaven is a "membership" thing. As it happened, the very sincere believers in Heaven as a community won that debate - if you want to call what happened "winning."

Who knows, though? I may well have been among the "winners" of the debate that raged so long ago. I may have been one who considered "organization" to be absolutely essential for any community - let alone a community that prided itself on being all about getting to Heaven. I may have been one to have been outraged that some "others" tried to teach otherwise; and I might have been one of the eventual order of bishops who chose to "outlaw" all thinking of Heaven as being "awareness" oriented simply because such an approach would have left no room for "law and order" - and "authority." Yes, I might have been one of the ignorant (and arrogant) had I lived in the 4th Century - and before that century - or even since that century.

And then again, I might have been one of the "losers" who were overridden and commanded to teach organization over awareness under the penalty of derision for failure to comply - or even some form of execution for challenging the status quo. Who knows? I might have been one of those stoned to death - or fired to death at a stake - or whatever.

In truth, I do not know about where I might have been in some distant past - and what views I might have held - *but I do know where I stand today - about this matter called "Heaven."* I know that if I had been born on some island on Jupiter and never heard of having to "belong" to a community to know my worth, I would have been just as worthy as those huddled in some community on Earth offering obedience to some "authority" in order to "know worth." It is in knowing that worth cannot be tied to any planet or nation or community that I "know" that sainthood cannot be dependent upon any "law and order" to achieve sainthood.

Am I crazy? Why not come to my little tent on Jupiter and find out for yourself? Keep in mind, though, that I might not stay on Jupiter. I might even leap on to Mars or Saturn or Neptune or even some far out distant planet of another universe. Infinity has no boundaries. Does it? No matter where I might go, though, I will be in "Heaven" because no matter where I might go, God, being Infinity Itself, will be there - and that is what Heaven is all about for me.

Again, I think it is wonderful that two of my fellow saints - Pope John XXIII and Pope John Paul II - are in Heaven. They deserve to be there - and "here" - just like everyone ever born deserves the same. None of us deserves to be "excluded" from Heaven when Heaven is really everywhere. I wonder when people on Earth will ever realize that, though - and stop looking for Heaven someplace else.

I am reminded of a passage in one of my favorite gospels - *THE GOSPEL OF MARY MAGDALENE* - a gospel, by the way, that was "out-lawed" by the "winners" of the 4th Century who insisted that law and order must be the rule of the day lest chaos ensue and a Heaven of Law and Order never be realized.

Of course, the story can be pure fiction - as any story about Jesus might be because all gospels were written by men subject to telling tales as if they were truth - but it seems right to me. That is why I believe it. When the Jesus of that tale commented about "the good news of the kingdom" in the 1st verse of the few verses that remain in *THE GOSPEL OF MARY MAGDALENE,* he commented as such: *"Be careful that no one leads you astray by saying, 'Look here' or 'Look there.' The child of humanity is within you. Follow that. Those who seek it will find it. Go and preach the good news of the kingdom. Do not lay down any rules other than that which I have given you, and do not establish law, as the lawgiver did, or you will be bound by it." When he said this, he left them.*

As it turned out, that idea was demonized as "heretical" - and that is pretty much the way it has been since then. I wonder what Pope John XXIII or Pope John Paul II thought about it - or did they even know about it? It was outlawed long before they reigned as popes and they may have never been given a chance to review it; or they may have known about it and agreed with the many bishops of the 4th Century that decided it could not stand. Who knows?

In any case, *Welcome to Heaven - John XXIII and John Paul II!* You will find life here rather amazing and fulfilling! I am so glad you finally made it!

Gently,
Saint Francis (of Laramie, Wyoming)!

Was Jesus A Messiah?

By
Francis William Bessler
Laramie, Wyoming
5/17/2006
(A Poem – though I have sung it Free Style)

Was Jesus a messiah – or was he just like you and me?
Did we give him all his power – to avoid being free?
Is Heaven another place – or is it just knowing God inside?
Is Hell only insisting – on following the blind?

Was Jesus a messiah – or was he just like you and me?
Have we turned away from the truth – of our mutual Divinity?
Did Jesus really tell us – that the Kingdom is within?
Did he really say – there is no such thing as sin?

Was Jesus a messiah – or was he just like you and me?
Have we known Jesus all along – or have we been deceived?
Did Jesus really tell us – that we should all be as a child?
Does that only mean – we should be equal all the while?

Was Jesus a messiah – or was he just like you and me?
Did he really tell us – to find our child of humanity?
Is life nothing more – than endless mystery?
Is worth only knowing – all are of the same Divinity?

Was Jesus a messiah – or was he just like you and me?
Was he only more aware – of what allows us to be free?
Is it really true – that to be a part of his family,
all I have to do – is live my life shamelessly?

Was Jesus a messiah – or was he just like you and me?
Did he only realize – God is in all equally?
Did he really say – we should take off our clothes
because we should have no shame – for the life God's bestowed?

Is Jesus a messiah – or is he just like you and me?
Is he smiling now – because the truth is finally free?
Is virtue only knowing – that we are all the same –
and that we need no messiah – when we live without shame?

Socrates, Jesus, & Me

By
Francis William Bessler
Laramie, Wyoming
7/7/2002; modified a bit 5/8/2009
(A Poem; though I have sung it too.)

What is the meaning of life?
It's a question we all should ask.
Asking that question and searching for answers
should be our greatest task.
It seems to me it's the only way
that each of us can be free;
and if you don't believe it, just ask the likes of
Socrates, Jesus & me.

Socrates was a questioning gent
who lived 400 years before Christ.
He led the way for Jesus, I think,
to find his life quite Divine.
He said, question everything, my friend,
to find the truths of Divinity;
and I must say that has been the way of
Socrates, Jesus & me.

255

Don't be afraid of life, Jesus would say,
take it and cherish it bold.
Don't fear what you can't see –
just love all that you can hold.
Know what is in your sight
and what's hidden you will see;
and that is the key of knowing life by
Socrates, Jesus & me.

If you do not love what you can see,
then how can you love what you can't?
Just embrace life for all that it is
and ignore those that say, thy shan't.
Life is meant to be lived and known
as much as we can allow it to be.
You can know life as much as we –
Socrates, Jesus & me.

Life is a mystery and always will be
and there's much we can never know,
but as long as we love the mystery,
we cannot fail to grow.
Generously question while searching for answers.
That's the key to being free.
Enjoy your questioning and your answers as we have -
Socrates, Jesus & me.

Be not subdued by the questions
for which answers do not come.
Enjoy the rays of light that shine
even as you may never understand the Sun.
Ask why there is light, but be not discouraged
if the answer you never see.
Love life as the gift it is – that's what we know –
Socrates, Jesus & me.

I have only a little more to offer
and then I will let you go.
Ask what you will, but never allow anyone
to dictate what you must know.
Love what you know and also that
which you would like so much to see;
and you will be hitching a ride with the likes of
Socrates, Jesus & me.

Become A Child

By
Francis William Bessler
Atlanta, Georgia
1983
(A Poem)

It's time, My Friends, that we took a different look
and begin to see life in a very different way.
It's time, My Friends, that we read a different book
and begin to be as children, each and every day.

It's time, My Friends, that we stopped listening to fools
who know not of wisdom, but claim to be of God.
It's time, My Friends, that we opened another school
that teaches not of swords – and offers guidance with a nod.

Look at the love of a Child – and let it be your own.
Don't pretend to be a master because you have grown.
A little girl or a woman – why should there be a difference?
A little boy or a man – there's no change in essence.

It's time, My Friends, that we begin anew –
Close your eyes and forget the sins of the past.
It's time, My Friends, that another picture we drew.
Open your eyes again – to see a Truth that will last.

It's time, My Friends, that we learn to admire the Child –
Forget the line of arrogance we crossed when we matured.
It's time, My Friends, that we embrace the kind and wild
so that we can finally say – Truth and Peace will endure.

It's time, My Friends, that Virtue, not sin, survives.
Yes, My Friends, it's time – that each of us becomes a Child.

Little Blackie!

By
Francis William Bessler
Laramie, Wyoming
June 19th, 2014

This is a story about a little fellow - without a beginning - and even without an end. That is, I do not know how *"Little Blackie"* originated; and even though I was within a few yards of Blackie when he (or she) died this morning in the back yard of my dear friend, Nancy, I do not know about its ending either. Blackie died alone - perhaps as it lived alone too.

Blackie - as I chose to call a little black bird that came to my friend, Nancy's, yard - was probably only a few months old when we first saw him (or her). For lack of knowing if Blackie was a male or a female, I will call "him" or "her" an "it". OK?

We noticed "it" about a month ago; and "it" was having difficulty walking - due apparently to a wounded leg - and unable to fly too, probably from an injury to a wing. Nancy and I guessed it must have fallen - perhaps from a nest - and hurt itself; but we do not know that.

All we know about Blackie is that it appeared in Nancy's yard about a month or so ago. A friend, Lynn, came by and told us he could provide a cage if we wanted. Maybe we could cage Little Blackie and provide it safety from the elements - and provide it food and water. If we did, maybe it would survive - and maybe grow strong enough to join its brothers and sisters out and about Nancy's yard. We even planned on nurturing Little Blackie through the summer if needed - and maybe bring it in for the winter if it lasted that long.

So, we took advantage of Lynn's offer and borrowed a cage and caged Little Blackie. Maybe that provided Blackie a little longer life than it would have had - or maybe it lessened the time it would have lived. We do not know. It is possible that caging Little Blackie led to an earlier demise. We simply do not know, but I think it is "probable" that we extended the little one's life at least a little by doing what we did.

In the daytime, we left Blackie in its cage outside on Nancy's lawn out back, though at night - because the temperature dropped below what is comfortable into the 30s - we brought Blackie inside. In the daytime, when it was outside, we opened a door to its cage to allow it to hop up and out of the cage if it wanted. One time, it did hop out and wandered quite a ways from the cage; but eventually I found it and put it back in its cage for that night. After that initial wandering from the cage, though, it stayed in the cage and never tried to hop out again. We were sorry for that because we wanted Blackie to be free, but it probably weakened from its injuries and never hopped out again.

Still, in its cage it seemed to be growing healthier. Other birds of its kind - probably of a "black bird" species - occasionally hopped into Blackie's cage and drank of Blackie's water and ate of Blackie's food and then hopped out again. Blackie did not seem to notice the visits, though, and just kept to itself - and the other birds seemed to have paid no attention to Blackie as such. They just hopped into an open cage, ate a little, and then hopped out - as if Blackie was not even there.

But Blackie was there - and here - for a little while - and Nancy and I are glad it was. This morning when I took Blackie outside, it seemed to be alright, looking up at me and wondering perhaps about the day ahead; but an hour later, Blackie was dead. Perhaps it was almost dead when I took it outside earlier - and I had simply not noticed. Within an hour of my taking Blackie outside this morning, however, Blackie died. I guess it was even weaker than I thought it was.

Nancy cried when she noticed Little Blackie without movement and said; *"I'm so sorry! I wanted him to live!"* I tried to comfort Nancy and told her something like - *"He did live for a little while and that is what we should be proud of. We did try to help it live, but life and death happens to us all - and we should not act like anything that lives can escape death. In seems rather harsh, but we all have to die in the end."*

Life Without Death

On the other hand, in the end, Little Blackie did not die near as much as he "lived to the end." That is how I see Blackie - and all my brothers and sisters in the air and on the ground and in the sea. Sure, death comes to us all, human and not human, but that death should not be our focus - even when it happens. Life should be our focus - even when it is no longer. It was once - and as I believe it - it will be again.

Who knows what happens when we die? Little Blackie did not know of a destiny after death - and neither do any one of us. We all speculate about "life after death," but none of us really know about it. Do we? Personally, having Little Blackie in my life for just a month taught me that life itself here and now is what is so precious - not some speculated life after death - though I believe that happens as well.

If we all have souls that occupy bodies while those bodies are alive - as I believe - then it is likely that those souls will simply occupy other bodies that are alive when one body does die; but again, the focus should be living - not dying.

But what if I had treated Little Blackie differently? What if Nancy and I had chosen to flip Little Blackie off and let it be without help? What if we had simply signed off the life of a "little one" and paid it no mind? What if we had simply left it on its own to die on its own? What if we had chosen to ignore Little Blackie and uttered some such words as "That's the way it is!" and let it go at that?

Well, for me, the answer is clear. Yes, I could have done that - or we, Nancy and I, could have done that - and yes, Little Blackie would have died on its own anyway - but if that had been so, I (or we) would have ignored the precious gift of life as if the life of one of us is somehow less worthy than the life of another. Because I (or we) chose to pay attention to Little Blackie, I (and we) chose to attend to life itself.

And when I die - as did Little Blackie this morning - maybe Little Blackie will be there to take my soul on a flight to whatever next life I may have; and when Nancy dies, maybe Little Blackie will be there to take Nancy on a flight to whatever next life she may have. It works that way, I believe, when we pay attention to whatever wonderful life we all have and treat one life the same as another.

Thanks, Little One!

So, yes, we did not save Little Blackie; but because of the way we treated Little Blackie, perhaps Little Blackie saved us. Suppose?

This evening, or maybe tomorrow morning, Nancy and I will bury Little Blackie in Nancy's yard somewhere, but very importantly, we will not be "burying us." *A funeral is only sad if in the process we think we are burying ourselves.* If we choose to ignore the living and the right to live - not by law, but by courtesy only - then when we bury someone, we are really burying ourselves. That I do believe.

As we live, we will die - and as we let others live and not insist on providing some means of death or punishment to them - even if deserved - then we will "live forever."

Meanness, I believe, is a certain form of death for a spirit - just as kindness is a form of life for a spirit. If we are mean, even if we think we are being just, we are really into a form of "living death." Kindness to all - and everything - then, is the only certain form of "eternal life" - be that life one mortality or a continuous series of mortalities.

Little Blackie is flying now - in some ethereal way - and because we treated Little Blackie like it was one of us, Well, Friends, we, Nancy and I, are flying as well!

Thanks, Little One! I (and we) appreciate your stopping by! Have Fun Flying Wherever You Are! We are so Glad you were Here!

Go, Little One, Go!

Thanks! (FWB)

Epilog

By
Francis William Bessler
Laramie, Wyoming
3/7/2014

I Am!

Who am I? I do believe that is what I am living in this body to find - the answer to that. Who are you? That is what you should be living in your body to find - the answer to that.

When I was younger and was quite entrenched within the Church of my youth, I thought I could only answer that question by "being told" the answer by someone much wiser than I am; but now I have come to believe that the answer lies within what might be called "science" rather than "faith." I do not believe that "faith" can provide any real answer now because I think that "faith" is really other oriented. Being so, I cannot rely on any answer that another might be offering. I have to know myself - and that means, I have to rely on myself and my own research of mind, so to speak.

But I find that prospect absolutely wonderful! Why? Because I see Life itself as being wonderful; and all I have to do to find myself within that wonderful world of mystery is to look at that wonderful world in general - and then realize that I am only part of it. I guess you could say that I can find the answer to "who I am" nestled in Nature. All I have to do is look at Nature - and there am I.

It is really amazing! I am not so mysterious after all. I am just one of the gang, like one of my songs of the '80s says. I'M PART OF IT! If I really want to know who I am - or at least what I am - all I have to do is look about and scan all of Creation - and presto - there I am!

But who is the "I" in all of this? Am I who I am related to a body - or a soul? Who are you? Do you define yourself related to a body - or a soul? Are you equivalent to your body - or your soul? Or do you even believe you have a soul - or more importantly, do you believe you are a soul?

As for me, I do believe I AM A SOUL! I am not a body. I am a soul. I am something that dwells in a body, but I am not my body. Someday, my body will die, but the real me that dwells in that body will not die. It will just go on to dwell in another body just like it chose to dwell in this wonderful one that is typing these words.

I decided long time ago to love my body, but it is I as a soul who is doing the loving. This soul, this I AM is who is loving this life and this body. I came into this world with my eyes wide open, as it were, and wanting to love life as a measure to prove that I see life (Life) as an expression - or expressions - of a Divine Creation.

One of the gospel writers mentioned that Jesus once said that BEFORE ABRAHAM WAS, I AM. I think Jesus was really saying the same thing as I have learned from life. Before Abraham was, I am too; and before Abraham was, you were. That is maybe you were - if you existed as a soul before Abraham entered into the world - if indeed, Abraham is a real person and not just a fiction person invented to start a faith.

But whether I began before Abraham or after Abraham, I AM as a soul - and so are you. The important thing to note is that it should matter nothing at all that Abraham did or did not exist before you as a soul; and it should not matter one iota if Abraham did or did not exist before I began as a soul. My being a soul has nothing to do with anyone but me - as your being a soul should have relevance only to yourself as a soul.

That is not to say I do not have a "parent soul." Oh, yes, I do! That is the evidence of Nature. All things come from something else - no exceptions. Of course, I had to begin as a soul from a "parent soul" in some way - and I will probably "beget" a soul myself in some way. That is the Natural Way; but once I have been begot, my journey should be my own. I should be grateful to my "parent soul" - or souls - for begetting me, but I should not lose sight that I have a right to be.

NONSENSE! Some are responding that way. Nonsense! I am not a soul in the first place - or I was "created" by a God - or whatever. Only God can create a soul. *My answer to that is that there is NO EVIDENCE to illustrate that is true; but there is plenty of evidence to suggest that all beings come from other beings. In that light, the "evidence" of reality would indicate that as a soul, another soul was my parent just like another body - and bodies - was the parent - and parents - of my body.*

But therein is a wonderful idea! I AM NOT ALONE! Or, it is likely I am not alone. That is, my soul is not alone. It came from another soul - or souls - and it is very comforting to know that it is likely that the "parent soul" or souls of my soulful origin will be there for me - their child - just like as a parent soul one day, I will be there for my children souls. That is just the way it is - and isn't it wonderful?

Some think that God is their "Providence." I believe that God is only the Source of all reality; but my true "providence" comes from other souls just like me. My providence is my own, however, as your providence is your own. I can talk to my folks and you can talk to your folks - providential folks, that is. And as we live and experience as souls within bodies, we can all know that because we come from another - like us - we can never really be alone.

Can We?

Well, Folks, that's it! Let me end it with that song I wrote in 1984 called *I'M PART OF IT.* If you have lived unaware that "you are part of it," you can pledge to pay attention to your own mystery and your own "probable reality" - and then begin to live a Full Life - full of wonder and respect for the awesome reality in which we live. Know you are a soul - and not just have a body - and then go forward to love that body as you love your soul - and cry out every single day of your life - *ISN'T IT WONDERFUL!*

Then I will end it with a brand new song - appropriately called *WILD FLOWERS.* Perhaps that little song will capture this entire work in one song. Life, as I see it, is literally Miraculous. I see magic in it everywhere I look - that is, in life itself - or a life itself. One life is the same as another, though - in terms of worth. So if we just look at a "wild flower," Life itself should be clear. I will leave you with that thought!

ADIEU!

Francis William Bessler

I'm Part Of It

By
Francis William Bessler,
Atlanta, Georgia
1984

Look at the little bunny – hoppin down the lane,
twitchin its nose and lookin for love and seein me on the way.
Look at the little chick, peckin at the ground,
finding the grains of wheat that make it grow so sound.
Look at the little kittin, purring on my lap,
finding joy in all it does and never finding lack.
Look at the little puppy, jumping about for joy,
sucking on its mama's tit and tagging behind the boy.

REFRAIN:
No, friends, I'm not above it.
God didn't make me to be a summit.
I'm just one of all the gang.
I want to be found within the range.
Yes, friends, I'm part of it –
not better or worse, but equal to it.
Why should I leave God's friends behind?
All life is God's and God's all life.

Look at the older rabbit, squatting on its heels,
nibblin away at the carrot, amidst banana peels.
Look at that ole rooster – a cock that is so proud
as he struts around the yard as if it is his town.
Look at that ole cat, set in all its ways,
growing more independent as it sleeps the days away.
Look at that ole dog, still waggin its tail,
still lickin its friends and growlin at those it hates. *Refrain.*

ENDING:

Look at the little bunny, hoppin down the lane,
twitchin its nose and looking for love and seeing me on the way.

Wild Flowers

By
Francis William Bessler
Laramie, Wyoming
3/4/2014

REFRAIN:
Wild Flowers - are so very pretty.
Wild Flowers - to help us see.
Wild Flowers - to inspire the soul.
Wild Flowers - to help us know.

If you want to know life,
then march up a hill.
Find a wild flower
and admire it until -
you've realized that Heaven
is where you are;
for Heaven, my friend,
is both near and far. *Refrain.*

In a wild flower, my friend,
there is no sin.
Take some time to study it
and you'll always win.
Just look at it and know
it's full of majesty.
Put one in your hair
and you're a king or a queen. *Refrain.*

The magic of a wild flower
is so very fine.
And where it grows,
life is so Divine.
So, consider yourself one
and love yourself in time;
and know that Eternity
is only a step behind. *Refrain.*

ENDING:
Wild Flowers - are oh so sweet.
Wild Flowers - bloom Eternally.
Wild Flowers - so very pretty.
Wild Flowers - for you and me.
Yes, Wild Flowers - are you and me.
Wild Flowers - are you and me.
Wild Flowers - are you and me.

WILD FLOWERS

The End

Books
by
Francis William Bessler

(Main Theme: Life Is Divine, Sinless, Sacred, & Worthy)

See www.una-bella-vita.com
or enter "Francis Bessler"
in the search bar of Amazon.com
for availability.

Prices vary from $14 to $28 -
depending upon size of book.

All books also available via Kindle

1.

WILD FLOWERS
(about 270 pages)
(essays and songs mostly written as website blogs from 2012 to 2014)
Printed in a smaller font 2 type.

2.

FIVE HEAVEN ON EARTH STORIES
(about 420 pages)
(Featuring 5 philosophical stories written from 1975 - 2007)
Printed in a larger font 4 type for the benefit of an easier read.

3.

EXPLORING THE SOUL -
And BROTHER JESUS
(about 200 pages)
(Featuring an analysis of several theories about the
origin and destiny of the soul - and supplying an
original idea too - originally written in 1988.

Also, featuring a new look at Jesus via an
essay series written in 2005)
Printed in a larger font 4 type for the benefit of an easier read.

4.

JOYFUL HAPPY SOUNDS

(about 470 pages)
(featuring all of my songs and poems written from 1963 to 2015; total: 197)
Printed in a smaller font 2 type.

5.

LOVING EVERYTHING
(WILD FLOWERS # 2)

(about 350 pages)
(essays and songs mostly written as website blogs from 2014 to 2015)
Printed in a smaller font 2 type.

6.

JESUS -
ACCORDING TO
THOMAS & MARY -
AND ME

(about 240 pages)
(Featuring The Gospels of Thomas & Mary
and a personal interpretation of each)
Printed in a larger font 4 type
for the benefit of an easier read.
Compiled in 2017.

7.
IT'S A NEW DAY
(WILD FLOWERS # 3)
(about 250 pages)
(essays and songs mostly written
as website blogs from 2016 to 2019)
Printed in a smaller font 2 type.
To be published in early 2019.

Made in the USA
San Bernardino, CA
26 July 2017